Alien Contact

Alien Contact

✦

The messages they bring

Bonnie Meyer

iUniverse, Inc.

New York Lincoln Shanghai

Alien Contact
The messages they bring

iUniverse books may be ordered through booksellers or by contacting:

iUniverse
2021 Pine Lake Road, Suite 100
Lincoln, NE 68512
www.iuniverse.com
1-800-Authors (1-800-288-4677)

Cover Design by Marie Meyer ©2006
Original Artwork of Alien by Amanda Aquino

ISBN-13: 978-0-595-38404-4 (pbk)
ISBN-13: 978-0-595-82778-7 (ebk)
ISBN-10: 0-595-38404-8 (pbk)
ISBN-10: 0-595-82778-0 (ebk)

Printed in the United States of America

Contents

Acknowledgments

I would like to give a special thanks to R. Broadtke, who has always been there for me, pushing me along, helping me in any way he could. Russ has taken my words, the aliens words and made them easier to read.

I would also like to thank H. Hollis for giving me a push to get the alien messages out. Having spoken to her many times made me realize that the aliens she speaks to say almost the same things that the aliens I talk to do. Also I would like to thank the people who attended these sessions and were willing to ask questions so we could receive the messages the aliens shared with us. The core group has been around for a long time, with people coming and going over the years. This is not a club where membership is required. Anyone is welcome if they are truth seekers and true believers..

I would also thank my husband Gary for being so understanding and allowing me to have the time to write this book.

I would like to say a special thanks to D. Dobberke for looking at and giving me suggestions for the book from the aspect of a person who is not involved in the UFO topic. A big thinks goes out to D. Fieldhack, D. Shurburn, and K. Baier for helping in the compilation of the book.

The biggest lesson I have learned over the years is that a closed mind places a limit on what one can experience and learn. This is my journey into what I believe is a better existence because of what I call the good aliens. I ask only that you keep an open mind.

In the love and Light of the Creator
Bonnie Meyer

Prologue

Most of the UFO stories that have been told to the public are about terrifying alien abductions. Believe me when I say that there is another side to this story that has been overlooked by the media and publishers. I believe that there are a lot of people, who have had contact without being taken against their will, probed, impregnated or traumatized by aliens. It is time for those who have had positive contact to speak up and not be silent about their experiences. I am tired of having people tell me that I am fooling myself when I share my positive experiences with them.

Keeping this story to myself over the years has not been easy, but I knew the time was not right for me to come forward with my truth until now. To tell my story I have changed the names of some people who were part of my experiences because I no longer have contact with them. Some of the characters in my story are composites of people, with the hope that my story will be easier to comprehend. The names of most cities have also been changed to protect those people who do not want to be recognized. The order in which some of the instances occurred have been rearranged so that my growth and progress can be better understood by the reader.

I can truthfully say that I went kicking and screaming into the UFO and alien issue. After all, who in their right mind would set out to make themselves look like an oddball? It has not always been easy, but luckily I have been blessed with a wonderful husband who has always been willing to listen and not think that I am completely crazy. My husband is a very strong person, and every time I get too involved or way out of line he is not afraid to tell me to get back to reality. He is my anchor, the one who always knows when to pull me back to Earth, so to speak.

Never did I believe that I would become involved with UFOs, let alone anything spiritual or having to do with Jesus Christ, God, or, for that matter, what they stand for. The only thing I wanted to learn about UFOs was, if they were real and where their ships came from. After realizing that UFOs were real, the next thing I wanted to know was who was piloting them. I came to the realization that whoever was driving them had to come from some place and I wanted to know if they were from Earth or someplace else. When I first heard about UFOs, I believed that anyone who felt that life existed anywhere but on Earth was nuts.

Over the years our home has been illegally entered many times. Some strange items were left in the house, which I think might have been done just to let me know that someone was there watching. One time someone left a pair of brown cotton garden gloves in a size smaller than either my husband or I wear. Another time a man's Gray short sleeved work shirt was left on the bed. The shirt was too small for my husband to wear. There was no other male living in the house at the time. Another time I came home and found a bouquet of dead flowers on the back porch. I took that as a warning to back off from what I was doing, and I took that message to heart. For years I didn't speak in public on these topics but did keep reading and talking to people privately.

Another time I was at a meeting in a small town about sixteen miles from my home. Traveling country roads to get to a meeting was not unusual. There were not many houses, so it was a lonely ride. On this particular night I had picked up a friend in Appleton to go to the meeting, and the drive to the meeting was uneventful. After the meeting we went out to my old full-sized van, which was still in good condition, especially the engine. As we started the drive home I noticed that the generator light was on. I knew that if I let my foot off the gas, the engine would probably quit and I would not be able to get it started again. So whenever we came to a corner or curve in the road, one foot went to the brake and the other one went to the gas pedal. I was afraid that we would get stranded on one of those lonely country roads in the middle of nowhere; this was before the time of cell phones. I decided to go right to my house and get a car that we also had as I felt it would be safer for the rest of the trip. My house was half-way between where we were and my friend's house. When I got home to trade cars, I woke my husband up and told him what had happened and that I would be home soon.

The next morning before going to work my husband checked the van. As he came back in he was shaking his head, saying he was taking the car and not the van to work because the van was not safe to drive. The fan belt had little squares cut out of it all the way around. My husband could not understand how I got home without it breaking. Ever since then I have always wondered what would have happened if it had broken. Was someone waiting for me to have car trouble? There I go sounding paranoid, but maybe after reading rest of my experiences it might not sound so paranoid after all.

Even with all of the surveillance and interference in my activities I knew in my heart that there was a higher power watching over me, keeping me safe. I just did not realize who or what the higher power was.

Part One

My Journey, How It Began

Many people say an adventure begins with a single step mine began with a 1200-mile road trip. My husband traveled with his job and was sent to Connecticut in 1973. He went ahead so he could find a place for us to live; meanwhile, I was trying to get our red 1966 Volkswagen fixed so it could be safely driven that distance. Our neighbor across the street volunteered to fix the car and that made me happy, as we did not have much money. I bought a car-top carrier to hold our clothes, bedding and cooking utensils. While putting it on the car, I realized that it was actually too large for the car. However, on the plus side it carried everything we needed.

My parents did not want me to drive that distance alone with two small children, so they followed us in their pickup truck. As we set out everything seemed to be okay until we entered western Pennsylvania. The car did not have enough power to maintain speed when going over the mountains. Many people call these rolling hills, but to me they were tall mountains. When I was on the downgrade, I pushed the gas pedal to the floorboard, passing most of the semi tractor-trailers because this was the only way to gain enough speed to get up the next hill. While going up the hills we slowed to a crawl, the truckers were passing us, but as we were going down, we would pass the trucks. After passing us a couple of times the truck drivers started waving at the children and they would wave back. This continued all the way through Pennsylvania, and I tried to make a game of it so the children would not be frightened. Finally, my parents had had enough and convinced me to put the car top carrier in their pickup truck, so the car would be easier to drive. The rest of the trip was uneventful, although my dad made a comment about how the "bug" got over twice the gas mileage as his truck.

When we pulled into the driveway of our new home, I was very pleased. It was an acre of land with a river flowing through the backside of the lot. Then I noticed the eight by forty-eight foot trailer, blue in color with a large porch on one side. The only problem with the porch was that it had no insulation and could be used only in the summer. You have no idea how small the trailer was in the winter. When it was cold we spent almost every evening and weekend at the local malls just so the walls did not close in on us.

My mom and dad stayed for about a week and then decided to go back to Wisconsin. While at work, Gary met a man who had just started working at the mill. Because he was alone Gary asked him to our home for a home cooked meal. The first thing he did when he entered the trailer was go to the fridge and help himself to anything we had to drink. I thought that was quite odd, but he was otherwise very likeable. Trap, as he was called, was about five feet six inches tall, dark skinned with long, black hair. Many a night after supper all of us would go outside and sit under the stars. He would talk about how, "There had to be life out there, after all, God would not have stopped at making just us. Talking like we are the only ones in the universe is egotistical, isn't it?" This was the first time I had ever heard anyone speak like that.

One night we mentioned to Trap that the car could not get up Second Hill Road with all of us in it. He asked if we had a screwdriver, and my husband went to get one. He then went to the rear of the bug and in about five seconds said it was fixed. I giggled to myself, "Sure, sure who does he think he is?" The next day as I drove the car to the grocery store and stepped on the gas to get up a hill, I realized that the car had never had so much power nor run so well. I had heard that Trap could fix anything and now had to agree that he could.

During this time the kids were missing their friends and someone we knew had a dog which had a litter of puppies. We talked him into letting us have one of the four-week old beagle puppies. The kids picked the runt of the litter and called her Sandy. She was so small that my son carried her home in the pocket of his army fatigue jacket. She did not even know how to eat out of a dish so we had to teach her. When Sandy got older she thought it was great fun to be chased and would run away every chance she got. The kids would take a piece of baloney put it on their chests and lay on the ground until the dog would come and try to take it. As Sandy grabbed the baloney they would grab her. This was great fun until the middle of winter, when we had to lie in the snow to catch her. Trap saw what was happening and called the dog over to him. To my surprise she went right up to him and wagged her tail. He picked her up, held her level with his face, locked eyes, and said, "You are here to be a companion and protect this family, you should not run away." Trap put the dog down and she never ran away again. We had her for seventeen years and she was the best, most gentle and protective dog we ever had. She seemed to understand everything we said. The kids would often sit on the living room floor eating cereal and watching cartoons in the morning. Many times they would get up to leave the room and tell Sandy "NO," and she would not touch the food. Many times they left their ice cream dishes on the floor over night and she never touched them.

We included Trap in our holiday celebrations and at Christmas we wanted to include him in our picture taking, but he always avoided having his picture taken. This seemed odd, so I began asking him questions about his past. He told us that he was left on the doorstep of a woman and that she had raised him. Outside of that we did not get much more information from him or about him. After my husband's job was finished we were sent home. However, six months later my husband was sent back to Connecticut. He tried to look up Trap but learned that he had left immediately after we did and no one knew where he was.

Trap had been my introduction into the possibility of life existing in space. Is he an alien or isn't he? I don't know and I don't care because he opened my mind and heart to the possibility of life in space.

My Introduction To UFOs

With my husband traveling for his job we realized that the only way to keep our family together was for all of us to accompany him whenever we could. In 1974 Gary was sent to another small town in Connecticut with a co-worker who was dating a divorced woman with five children. This is where I met Edna. She became my closest friend and partner in my early UFO escapades. My husband found an apartment for our family, and Edna, who had always been fond of camping, spent a rainy summer in a tent with her children just to be near her boyfriend. The really funny thing was that Edna and I lived five blocks apart from each other in Wisconsin but had never met and probably would not have because we did not travel in the same social circles.

Later we were sent to Connecticut, and while we were gone a large bridge was built over a lake in our hometown. It was during the construction of this bridge that strange lights were seen in the construction area. It was reported in the local newspaper, and many people would go down by the construction site near the foot of the bridge to see what was going on. They were often treated to sights of strange objects and lights over and under the bridge. Edna and her family often went down to look at the lights and this got her interested in the UFO topic.

It was not long after our return to Wisconsin that I saw my first UFO. This took place in my backyard. I saw three lights about the size of a quarter making unusual maneuvers in the night sky. They flew in a straight line across the sky; then they reversed direction, exchanged places, and flew three abreast. When they zigzagged across the sky, they looked as if they were playing tag. I knew in my heart that we had nothing on Earth that could accomplish either of these maneuvers or had anything that could go the speed they were flying. This was amazing to me, but it was all the proof I needed. I was off and running going to at least one and sometimes three meetings a week, reading every book that I could get my hands on and spending every opportunity I could sky watching. For some reason my husband knew that this was very important to me and didn't make a fuss when following my dream of finding the answers that I needed.

Edna and I started riding around in the car most nights, following any light we saw in the sky, often finding out that they were only red lights on radio or water towers. We found every light associated with our local airport. After awhile we got to recognize where the stationary lights were so that we knew when we were seeing something that should not be there. Many times we reported what we had seen at the local UFO meeting place and were frequently ignored. I often wondered what they thought of us because we saw so many strange things in the night sky and they used to sit outside all night long, hardly seeing anything.

Edna and I attended many UFO meetings together, often traveling far from home. One night, on the way home from a meeting there was a UFO in a farmer's field alongside the road between Appleton and Menasha. It was early spring and the ground was freshly plowed with a single large tree, bare of any leaves, in the middle of the field. There was a round silver craft about one hundred feet in diameter, hovering and wobbling just above the field. It was about fifty feet in the air and there was no sound. About in the middle of the craft was a row of different colored square lights circling the craft. I thought the squares were windows, even though each was a different color. The colors of the squares from left to right were; white, yellow, orange, red, blue, dark blue or purple and green. All of a sudden the lights started blinking from my left to right as the craft started to move. The faster the lights blinked the faster the craft moved. As it started to move faster and faster the lights became blurred into a solid single colored light. The craft dipped, looked as if it just missed the top of the tree in the center of the field, and headed south. It looked like it was going directly to the north end of Lake Winnebago. We tried to follow the craft, but it was gone in a few seconds.

Edna did not have much money at this time and wanted a camera to take pictures for her business and the UFOs she was seeing, so she bought the only camera she could afford. After taking some pictures she took the camera back because it did not do a good enough job. By that time she had a little more money and got a better camera. This happened again and again until finally she ended up with a decent 35-mm camera. Now she felt confident that if she saw anything she could get a picture of it. One night Edna's family and mine decided to go out into my backyard to look for strange lights in the sky after the 10 p.m. news. So outside we went. We were out there for only a few minutes when we saw some high flyers. These are craft that look like stars except they move very quickly and often make quick, almost square turns or zigzag across the sky. Edna grabbed her camera and took a picture. When the photograph was printed there was a streak in the sky that we did not see with the naked eye.

We took the picture to a few photographers and asked their opinion of the streak. We were asked questions and they realized that we weren't knowledgeable enough to fake the picture. They said they did not know what we had but that whatever was on it had to be moving thousands of miles per hour to make that much movement for the amount of time the shutter was open.

A local TV station was contacted about the photograph and they came to do an interview with us. While the bright camera lights were focused on the photo we could see a circular craft at one end. Even the cameraman was impressed with what he saw.

Our neighbor across the street did not believe in UFOs and he often snickered at my beliefs. One night he and my husband were outside talking. All of a sudden my husband came rushing in the back door all excited and out of breath. When he could talk, he told me that there was what looked like a carnival carrousel in the sky. It was circular and had lights blinking off and on all around it. By the time I got outside it was gone. The neighbor said to me that he had no idea what he had seen but now felt there was a possibility that there could be other life forms in the Universe. That made me feel good because now there was at least one person in the neighborhood who did not think I was crazy.

UFO Meeting Place

There was a place in a town near me where anyone interested in UFOs could come and meet with like-minded people. Because of her sightings Edna became involved with these people who believed in UFOs and the aliens who drove them. When my husband, children and I got home from Connecticut, Edna told me about the lights that were seen in the sky and that she wanted me to go with her to the UFO meetings she had been attending. Edna also told me they even believed that human-looking aliens were on board the spacecrafts. I was not happy with what she was telling me as I thought they were stringing her along. As a matter of fact, I thought she had flipped her lid. She decided her non-believing friends needed to see the slide presentation this group gave during lectures, so she arranged for us to see the presentation. The meeting was to take place over the

Christmas holiday, but there was a big snowstorm that night and the slide presentation was cancelled. About a month later Edna arranged for another presentation, and I was the only one who showed up at the meeting. I did not believe everything they presented but decided I had to investigate for myself and find my own answers. The person who owned the house was very interested in George Adamski and his material. They talked only about aliens with blond hair and blue eyes. Any attempted we made to discuss the possibility of being other types of aliens in the Universe were quickly squelched. I went to the meetings at least once a week and sometimes as many as three times a week because these people were intriguing and I enjoyed looking through their telescope.

One night Edna and I were on our way to a meeting in Appleton and we saw six red circular lights over a farmer's field. They were the size of a nickel held at arm's length and seemed to dance in the sky. The six red lights were only a few hundred feet off the ground. Edna stopped her van and we watched for a few minutes until we decided to drive the rest of the way to the meeting and see if anyone else had seen the same red lights in the sky. When we arrived at the meeting we told of our sighting and no one seemed interested. After a few minutes a couple came in all excited, talking about six red balls of light they watched dancing in the sky as they came from the west. As soon as they told their story the host of the meeting got sighting reports out of the filing cabinet and had us fill them out. We were glad that someone else had seen what we had because finally we were believed.

You never knew who would be at these meetings and everyone who came had a story to tell. One time a couple came to a meeting and told about an experience they had when they went for a Sunday drive. Looking into the rear view mirror, the husband saw an old car that looked like a Model T. It was black and shiny, looking as if it just had come off the showroom floor. All of a sudden two men dressed in black jumped out of the car as it went into the ditch and passed the couple on their right side. The two men were in the ditch on the opposite side of the road running fast enough to keep up with their car. Much to the couple's surprise the men and Model T were moving so fast that both car and men passed them. They slowed down their car, watching this peculiar sight of the men who ran so fast their legs were just a blur and a car that steered itself as it went past them. They watched as the men jumped into the car, which was now ahead of them on the road. The couple slowed down even more to watch as the men and car were beamed aboard a UFO which had suddenly appeared over the middle of the road. As soon as the car and men were on board, the craft took off. I thought this interesting story needed to be included because it was years later that I heard other stories of men in black who often drive old large black cars.

Years later the people at the UFO meeting place moved out of the area and we no longer had a place to meet. Many of the people there went only by first names so we were left with no way to find them. Edna, Dale and I met by ourselves for quite sometime before people found out that we were meeting and they joined us. At one point there were a dozen people coming to the meetings and you never knew who was going to be there or what type of story you were going to hear. At one meeting an elderly gentleman showed up wearing a coat and tie. He shared how during World War II he was an interpreter between the Americans and the Russians after the two armies met at a German river. He had to cross this river each day and a driver would take him where he needed to go. One day his Russian driver picked him up and drove him to a large warehouse type building and took him inside through a side door. Inside he saw three circular metal craft on tripods. He actually touched one. As he and the driver passed one of these round discs, a Russian General saw the American interpreter and gave an immediate order for him to be taken out of the building. The next day there was a new driver assigned to him. I do not recall him giving us his name, only vague hints such as, "When I returned home after the war, the mayor wanted to give me a parade but I declined." He never came to another meeting but I placed what he shared into a file for future confirmation. It was an exciting time for all of us.

This was a very interesting time in my life, the excitement of always being able to learn new things and meeting people who were interesting. To this day I still have contact with a few of these people. This was when I met Dale, one of my best friends, and I feel very fortunate to have been able to call him a friend for over thirty years.

Door County

The local technical school invited a well known UFO speaker to the area to give a lecture. Edna and I went and while waiting for the lecture to begin talked to some interesting people in the audience. A woman there told us about a man in Door County who was meeting with aliens almost daily at his place of employment. After the lecture we got his name and telephone number because we had decided to call him the next day. We set up a meeting for the following week and decided to make a day of it as it was a couple hours drive each way.

It was February and very cold, slightly overcast as it often is in Wisconsin during the winter. Door County, Wisconsin is the area that looks like a thumb that points out into Lake Michigan. We were going in Edna's van because my husband needed the car for work. My husband dropped me off at her house and for the first time we learned of the problems that can occur when you get involved with UFOs. The van would not start. Edna called a friend to start the van and he did it by bypassing the battery. I have no idea what that means, but we were on our way. Next the hot light came on so we decided to stop at a mechanics garage and see if anything was wrong. He said he could not see any earthly reason for the light to be on and to go ahead. He also said we should not shut off the engine until we got to where we were going. So off we went, hot light still on, but very determined to get to see the Door County man.

As we were getting close to our destination, Edna decided to stop and get a new tape for the recorder that she had just gotten from her son on her birthday. We stopped at a store and I stayed in the van so that we could keep the engine running.

When we got to the house, we were welcomed with open arms by both the man and his wife. We wanted to tape what was said so we could listen later and review what we had learned so we asked permission, and they both agreed. Edna and I enjoyed an afternoon discussing our favorite topics; UFOs and aliens. He said the aliens had given him a triangular stone and while holding it in a specific position it would give a signal, letting him know when aliens were in the vicinity. He showed us the stone and wouldn't you know it, it gave him the signal the aliens were in the area. He showed us a pair of interesting gloves the aliens had given him and when we looked inside there was a J. C. Penney's tag. After that we were shown a photo of footprints the aliens had left behind. It was strange because one footprint was different than the other; our shoes have the same design on the bottom of each shoe, so why didn't these?

The afternoon was getting late and we would have to drive part of the way home in the dark so it was time to leave. You never knew what the winter roads would be like in the evening hours. After we were in the car for about ten minutes, I saw a shiny silver UFO off to the west and a little ahead of us. Just after I saw the UFO we decided to play the tape recording because we did not believe everything the man had said. The tape started off all right, but after a few minutes it got all garbled and full of static. We could not understand what had happened to the tape because the recorder was only a few weeks old. The tape recorder worked perfectly after this one incident. We did not talk for a long time as we were lost in our own thoughts.

As we neared Green Bay hunger overtook us, so we decided to eat at the local Ponderosa restaurant. While still in the car I looked at Edna and realized that her face was all red, it looked sunburned to me. I did not say anything to her at the time because I had to use the bathroom and decided I would tell her later. Little did I know that she was also looking at me, thinking the same thing. In the restroom we looked into the mirrors as we were washing our hands and got our first good look at our red faces. We looked at each other and pointed at our faces, unable to say anything or come up with any explanation as to what had happened.

We had on blouses with different necklines, and where our necks and chests were not covered the redness was very evident. It did not hurt and went completely away after three days, or so we thought. We decided we needed some answers and felt that those at the local UFO meeting would surely have our answers. At the next meeting we told them what had happened to us after seeing the UFO on our way home. The answer we got from them was that we had sunburn off Lake Michigan as it reflected through the van windows. Well now you have to remember that this was February in Wisconsin. The air temperature was in the teens and there was snow on the ground. We never got any closer than a couple of hundred feet to the Bay of Green Bay which was only partially frozen over. Now how could we get sunburn under those conditions? My husband and I have owned a number of vans since this happened and we have never been sunburned through the front window in Wisconsin or anywhere else for that matter in winter or summer.

After looking back at this incident these many years later and reading and talking to other people who have had similar experiences, I believe the UFO got to close to us and we got a burn from it. I also believe that somehow the UFO affected the tape in the tape recorder. As a follow-up to this whole story, it is now approximately twenty-five years later and whenever I get hot or excited the red face and chest is still there; you can even see the line where my blouse was open. The last time Edna and I spoke about this incident she confirmed that she also has the redness on her face and chest when she gets excited or hot.

Camping: Huckleberry Campground

During this period of time we began to realize that strange things were happening. We often wondered how we could go out night after night chasing lights in the sky and not use much gas. Many times we would go out and think we were gone for only a few hours, only to realize that we got home in the early morning hours. Still the strangest thing happened on the July 4th weekend of 1976. A group of us decided to go camping near New London. The entourage consisted of Edna and Sue a close friend of ours, their children, myself, Gary and our two children. On Saturday night Edna and I decided to go to the UFO meeting in Appleton which is thirty-two miles from the campground. We left all the children in Sue and my husband's care. This was not an easy task because there were eleven children total from the age of about six to about sixteen.

We had promised to leave right after the meeting and be back early. The meeting usually ended about 10:00 p.m. and we did not stay to enjoy conversation nor the coffee and cookies that were usually served afterwards. We left the meeting at about 10:10 p.m., and I planned to drive back to the campground using the usual route. For some reason I decided to go the back way into the campground; I turned on a side road and remember seeing a sign which said Bean City ahead. A little ways down the road I could see a UFO hovering over the small country road. The craft completely filled the road from side to side, even covering the ditches on both sides. I remember seeing a UFO but I did not remember anything until we were on a road that I did not recognize. We drove around for some time until I realized that we were on Highway 54. To get to Highway 54 we would have needed to go through New London but a river divides the city and there are only two bridges to get from one side of the city to the other.

We never did see the Bean City tavern, which we should have seen as we drove past it. I could not figure out how we got to Highway 54 as I did not remember going over any bridge to get there. Finally we got back over one of the bridges and found our way back to the campground. When we got there Sue was very upset she said, "Do you know what time it is? You said you would be back early." Looking at a clock we saw it was approximately 1:30 a.m. I could understand why Sue was upset with us; after all, watching eleven children was not an easy job. Needless to say my husband and the children were sleeping and did not even know we were among the missing for a period of time. This was the first time that it was evident to us we had missing time. I checked the gas gauge the next morning and we had plenty of gas left so we could not have been driving around for over two and a half hours. If we had driven around for that amount of time, we should have been almost out of gas, but to my surprise there was still over half a tank. I have driven the same route many times, trying to figure out what really had happened. It is 32 miles from the campground to Appleton where the meeting was held. On these trips it has taken from 32 to 45 minutes to drive the distance depending on the amount of traffic. So where were we and what happened during the missing time?

After discussing this incidence, Edna and I decided we should investigate what had happened to us. Missing time was starting to be discussed in the UFO community so we figured the only way we could find out what happened was to be hypnotized. We knew no one who would do it for free and neither of us had any extra money to spend on such a notion. Edna had broken up with her boyfriend and my husband was once again laid off from work. We had a hard time meeting the necessities for survival and certainly had no money for such an expense. We decided to keep our feelers out for anyone who would be willing to work with us for free. We knew that it would probably be next to impossible but we had faith that if it was meant to be, it would happen. Years later we did find someone who was willing to work with us pro-bono. This will be discussed in the hypnosis section of the book.

About this time Edna contacted a very popular tabloid magazine about our sightings. They came and talked to us for a long time. The magazine brought an artist along and she drew pictures from our descriptions of the ships and what the aliens looked like. They also flew in a hypnotist that they knew so she could hypnotize Edna and me separately. The hypnotist took me back to where a contact had taken place so I could relive what had occurred. After the hypnosis was over she told the magazine that she believed my story and felt that I did not make up any of my experiences.

After the reporters left I got a call from them and they read the story to me. To my surprise the magazine reporters took a couple of our experiences and put them together into one story. Luckily the reporters were relatively new and let us sign a contract with them that would give us the final O.K. on the story. They put many of our experiences together as one experience and made us look foolish; maybe using only one experience was not exciting enough for their tabloid. I believe that if the story had been printed as they wrote it, we would have been the laughing stock of our friends and family. I told them the story was wrong, what they had written was not how things had happened, and they were not to print the story. I have to give them credit, they did not print the story nor did we ever hear from them again. I will always be grateful that the article was not printed as it had been written.

Another UFO Investigation

A telephone call came to us from a woman I will call Caitlin. She had been having experiences on the family farm in the northwestern part of Wisconsin. Having no local contact to discuss her experiences she went to her local public library got our phone number from the library and gave us a call. She and her husband had been happily married for twenty years; however they had started fighting about a month before her telephone call and she could not figure out why they were fighting.

When Caitlin described on the telephone what was happening to her, we knew we had to see her so we could hear the whole story about what she was experiencing. Edna and I waited for Dale to get out of work and then proceeded with the five-hour drive. Caitlin thought it would be better if we met her at her parents' home because she believed she was safer, and I certainly can't blame her for not wanting strangers in her home. The farm that she and her husband worked was back to back with her in-laws. Caitlin did most of the barn work and took care of the animals, often spending nine hours outside each day.

Caitlin knew that there were aliens on the farm and felt they were messing with the animals. She explained that after a while one gets to know how the animals should act, and lately they seemed to be very upset. Often the cows were very uneasy as if someone else had been in the barn. Caitlin also believed that they marked the cows for some purpose, but she didn't know why. We asked if there were any cattle mutilations on the property and she said no. Caitlin also explained how she felt they were messing with her house cats and the family dog. All of the kittens were freaked out and it seemed the dog was shy and often hid under the kitchen table, growling as if he could sense that something was outside.

Caitlin had been seeing UFOs regularly for some time. Once she saw a silver ball come out of the sun; another time she saw a silver craft with red lights on the bottom. She also described seeing three craft moving in a straight line. Sometimes they even landed in the wooded area on the farm. When that happened she could see lights flickering in the woods.

One of the main things Caitlin wanted us to know was that she did not drink and that she enjoyed her home life and family. She talked openly around her children about what was going on and explained that they had become very frightened and would not talk about it anymore. The children had weird dreams but when they tried to describe what they were they couldn't remember them.

This woman told of seeing a tall "being" more than once. It was strange because it had what looked like a mask or motor cycle helmet on, so she could not see his face. (I also have seen this type of helmet on beings more than once although I did not have a negative encounter with them.) It, appeared like it had on a long fur coat that covered it from neck to ankles. One time she saw him on her deck kneeling as if it were praying. Sometimes she tried to wake up her husband so that he could see what was happening but he always seemed to be in a deep-sleep almost as if drugged. This incapacitated spouse phenomenon is a common event I have read about.

If you look at only this part of the picture you know that she has had alien experiences. But there was much more to her story. When she went into the barn she could see pictures on the frosted windows. Most often she could see the word "Hi" written in the frost. She could see pictures on the wood paneling, the ceiling or anyplace she looked; however, no one else had seen the writings or pictures and she thought her husband and in-laws wanted to institutionalize her. They even had a minister come over to talk to her and he gave them the names of two good psychiatrists. She was afraid to leave her children alone in the house and she did not want them to travel to school alone. Caitlin appeared unstable to family members, but then who wouldn't be with the things that were happening to her.

She also knew that everything in her house had been gone through. Things had been moved around and some items were missing for a short period of time only to be found again later. One time a new peanut butter jar was left open on the kitchen table and looked as if it had been sampled. No one in the house said that they had gotten into the peanut butter. Many times since then I have heard stories about no one believing what was happening to an individual who had encounters with aliens.

Often Caitlin heard what sounded like small feet scurrying around on the roof of the house. Other times she saw a big black dog moving around the farm. This dog was seen with something that looked like a little woman. Once she even saw something that looked to be the size of a child with a mushroom head, big black eyes and long skinny fingers with points on the ends. Another time she saw footprints in the barn that looked like a raccoon's but much larger with big wide toes.

We asked about her sleeping habits and the answer she gave us was not a surprise. It seemed that even when she had a good nights sleep she was always tired the next day. No matter when she went to bed she usually woke up tired. There were times when it was warm outside she felt instantly cold and when she had this chill she knew the aliens were around.

We told Caitlin that there was a light of protection that God and Christ has given everyone and that she should use it to protect herself and her family. We explained that some of the aliens feed off negativity, anger and fear. We could feel all of these negative emotions in the house. We asked her to believe in the light of protection with complete conviction or it would not work. Without that belief the aliens would have permission to intrude on her and her family.

As we were leaving we asked Caitlin to let us know how things were going but we never heard from her again. I have included this story because it has baffled me since the first day I heard it. Because I have had a hard time getting people to believe what happened to me during my encounters part of me wants to believe this story and yet I have a hard time with everything she said had happened to her.

Unusual lights

At the UFO meetings many people talked about very unusual things going on in their lives. Sometimes while out watching the night sky they would feel as if someone were watching them. At times the family pets would sit and watch something that seemed to walk through the house. This made them feel uneasy, and the hair on the back of their neck would stick straight up. I said to myself if the aliens are really out in space, they should show themselves to me; little did I know that they would try to influence me in strange ways.

During a period of about four months when I was home alone, balls of light would show up in the house. These balls of light looked like the soap bubbles children make outside. They looked like a bright light was shining inside and they seemed to radiate many different colors. They would bounce around and sometimes it looked as if they were playing tag. When I asked at the meeting place what they were, no one had an explanation for me, although I felt in my heart that the aliens were answering my request to show me of their existence.

One night we were having a bad rain storm with great claps of thunder and lightening. It was so bad that the lights went out in the area. I looked outside and the street lights were off and all of the neighbor's houses were dark. But there I stood in the window with all our lights on. How was this possible? About a week later something even stranger happened. We lost the electricity to our house, but everyone else had lights on and the street lights were shining brightly. I was going to wait for my husband to come home so he could see what was wrong with the lights but being impatient, I checked the fuse box and everything was okay. My husband checked when he got home and also found no problems. Maybe the aliens were trying to get my attention, so I said out loud, "If the aliens are doing this, it is not funny, and would you please turn on the electricity?" After about five seconds the electricity came on, and I thought, "My goodness, if they have this kind of power, they certainly could do anything they wanted to do. Maybe the ones that are doing this were not bad." Suddenly the lights blinked on and off three times as if to signal I had the right idea.

The electricity in our house would go off and on frequently when no one else's in the neighborhood did. The children saw this happen time and again but they were so young I don't think they remember what happened. Neither one has ever spoken about it. I now believe this was the alien's method of introducing me to them.

Strange happening were also occurring with street lights. One night it occurred to me that the street lights were going out way too often when I passed them; sometimes the lights turned on if they were off. This seemed to happen only when I was thinking about aliens. Then I tried to turn them off and on with my mind power, but it did not work. This hasn't happened often but has continued to the present. I can't remember when this all started, but I mentioned it to Dale, and he indicated it was also happening to him. Dale and I got together to talk about the street lights, and he explained that one night as he was walking to the Dairy Queen about a mile from his home, he also had street lights blink out. As he got about three blocks away from his home, a street light would go out. As he continued walking they continued to blink out, he would turn around occasionally to see if they stayed out, and they did. This continued the rest of his walk to Dairy Queen; but on the way home, as he got near a street light, it would come back on. Now that was weird!

Street lights are supposed to go on at dusk and off when the sun starts to affect them. I know many people who have had a street light go out when they are near but I have never heard anyone claim to have this happen year after year, no matter where they are. So what was affecting the street lights, why only certain people, and why so often? I knew it had something to do with the aliens, but I never suspected how they would answer the question when we finally asked. Many years later we finally asked the aliens how they knew who we were. They explained that each person has a light that shines within them, the brighter the light, the closer we are to God and Jesus. They could see this light because it shined like a beacon from our heads from great distances. This is how they knew who we were and where we were. They explained that was the reason the street lights go out. Our lights at times were so bright that they turned the street lights off. Then I wanted to know why the street lights sometimes went on, and it was explained that the aliens sometimes did it just to see what our reaction would be.

My husband noticed how often the street lights would go out when we were driving, and I asked him if he knew what was happening. He explained how we had a car-top carrier that was shiny and reflected the light back to the street lights and turned them off. Years later we traded the car and got a different car that did not have a car-top carrier and the lights were still going off. So I again asked what he thought was causing the lights to go off, and he told me to, "turn your light down because it is too bright." Where did that statement come from? I was shocked! Now, all these years later, when the lights go off, Gary still tells me to turn my light down.

Meeting Ike

I had decided that if I were going to continue in this field, I should look into other paranormal topics. It was fall and the new schedule came out for the Fox Valley Technical School. They had a class listed for Energy Focusing and what you could do with it. I thought that if the school were sponsoring a class like this, it would not be taught by a crazy person. I went to my first class and that is where I met Ike.

When I first saw him he was wearing a pyramid on his head. I thought what a weirdo, but what did I expect in a class like this? The teacher explained how the pyramid had energy that we are just now learning about. So we experimented in class with a dull razor to see if it would get sharp and to my surprise it did. Next we put a glass of water under a small tabletop pyramid and it tasted fresher. We were given the dimensions to make our own pyramids so we could experiment at home. I put a glass of milk under my home made pyramid for two days and it did not sour. Even the kids got involved; we had a lot of fun experimenting trying to see if we could keep cheese from molding. We also put a can of moist dog food under the pyramid to see if it would stay fresh and it did.

The next week Ike came to class with a pair of black glasses with tiny pinholes. Ike explained he was wearing them to improve his vision. I really was surprised with that one, but he said it improved his vision.

During the last class we were told the students as a group were going to raise a person from a sitting position on a chair into the air with two fingers. All we had to do was learn to focus our minds in unison to accomplish this. What we did was take the heaviest person in the class and put him on a chair in the front of the classroom so all of us could see him. Then we were told to concentrate with our minds to make him lighter and lighter. Two people were chosen from the class to lift him and I was one of them. He was told to think of himself being as light as a feather. I stood on his left and the other classmate stood on his right. We took our index fingers and placed them under his thighs close to his buttocks. As everyone was concentrating the instructor told us to lift him with our fingers and we did. We managed to get him a few inches off the chair before our concentration was broken. So now I knew the mind by itself or in a group is a strong instrument that can be used in many different ways.

I talked to Ike during our breaks and once I got to know him I liked him a lot. We talked of many metaphysical topics including ghosts. He liked to go ghost hunting, he called himself a ghostbuster, always trying to prove if they were real or not. Ike was the first person who introduced me to the concept of different dimensions, even if we cannot see them. I asked him if he would like to come to our UFO meetings and show us some of the things he was interested in. He accepted, came to our meetings, and became interested in what we were learning. Ike came to the meetings for awhile until he felt he was being drawn to the southwest, almost like he had something very important to do there. We said our goodbyes to him with heavy hearts because we knew we would miss him.

Curious Greetings

After seeing the first few UFOs, I realized that almost every time I would go out into the country there seemed to be strange objects flying alongside my vehicle. The country roads I traveled had a ditch on each side and most of the time the objects were just beyond that, about twenty feet from the side of the road. Some of them looked circular or round and silver colored, but most were black or very dark in color. Most were about the size of a basketball and paced the car. All of a sudden they would be there, keeping pace with the car. If I went faster, they would go faster; if I slowed down, they would also slow down.

They seemed to be watching, never getting any closer or farther away. This would last for a minute or two, and then they would shoot off in a direct line away from the vehicle. There was never a feeling of fear. I never felt threatened, just a feeling of well being. I felt more inquisitive and went searching for answers. It seemed as if someone were checking up on me, saying hi, and then moving on. After I came to the realization that I was having contact with the aliens, this phase gradually ceased. At the time I did not understand what was happening; all I knew was that it was a safe, secure feeling.

Self Hypnosis Classes

Edna, Dale, and I wanted to find out what was happening to us, but we weren't having much success in finding anyone to hypnotize us. When we found out Fox Valley Technical school was offering a class in self-hypnosis, we thought if we could learn self-hypnosis, we could hypnotize each other.

The three of us took the hypnosis class and then an advanced hypnosis class. We were taught how to relax the mind and body, how to breathe and to slow down the body functions. The teacher emphasized the importance of achieving deep relaxation and how not to allow things around you to interfere with the relaxation. We worked in the classroom with most of the lights off. He had a very soothing voice and I could follow his instructions easily. He had a way of making the students at ease in his presence. During the class he kept getting us to go into a more relaxed hypnotic state with each succeeding week.

The thing I remember most about the class was the night he wanted us to leave the classroom and fly like a bird over a fenced-in field. We were to look around so we could come back and tell everyone what we saw. I don't remember how it happened but as I flew over the field, I looked at the sky and decided that I wanted to go out amongst the stars and see what was there. I visited the stars and looked over a few planets. I was soaring like an eagle, going up higher and higher, diving at the stars and planets. I could feel the wind as it rushed past my face, feeling like I could do this forever and did not want to stop. As the teacher brought us back, I fought to keep going, but his voice was pulling me back ever so gently and slowly.

When we were all back and fully awake, we were asked to describe what had happened. As everyone described how they flew around a field and looked at the ground or at the fence, circling the field and waiting for more directions, I realized something had happened to me that was different. Why did I take off like that? Why did I not follow directions? This was the first time I felt more connected to the stars than to Earth. The teacher was amazed that I did not follow his direction and that I went on my own out into the sky while the others were bound only to his direction.

We never did use what we learned in this class to hypnotize each other. The self-hypnosis class has helped me over the years in many stressful situations such as pain from difficult surgeries. I now realize that this was one step in my learning process, and this made it easier when my hypnotherapist helped me learn what really happened in the missing time experiences. I also use the self-hypnosis that I was taught to put myself into a relaxed state when I let the aliens speak through me, but more on that later.

Meeting James Earl Carter Jr. the Future President

I had read that Jimmy Carter saw a UFO while he was Governor of Georgia, and I wanted to ask him about his sighting but never thought I would get the opportunity. In the fall of 1975 while campaigning for the presidency, he was to make a stop in Appleton, Wisconsin, so Edna and I decided that it was our opportunity to speak to him about bringing forth everything the government had on UFOs. We figured that because he had a sighting, he might be willing to get the material about UFOs released.

Many of the people at the UFO meeting place also decided to try to speak to him and, we all felt it would make more of an impact if one of us talked to him at each place he planned to make a stop. There was a K-Mart store on College Avenue that was close to the airport, so I decided to try to talk to him there.

It was in September of the year that he was running for president. I got to the store early so that I would not miss him. There were plenty of men in suits already in the store looking everyone over. When candidate Carter came into the store, I got to talk to him for only a minute or two, and then the security personal were moving him on. I did ask if he would look into the UFO issue and try to get the information out. He promised to look into it and get the information out, and then he was gone, moving on to the next place he was to visit.

I really thought he would and could do that, but to my surprise he never released any information. I have a feeling that once he was in office he realized that he could not get the information. Many investigators claim that even the president does not have a high enough clearance to find out about space ships or aliens. After he was elected president we waited patiently for the information before sending a letter asking when we would be hearing about UFOs, and a letter came from a secretary stating Mr. Carter never said he would try to release the UFO information. So I was disappointed again, but never was I willing to give up searching for answers.

Local Abductee

In the early 1980's we heard about a local man who had a frightening encounter with aliens in the mid-seventies. It took Dale, Edna and I some time to track him down, but we finally located him and realized that he had more than one encounter.

We had to talk for quite awhile before he finally agreed to meet with us. At first he shared what had happened to him with friends and received ridicule. Some investigators from a very well-known UFO organization had previously told him not to share his experiences with anyone even though they did not seem to be able to help him come to terms with his abductions which made him feel helpless.

Harry lived in a farmhouse with his dog just outside the city limits. When we got to his house, we made introductions and then proceeded to the living room where he told us his story. It did not take us long to realize that his experiences were not good. He had been out duck hunting one fall day when it happened. He had retired for the evening, leaving his gun in the bedroom to clean it for the next day. His large dog always slept in the corner of the bedroom with him.

During the night the dog awoke him by whining and making a fuss. As Harry awoke he realized that his body was paralyzed; he could move only his eyes. There in his bedroom were small beings, who did some experiments on him. These experiments were very painful and scary. They used some strange instruments that he had never seen before.

Harry struggled to break free of whatever was holding him in bed. He could see his normally a good watchdog, cowering in the corner. He could see his gun and tried to reach it to protect himself and the dog but could not move. He wondered how these things had gotten in the house because there was a light outside the bedroom window which allowed him to see anything in the yard. Suddenly they were gone; he could move and the dog fled the room, never again to be coaxed into it. He showed us the bedroom where all this happened and tried to get the dog to enter the bedroom, but the dog refused.

We shared some of our experiences with him and realized that Harry's life was now being controlled by his experience. He showed us the burglar alarms he had put on all his windows and doors and he lived in fear of the aliens' return. I have never seen anyone so terrified.

The meeting went as well as could be expected, and the man from the UFO investigation group seemed to be interested in our experiences. When the meeting ended as we were walking toward our cars, the investigator said, "Oh, by the way, I recorded everything that was said tonight," and showed us the recording equipment he had in the trunk of his car. We were all so shocked that we could not speak. We just got into our cars and left, thinking quietly to ourselves about what he had done…recording our conversations without our knowledge or permission.

We later discussed what had happened and became very angry. After all, who was he to record us without our consent? If he had asked permission we would have said yes. We were disillusioned because of the tactics he had used and decided we would not become members of any UFO organization.

We met with Harry several times after this initial meeting, and he had not recovered from his experience. Since that time he had more contact with these beings. Harry saw a UFO in the sky while fishing on a local lake with his girlfriend. As he bent over to get more bait, a ball of light came towards them. It passed over Harry's head, hit his girlfriend in the chest and then passed through her body. She was not hurt but had a medical problem that was cured after this experience. It seems that she had a very serious diabetic problem and had to take shots for it. After this happened there was no sign of the diabetes. Because of what had happened to him and people's reaction to it, he unfortunately retreated from society.

This made me question if both the spiritual and negative aliens could use superior knowledge and technology to perform miraculous healing. So here we go again, why are my experiences so different? I have never been experimented on or felt threatened. It has taken many years for me to realize that I was fortunate that the abducting aliens had not gotten to me first or maybe I had faith in God and He was protecting me from that kind of contact.

Seattle, Washington, Jorpah Conference 1986

I attended my first UFO conference in Seattle, Washington on the 1986 Labor Day weekend in a park in the center of the city. Edna drove out with her husband and son. They had a van that converted into a small camper with a stove and refrigerator in it. Edna's family left early because they were going to make the trip a vacation. It turned out to be a vacation from hell and is one that they will talk about for the rest of their lives. First their engine blew up and they could not get it fixed, so they had to get a replacement. But that was not right so they had to try another engine. Then anything that could go wrong did go wrong. I remember Edna being mad at the aliens for a long time because they did not come down and fix the problems they were having. In one of the sessions she asked why they did not help. The aliens answered that what happened was an earth problem and they were not allowed to help or interfere because she had made the decision to drive. Over the years they have told us repeatedly that they will not interfere in our lives. We must learn to live with the decisions we make and the consequences of those decisions.

Dale and I flew out from the local airport. We had to take our own bedding and any food we wanted to eat with us because we had no transportation to get to a restaurant and there was no food available at the conference building. There were no restaurants or grocery stores within walking distance of the conference. Bachelor Dale took only sunflower seeds to eat. He claimed he could survive on sunflower seeds for a long time. Needless to say, when anyone offered him real food he ate it. I took a large suitcase for my sleeping bag and pillow. Fitted in-between these items was a canned ham, some crackers, and a jar of peanut butter. I took the peanut butter because it needs no refrigeration; even to this day whenever I travel I can always be found with a jar of peanut butter. In a small carry-on bag I carried my clothes for the weekend. Our flight was very pleasant and uneventful, and to our surprise Edna and her husband picked us up at the airport.

The park where the conference was held was beautiful with many cabins among the tall trees and green grass. I was pleasantly surprised and certainly did not expect to see anything like that in the middle of a large city. There were no bathrooms or showers in the cabins, so we had to go across the compound to the building where the showers and the bathrooms were located. The cabin Edna, her husband, Dale, and I were assigned to had three very large bunk beds about the size of a king-size bed.

Here we were in the city of Seattle, in the middle of a wooded area, surrounded by a high fence, which was locked at night. If we were outside at closing time, we were locked out for the night. We were from small towns in the Midwest, so this made us feel safe. The conference was held in the large main building. Everyone was so nice and friendly. We met some people that we corresponded with for years afterwards. One woman in particular that I remember was from Canada. She was wondering what she should do about a boyfriend she had. She asked us to speak to the aliens about her situation and we did.

Aileen Edwards, who put on the conference, was the editor of "The Missing Link" magazine and director of The UFO Contact Center International, which was a nonprofit organization. We had been corresponding for some time with Aileen, and she asked us to speak about our alien experiences. We agreed after all how hard could that be? Edna and I spoke on Friday evening, and, because there were not that many people present, we were asked to speak again later during the conference, which we gladly did. Because this was the first time I spoke in public, I saved the speech and every once in awhile get it out, look at it, and wonder what I would have said if I knew then what I know now.

We met a man at this conference who was also interested in aliens; he thought he had to find an Indian artifact which would help explain the alien connection. It was so important to him that it contributed to the breakup of his marriage. This was the first time the realization came to me that the alien topic could became so important to some people that they gave up their marriages and children just so they could devote their whole lives to the subject. I believe this is wrong; after all, couldn't you have both? There had to be a middle ground that could be reached. I knew then that I had to find that middle ground because my family was so important to me.

While in Seattle at the UFO conference we met a woman who told how she had had cancer and the doctor sent her home to die. Feeling terrible and in pain, she slept on the sofa because it was a lot closer to the bathroom. One night while on the sofa she got a very distinct feeling she needed to meet someone. Eventually she couldn't ignore the feeling so she crawled on her hands and knees through the house, down the front steps, and into her car.

She drove slowly through the small town and crested the hill outside of town where the road turned to the right; however, she drove straight ahead into a grassy area and turned to the left. There was a deep gully in front of her car. She looked across the gully and saw a UFO on the ground with two beings in front of it. She felt her car slowly move forward down, into, up and across the other side of the gully before it came to a stop near the two beings.

These beings gently helped her out of the car and into the craft. She was placed on a table and another being did a complete medical examination of her. When he finished she was told they would help her fight her illness but she had to promise she would follow their instructions about the treatment. She agreed, and the medical examiner then produced a large syringe with a long needle that was filled with a green liquid which was injected into her stomach. Removing the needle from her abdomen, the alien physician told her she was not to take any food or liquids for three days, after which she could eat or drink anything.

A short time later she was placed inside her car, which did not have the lights on or the engine running. As she sat in the car she felt something push her car back through the gully into the grassy area near the curve. She started her car and drove back through town toward home. When she drove into the yard and parked next to the front steps, her son, who had been frantically searching for her, came out and helped her into the house while asking many questions about where she had been and why she hadn't called anyone. Because she had left home without telling the family, he thought she needed to go to the hospital for observation and treatment.

When he mentioned treatment, she became very insistent that she would not go unless her children promised they would not allow anyone to give her food or fluids for the next three days. When they agreed that someone from the family would be by her bedside making sure that no one gave give her food or fluids for the three days, she agreed to go into the hospital.

The doctors checked her out and told her that she could go home and prepare for her last days. As she left the hospital she was as sick as ever and felt as if she were going home to die. But as the days went by she got stronger and stronger, feeling much better each day. Six months later the doctor stopped by to pay his respects to the family at her passing. When her son heard what the doctor said, he called his mom and she answered him from the roof where she was making repairs?

Needless to say, the doctor was speechless. She was checked over, and they found no cancer and she was given a clean bill of health. Since she was fully recovered and had regained her strength, the doctors asked if she would be willing to give a small vial of her blood to other cancer patients that were given no hope of survival. I remember her saying that she had given her blood to six or seven people and they had all recovered except for one woman who had committed suicide. The doctors were very interested in her blood, and she was willing to help in any way she could. However, after the suicidal woman episode she refused further participation in the cancer research project because she was linked emotionally with those people who received her blood, causing her an additional burden.

I wondered whatever happened to her and this cancer treatment. I had looked for years to see the story in the newspaper or on television but never found it. It seemed to me as if the aliens had given us a cure for cancer, so why, wasn't this looked into further? Who would benefit the most if this were not brought forward? This was the first time that we had heard of the aliens healing contactees, but it would not be the last.

I enjoyed the conference and wished I could have gone back again but never did. The conference was over on Sunday, but our flight did not leave until midnight because we were on the red eye express. Aileen was so nice she offered to take Dale and me back to her home and then made sure that we got to the airport. I don't think I ever thanked her properly for being such a wonderful hostess. Aileen did "The Missing Link" magazine from her home so we got to see how the operation worked. Dale and I got home early in the morning on Labor Day so we had the full day with our loved ones. Edna got home a few days later without any further complications.

Cleveland, Ohio Conference 1988

Edna and I read about an upcoming conference and decided that it was time to get our feet wetter by attending another UFO conference. It was close and not expensive, so we made our plans and decided to take Edna's smaller car because of the good gas mileage it got. We made a bed in the back so one could drive while the other slept. We started out about 3 a.m. on a Friday so we would get there in time for the opening supper and to meet the speakers. Many of the speakers gave a summary of what their lectures would be about.

I especially remember the gentleman at the conference who gave a talk about there being two types of Sasquatch in the Ohio area, one with red eyes and one with yellow eyes. This was the first time I had ever heard about them having different-colored, glowing eyes. He also talked about many Sasquatch being seen around city dumps.

He told another story about a woman who lived in the country and was romanced by a Sasquatch. Her husband was not home a lot, and almost every time she was home alone one would come around in the evening. He often left her flowers on the front porch. She was very frightened and told her husband what was happening. He, in turn, told his friends and they decided they were going to kill this thing before it could do any damage. So the group of men got together with their guns and sat in a car one evening waiting for it to show up. They did not have to wait long as it came lumbering out of the woods, stopped in the garden, and picked a handful of flowers. As it came near the house, they proceeded to get out of the car and take aim at the creature. They shot and heard a howl from the creature, which made them all shake in their boots. It turned on them and they fled to their car where the creature walked around it making awful noises. It actually made marks on the car while shaking it like a toy. The Sasquatch then turned and strolled towards the woods limping as it went. As it entered the woods, it again let out a terrible howling sound. When the Sasquatch was out of sight, the men got out of the vehicle and proceeded with their guns drawn to follow it. When they got to the point where it had entered the woods, they looked for a bloody trail to follow but could not find any. They knew they had hit the creature but could find no evidence of it. That ended these experiences as the Sasquatch never returned.

On Saturday night we were invited to the hotel room of the group putting on the conference. It was fun talking to everyone and being able to hear what the speakers talked about when they were not on the podium. The group had drinks in a tub filled with ice. The group had past newsletters for sale and I bought only a couple of them. Everyone seemed to be drinking except me; and as the night went on everyone got happier and the newsletters got cheaper, so I bought a few more. I still have these newsletters and often get them out to reread.

An interesting part of this whole trip happened on the way home. We had been keeping track of our gas mileage and at one point realized that we got extra good gas mileage. Now Edna and I both drove like little old ladies and made no quick starts or stops so we always got good gas mileage, but this was almost impossible. It was something like five more miles per gallon on one tank of gas. It also seemed as if we got home quicker, taking less time to get home than it did to get there.

After going around Chicago and heading north toward Wisconsin it was getting dark; we turned on the headlights and realized they were not functioning properly. They turned on all right, but when changing from low or high beam they would go out. We had running lights so we drove slowly on the gravel shoulder of the road. We played with the lights and eventually got them to come on. We then left the lights alone so that they could stay on. After we got home the headlights were checked and nothing was wrong with them.

Much later during a channeling session with the aliens we learned we had an encounter with them on the way home from Cleveland. A UFO picked us up and took us on board. The beings on board looked very human. The captain or pilot had on a green uniform that looked very much like military army fatigues. He had short, dark, almost black, shiny hair and had what looked like a military type of haircut. He was about five feet six inches tall and stocky in build and had dark olive-colored skin. There were three other aliens in the control room, and two were dressed in the same military type uniform.

I was taken to another room that looked like a doctor's office. As I sat on a table a being entered, he was not human looking. I got the impression he wanted to look me over. I was frightened and he said with telepathy that they already knew everything about me from their soul computer and I should not be afraid because they only wanted to see how my body was doing. They would not do any experiments on me like so many of the abductees talk about. He promised that he would not hurt me and proceeded to look at how my knees were working. He straightened them out and then bent them many times. He seemed very interested in how they operated. He also put something around my arm, and I assumed that it was checking my blood pressure. After the checkup I went back to the control room and the same male was at the controls. I had the impression he was male as he had no shape like a female would. He looked at me and spoke to me telepathically and said that we have to work together to accomplish our jobs. I had no idea what he was talking about but nodded yes. He showed me a scene in my head of people holding hands in a circle; they were holding tightly to each other as if some force were trying to separate them. I realized he was trying to show me how working together as a team makes us stronger than working individually. This man then told me that he would be keeping watch over me and if I ever needed him, he would try to help me.

While this was happening I noticed another person in the room standing off to one side. This young woman (who had a very female shape to her body) was not part of the crew and looked as if she were observing. She was pretty and had blond, shoulder-length hair that was turned under at the bottom. She had on a blue uniform with a skirt. She never said anything but seemed to take an intense interest in everything that was going on. It was years later I realized that this female was Monn, the alien that was to be my contact and the one that I channel most often. This was my first introduction to Monn, I never spoke a word to her and she never spoke to me.

So I was never probed or experimented on with this or any other contact that I have had through the years. The aliens always respected who I was, and I also have a lot of respect for them. Many years later I realized why they were so interested in my knees. In 1991 I had to have a right knee total replacement, and in 2002 the left one was also replaced. I now realize they probably knew that I would have problems with my knees and were just checking up on me. Many people have asked me why the aliens did not take care of my physical problems, so I eventually asked them. They answered that I knew the body I was entering and the problems that it had, but it was the one available for my soul to walk into; therefore, they would not interfere with my life in that manner as it would go against the Law of Noninterference. This law does not interfere in our making our own destiny. We make our own decisions and are responsible for our own actions. The aliens have explained that they will not interfere unless our actions will upset the Universe. In other words, we can goof up ourselves but they will not let us destroy the planet as that would affect the Universe.

Channeling And The Reluctance To Do It

Like everything else in my life I went into channeling questioning everything about it. What I had seen of channelers made me believe that some of them were charlatans and I did not want to be like them. I felt that many of them did the channeling only to be important and have people look to them for their answers. Most channelers I have seen personally are very lovely people, but I feel they are tapping into their inner selves for the messages they are channeling. I believe psychics, channelers, and tarot card readers are all responsible for any message they give to people that might affect a life in either a negative or positive way. I did not think I was ready to take on that responsibility. Enough of this, I am getting ahead of myself.

About this time a mother and daughter started coming to our UFO meetings. They came from a town about 30 miles away. The nineteen-year-old daughter channeled a being that was not just one person but represented a group of beings that worked together. One evening in the spring of 1986 Edna and I went to their home specifically to hear channeling and to see what it was all about. I will call this being Anon because he said that he talked for a group of beings. A lot of questions were asked about a specific person. These questions were answered, and what was said sounded genuine. I was intently observing everything to see if it was genuine or not. However, I was still a little puzzled after the channeling but there was less resistance than before.

For the first time I looked at channeling in a different way. This young woman was not doing it for money and or glory because she was doing it very privately. Later we again went to hear more from Anon. I will tell you what happened that evening only as it relates to me, although many other people were discussed. This was what I now believe was part of my wakeup call, to my commitment for being here at this time. At this meeting Anon, told me that I was to let someone speak through me. He (they) said that I should go with it as I had made the commitment before I came here. Being the person that I am, I said to myself "NO WAY!" No way was I going to let anyone else take over my body and say all sorts of things over which I had no control. He also said that they were helping a being called Monn learn how to speak English and that she was doing very well with her lessons. She was just about ready to start her part of the mission. Again I said to myself, "NO WAY, not me." He again said that I had made this commitment before I came to the planet and it was very important that I keep that promise. My thoughts were how dare he, try to tell me what to do. After leaving their home I became reflective and very quiet. Edna asked if I really thought I could do this channeling. I said I didn't know if I wanted to do it because I didn't believe in channeling. What I find very interesting is this mother and daughter stopped coming to the meetings after giving us this information. People kept coming into our lives and then would disappear.

The only channelers and psychics that I had seen prior to this were on television, and I thought they all had help from the sidelines. I decided to go to a local psychic and see if she would say the same things, Anon had said. I would not to talk to her about myself, so she wouldn't have anything to use. She did not have much to say to me, and what she did have to say was wrong. She even had my children in the wrong birth order and told me about their marriages and what would happen to them; needless to say, most of these things never happened.

Did I want to become part of this? Did I want the responsibility of suggesting a path and sending people down a path that was not right for them? I knew in my heart that if you channel or are psychic, you are responsible for anything that is said. I also believe you are responsible for anything you say that could influence anyone who is listening. In other words, if anything is said that has a negative impact on anyone, you must at some point take responsibility for that. This is not something to be played with. I have seen many people asking for ways to handle their lives, but rarely do they follow what they are told. People just seem to go from psychic to psychic until they find one who will give them the answers they want. Many go to channelers who speak to the dead to get answers instead of looking into themselves for their answers. Most psychics and channelers do not think they have any responsibility when they speak to people. Psychics and channelers seem to have everyone's answers but sometimes aren't good at handling their own lives.

Now you can see the quandary I was in. I certainly did not want to channel the dead; they did not know any more being dead than when they were alive. What good would it do to talk to dead people, except to maybe help the person who was still alive to feel better about whatever was unsettled in their past with the dead person? I certainly did not want to let an alien talk through me for any reason. I felt people would think I was crazy. After all, aren't most channelers channeling information that is just garbage and aren't they trying to dupe the people around them into believing they are great? I believe many of these channelers feed their own egos while doing this. After all, what could inflate an ego more than to have people always asking you to give them their answers? The answers that the psychics give are very general and vague and could be for anyone. After all, what they lack in giving relevant useful information, they make up by giving the people what they want to hear. For example, one person kept asking questions about her children and who they were in a past life. She often told me what was said, and, if she did not like the answer she kept going back until she found one who told her what she agreed with.

I would like to explain a little about how much this was bothering me. I asked Hank who was my hypnotist to help me with a problem I was having with the channeling I was doing. There was some apprehension on my part. I told him I believed the channeler had a responsibility to the people who were listening. I knew that something might be said during the channeling to someone that was not right for that individual. I felt as if I would then be held responsible if what was channeled changed their path for this lifetime. Maybe I would not be held responsible in this lifetime but I believe I would be at some point in time. You have no right to interfere in the path people have chosen for themselves.

Hank asked if I thought that the messages I was getting were harming anyone. I answered that I did not, because I have a close relationship to Monn and the other aliens that I talked with. Hank said that all I had to do was remember that I had control of the situation; I could stop anytime I felt things were getting out of hand. He told me I had the strength to do that. He said that if I felt the messages did not seem right I did not have to pass on that message. Hank stated I was like a flower opening up. I previously sat in the background and let other people lead, and the time would come when I would probably take the lead. I knew that I needed to keep God as the pilot in my life's endeavors and then I would never go wrong. My thought was, "Why me, why did this come to me?" I only wanted to be a wife and mother and be the best one that I could. Now I had to face the fact that I had volunteered and promised to do more than I realized.

I find it very interesting that many people especially during the Y2K situation were interested in what to do to save their bodies. Meanwhile the aliens that we were speaking to told us that we needed to figure out how to save our souls, not our bodies. Don't get me wrong, they told us that everyone should have an emergency supply of food, water and medicine enough for about ten days. Humans should be ready for any type of emergency. One time the aliens asked us what we would do if we had a large supply of food and people came to us for help. Would we get a gun and kill them? That certainly would not be spiritual, would it? Now that made me stop and think, how far would we go to protect our bodies only to lose our souls?

Missing Time

On one of the last trips I made to see the mother and daughter in Fond du Lac who channeled Anon something very strange happened. Edna and I had already talked to Anon, who channeled through the daughter, and he had told me that I would be channeling. So this time we were going to talk to them about what was going on in our lives. I wanted to bring both of them up to speed on how the channeling was going.

The evening was very pleasant; the mother and daughter each explained how they were being bothered by Orion beings. A lot of things were missing from their home including a ring. They were upset and told the beings they wanted their things back. It seemed that everything showed up eventually, out in the open, where one or the other would have seen what was missing. I have had some of the same experiences especially since I have been working on this book. Sometimes parts or whole chapters are gone. It is really surprising to find that whole channeling sessions disappear off a disk. This makes me think I should work harder. I find it interesting that someone or something would try to stall the progress of this book.

As we were leaving we said our good-byes and got into Edna's van. The time was about 11:45 p.m. As we were driving down the North ramp onto Highway 41, Edna was eating salty snacks out a bag that was between the front seats. Edna always ate when she drove so she could stay awake. As we got about twenty feet from the bottom of the ramp I could smell the strong odor of cinnamon. It smelled as if there were a fresh apple pie in the vehicle. It reminded me of coming home from school and smelling the fresh apple pies that my mother baked in the fall with the McIntosh apples from our trees. Edna and I both commented on the smell and wondered where it was coming from. The next thing I remember was recognizing a local gas station on the south side of Oshkosh, which is about thirty miles from Fond du Lac. I commented to Edna on how quickly we got there and that I did not remember anything between the two cities. We had not done our usual talking about everything and nothing. As Edna reached into her bag of snacks for another bite she said, "This is strange; the bag is almost full, usually by now it's half gone."

The rest of the way home we talked about what had been discussed at the meeting and what we were going to do the next day. The conversation came back to the cinnamon smell in the car and we wondered if maybe something had happened. I felt unusually tired when Edna dropped me off at home. My husband was sleeping and I did not want to wake him up, so I went right to bed without turning on any lights. The next morning I got a call from Edna, asking if I realized what time we had gotten home. I answered no; I went straight to bed because I was so tired. Edna explained that her husband was up when she got home and he commented about how late it was. It was about 2 a.m. and he asked if our alien friends took us for a ride. That got us thinking that maybe we had missing time again. What happened during almost two hours of time? Could we have driven around for that amount of time and not remembered?

When we asked Monn later about the smell, she said that we had had contact that night with her and she wanted us to remember what had happened, so she used the smell of cinnamon to try to get us to remember. Needless to say, it did not work. For a very long time I waited for the smell of cinnamon to occur again, thinking that the aliens would use the smell to let me know they were about to make contact, but it never happened. We were not afraid of what had happened, just curious. We certainly did not feel violated in any way. I believe this was just another gentle step toward the realization of what was happening.

The Channeling Begins

Months later I realized there were other thoughts in my head beside my own and I had also started to feel a presence other than my own. This often happened when I was doing manual labor that needed no concentration, such as scrubbing the bathtub or washing dishes. It wasn't like someone talking to me; the best way I can describe it is like a ticker tape playing in my head that I could read. This continued for some time. I was very inquisitive trying to figure out what was happening.

Someone was trying to speak to me. One of the messages was that they, whoever they were, loved me and did not want to harm me. If I did not want to communicate with them they would leave. This intrigued me because if they wanted to harm me in any way, I believe they wouldn't have volunteered to leave. So if they loved me enough to leave, maybe I could trust them, maybe they weren't so bad after all.

Then there was a voice in my head that I knew was a woman. It was like I could hear and feel her. She explained that she had a solid body and a little more about herself so I would be more comfortable. I liked the idea that she had a solid body and that I could touch and feel her. It took me a while to become comfortable with the process. She spoke to me and told me her name was Monn and that I had known her before I came to Earth. She worked with a group of aliens who are here at this time to help the planet through a transition that was about to take place. She said, "We are your friends and we are here to help the planet in the troubled times ahead." I asked what they meant by times of trouble. She said that earth is now going through some natural changes and disasters such as a pole shift, which has happened many times before on this planet. The biggest problem today is man's ability to exterminate himself and destroy the planet with atomic weapons. I thought, "Holy cow, what would happen if many countries exploded atomic weapons at the same time?" It was then explained that there would be an immediate change in the climate, strong winds of over 200 miles per hour, and everything we knew would change in an instant. Monn explained that now there are more powerful weapons than the atomic bomb available to the people of our planet. If they should use these weapons, it would affect the rest of the planets in our system and even planets that are further out. That is what the aliens are worried about; therefore, many aliens have volunteered to come and assist us in any manner that they can. I found this information very interesting. Why would complete strangers to this planet be willing to help us when we aren't willing to help our neighbors? This surprised me and got me interested in what else they had to say. I wanted to continue this experience but was very careful because I did not want to be fooled by these beings. They could be using trickery to fool me, they could be someone or something that wanted to get me to do something not quite right or maybe something evil. So very carefully I moved forward, always with the idea that I could back away if anything seemed out of order.

Then one day we were both ready to do the channeling. I was ready to let Monn use my voice box and she was willing to speak through me to relay the messages. When the channeling first happened, we were not prepared and did not realize how important it was to keep track of what was being said, so some of these sessions have been lost. Later we asked some of the same questions so we would have a record of the alien answers.

When the channeling began, I did not know it was happening, I didn't remember anything that was said. The being coming through, suggested that we tape the sessions so that we would have a record of what was happening. This frightened me very much as I did not know how the channeling was to take place. I asked if maybe I should read some books and there was a message in my head, "Don't read anything, just let it flow, let it happen. You shall then know that it is not something you read about and you won't have any preconceived ideas of what should happen." Because this was so new and I was so shy about the channeling it only happened when Edna was present. We often asked people in the group to give us questions they would like answered. We would then ask Monn and see if she would give us an answer. Sometimes she would answer and other times she would not. When she answered the questions, we would relay the answers at our next meetings. No one around me seemed to realize that this was not an easy situation for me. Everyone wanted me to channel. They were not interested in my feelings, only what the channeling sessions would bring to them.

We started to tape every session so that I could listen and find out what was being said. It is very hard for me to listen to the tapes. It is strange to hear my voice on the tape and realize it is not me because the pattern of speech is different. The reason that I do not remember what happens during the channeling sessions is because my soul actually leaves my body and the alien's soul enters to use my voice box and keep my body functioning correctly. To this day I hardly ever know what is being discussed during the sessions.

In these first sessions questions were asked about our abductions. During this time we used the words abduction and contact interchangeably because we did not realize there was such a difference between them although we did realize our experiences were different than what was happening to most people and different from what was being talked about in the UFO community.

The other people in the group asked us to share what was being discussed with the aliens and as time went on the aliens asked to have more people join the sessions. The aliens were being very patient with me, allowing me the time to become comfortable with the process of channeling.

One day I realized that there were blank spots on the tapes and the title on one of the tapes read "edited". I could not figure out what was happening and suspected that Edna was doing the editing. My mind began to whirl; I began to wonder what was on the tapes that I was not hearing. This did not sit well with me. I felt that I should have full knowledge of what was coming through me. The control of the tapes had to be mine; after all, I was responsible for what was being said. I was very passive and allowed it to continue for some time; over the years I have gotten stronger and speak up more now.

Monn finally said that everything was to be shared with everyone in the group in its entirety. The tapes were not to be edited, and if anyone did not want someone to hear a question or an answer, then they should not ask it. The tapes were not turned over to me in a timely fashion, and when they were, there were blank spots on the tapes. Eventually I had to leave the group because it was the only way for me to regain control of the sessions. From that point in time I have all the original tapes in my possession. The channeling has continued to the present day and is done with whoever is present at the meetings. Sometimes Monn even asks for a specific person who is not with the group to join a session.

I have heard many channelers tell people what they "should do" with their lives. I heard one channeler tell a person to sell their home, another one their boat. Some were told what to do with their money. One time I heard someone tell the person they were talking to that she should divorce her husband. From what people had said to me, things did not work out as the channeler said it would. Many times when this was happening I wanted to scream at the channeler how they were going to be held responsible for what they were saying. Did they know who they were channeling? Did they know if this entity was spiritual or not? I wondered if they cared; my fear was that I could become like them and my channeling would deteriorate to where it would become a joke.

Because of our impatience and wanting to talk to the aliens more than they were willing to channel, we thought we could use a board to speak to the aliens. The aliens did not like us doing that, and the reason they gave for us not using the ouija board was because it could be infiltrated by negative beings who could fool us into believing they were positive. Because of the negative happenings that are associated with the ouija board, we thought we would be smart and make a letter board of our own. We used this letter board to speak to the aliens once a week or more. We were often scolded for using the letter board, and finally they told us how easy it was for the negative forces to infiltrate the process and give us bad information. Because we wanted to talk to the aliens more than they were willing to channel, we continued using the letter board. Again they explained that it was not a good idea because whatever the level of spirituality the people using the board are at, that is the level of the beings that would be drawn to it. This is scary when you consider that there are some very negative people out there who are calling on anything to come through the ouija board. Many years later I was told that a member of the group wanted to continue talking to the aliens on the letter board but wanted to exclude me from these meetings. This did not surprise me because I felt these people were getting together by themselves. By the time this information was shared the person who wanted to exclude me had already left the group.

To make the letter board we took an old metal TV tray and put the letters of the alphabet on it with a yes and no in the upper right and left corners. We used the top of a margarine container with a hole in the center so we could see what letter it would stop at. The aliens had trouble spelling our words; often spelling the words just like they sound.

I would like to explain how we proceeded with the letter board. The margarine top would be put on the TV tray upside down. After we would ask a question, it would move around the tray so fast that one person would call out the letters and another would write them down. After the margarine top stopped we would then try to figure out where the words were and then read the message. It would look like this, sixdayinaweektoyou; then we would put in lines where the words ended. Six/day/in/a/week/to/you. It was a very cumbersome process of deciphering the spelling and what they were trying to say. Even Monn had a hard time spelling our words; no wonder the aliens did not like this form of communication.

After using our homemade board for some time, we came to realize that each alien we talked to had a unique way of signing in so it was easy to tell who we were talking to. One signed by my making the margarine container lid go up and down about five times on the board. Another alien signed in by moving the lid so fast that it was almost torn out of our hands. Sometimes we could tell that the beings we were talking to were not the ones we wanted to speak to; there was a difference in the feel of how the margarine container moved. When that happened we got off the board and tried again later.

Radio Talk Shows

Edna and I foolishly decided that we knew everything there was to know about UFOs and aliens, so we decided to do radio talk shows. (Sometimes ignorance is bliss I now realize that I cannot talk with authority on the whole topic of UFOs and aliens, I can speak only on what has happened to me personally.) We did quite a few radio shows, and there is one that sticks in my mind. This was a local station about fifty miles from home. We had a good rapport with the moderator and had fun although I don't know if he really believed us or not. As we were going off the air Edna said something like, "If you don't believe us, look at the sky tonight and you will see all the proof you need."

The next day we went shopping early in the morning, and when we got home in the late afternoon, there was a message waiting on the answering machine. We returned the call immediately to the radio station, and the man who interviewed us said, "Where have you been? We have been trying to call you all day. The telephone lines at the radio station had been busy all day. People were calling telling us that they had seen lights all over the sky the night before just as you had said we would."

Many times we were laughed at during the radio interviews; I remember one incident in particular. I talked about how there might be other life in the Universe although they would not necessarily look like us or breathe air like we do. All the stars we see are suns and they could have planets rotating around them, which could have some form of life on them. I was laughed at by one of the fellows who called in and said that I was nuts to believe that way. I am very happy that some of our scientists believe that there could be life in space even if it is only microorganisms.

TV Show: At The Local Cable Access Station

I don't remember how it exactly happened, but in 1986 we did a television show on the local cable network channel. It was not seen by many but we believe it got to the people who were supposed to see it. It was fun but also a lot of work. The show was on every Friday evening.

We had to have all our own people to produce the show. This included making our own stage set, having our own camera people and someone in the control booth. Edna's children handled the cameras and Dale helped them out. Meanwhile Edna and I were in front of the camera scared out of our wits. The station had a support person available to help us when we were short a person.

After doing the TV show for about six months, it became increasingly difficult because we had to read and prepare material from books and magazines for each week's show. It was hard trying to talk for a half-hour show on the UFO topic and not repeat the same material. We even started to share some of our experiences with the audience. I did not want to share with anyone outside of the group that I channeled. Edna liked to share anything that was attention grabbing and I was afraid that she might spill the beans on the air, so I told everyone that if anyone mentioned that I channeled, I would walk off the air and not return.

Because the show was becoming very hard for Edna and me, we asked Dale to join us, and he agreed to be with us in front of the camera. Dale became a moderator and often headed off things that were not appropriate to talk about on the show. One time I remember Edna talked about ghosts doing odd things in her home. We were there to talk about aliens and UFOs, and nothing else. We tried doing a call-in show as it didn't involve as much preparation time. It worked out well for us, and we knew then what the people wanted to know. My involvement in the production of this weekly program has made me very respectful of anyone who does a television show, especially if you have to do all the leg work yourself. We enjoyed doing the show very much but it became apparent that we were getting a few nuisance calls each week. There was one young man in particular who called almost every week to ask some very ludicrous and embarrassing questions. Realizing that we had probably gotten to open people up to the fact that aliens existed, we decided it was time to give up the show. As the years have gone past I am surprised at the people who I meet that say, "I remember you, you did the show on UFOs at the local cable station."

I remember this time fondly; it was a time when I thought that I knew it all. Oh, to be back to those days when I thought I knew everything there was to know about the UFO field. I knew very little, and each and every day there was some new type of information coming our way. I had to read everything I could and then pick out the pearls of wisdom. It became apparent to me that there are many people in this field who tell stories with a half twist to the truth so it seems quite genuine, but it is not. I want to believe people are what they represent themselves to be, and I find it hard to understand why anyone would misrepresent themselves or the material they have. As I write this book I am still learning that not everyone is truthful. People tend to change; sometimes this is good and other times it is not. Oh well, time for me to get off my soapbox and on with the story.

Hypnotist, Finally the Answer:

Many years later a minister named Marge started coming to some of our meetings. Marge's interest was in healing, not UFOs or aliens. She was a wonderful healer who loved everyone. Her philosophy was that if God gave you a gift of healing or psychic powers, you had no right to charge money for that gift. If you charged money that gift would be taken from you. That got me thinking. Maybe some of these gifts did not come from God. If not God, I wondered, who could it be coming from? It was years later that I realized that the dark side of the force has the same powers as the light side of the force, they just use it in a different way. Reverend Marge said there was a woman named Tina who was staying with her until she could find housing in Oshkosh where she was attending college. Tina was very interested in UFOs and wanted to find out more about what was happening to us so they both came to our next meeting.

After telling Tina some of our experiences, we told her of our search for someone who could help us find answers and how we thought that could be done through hypnosis. We told Tina we were looking specifically for answers as to what had happened on our way to Huckleberry Campground after a UFO meeting. Tina said she knew someone who might be interested in working with us because he had helped her through a very difficult time in her life. He was a physiotherapist who used hypnosis in the treatment of his patients. The only problem was he lived and worked in Milwaukee. She thought he might be interested in seeing us, but she didn't know if he would do it gratis and would write to him the very next day. We were grateful for any help she could provide us. This meeting was on Sunday, and by the next week Thursday we heard from Hank. He said that he had no knowledge of UFOs or aliens but he would be willing to work with us for free. However, we would have to come down to Milwaukee for the sessions. We said yes immediately. Edna's husband happened to have an appointment in Milwaukee on September 9th of 1985; we dropped him off and then went on to Hank's office. As we entered his office, I was very apprehensive because I didn't know what to expect. After so many years of searching we were thrilled to have someone willing to work with us. I knew having him help us was good because he knew nothing about UFOs or aliens; therefore, he had no preconceived ideas of what questions he should ask or what could be remembered. Were we finally going to get the answers we were looking for all this time or would we find out that we were just fooling ourselves? The time for the truth was finally here, whatever it was.

Hank met us in the outer office. We each introduced ourselves. Hank took us into his office and while sitting there waiting for our first session I was scared. His office was a small room with no windows. Many photographs hung on the wall-papered wall and later I found out that he had taken most of them himself. The office had a small couch, a recliner and a straight chair. Hank sat in the straight chair, Edna was seated in the recliner, and I sat on the small couch.

Hank wanted us to tell him exactly what we remembered about the night with the missing time, in sequence. I don't know how I got up the courage but I asked Hank if we could tape the sessions, and to my surprise he said yes. I was very glad because I had already made up my mind that if he said no, I would leave.

We talked for a while; I know Hank was trying to create a safe zone/space for Edna and me. Hank thought we might be hiding our memories because it was traumatic, so he told us that he wanted us to view what had happened that night in cartoon form. That way we could view what happened as if we were not part of it.

He started to hypnotize us very slowly and took us back to five minutes before our missing time started. He purposely took us down a flight of stairs in a tree and we were to open the door and view what had happened to us that night. It started with Hank saying, "Bonnie is driving, what are you saying to each other?" I asked Edna, "Do you think we will see any UFOs," to which she replied, "I hope so."

I was driving my 1974 green Plymouth on the back road into a campground near New London, Wisconsin. As I turned down the side road that would eventually lead to the campground, I remembered seeing the sign that said Bean City. It was at this point that I saw the UFO. It was a mushroom shaped craft coming down over the road. It was silver in color and very shiny. It extended the whole width of the road and hovered about five feet above the road. A stairway came out of the center of the bottom of the craft and a "being" came down the steps.

Below is a drawing of the craft I had seen over the road on the way back to the campground near New London.

I stopped the car and was standing behind the car door for protection. The lights on the car were still on and the engine was running. Edna was crying in the front seat. I was afraid that if I went too close they would take me and not bring me back to my family. I could see the silver suit of an alien coming down the steps. The suit looked puffy at the sleeves and the ankles. The feet of the being had the same silver color covering. The being had a motorcycle-type helmet on its head with a black face plate in front so I couldn't see what its face looked like. (See drawing below.)

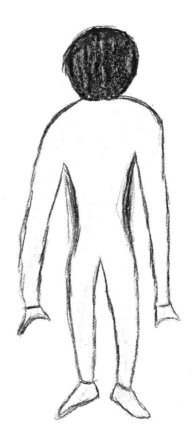

The alien made a motion for us to join him and I shook my head no. I looked over at Edna and saw that she was still crying. When he saw how scared we were, he made a hand signal like I would make to someone to "forget it." I knew they were disappointed that we did not want to go. I could feel deep inside my soul how disappointed this being was as it started up the steps. Somehow I knew he was going to leave. At that time I had been studying UFOs and aliens for approximately two years and here I was faced with the fact that, yes, aliens did exist. I decided it was stupid of me to miss an opportunity of my lifetime as it may never happen again. I don't know why, but I extended my hand toward him, palm up. I don't know how I got inside the craft but all of a sudden I was there.

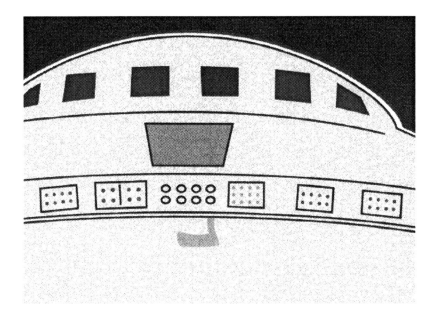

The first thing I noticed was how big it was on the inside, it looked so much smaller from the outside. The next thing I noticed was that it was all white in color and had a nice fresh, clean smell to it, not antiseptic like some hospitals smell. I could see that there were no seams in the whole ship; it looked like it was molded out of one piece of shiny metallic-looking material. There seemed to be one level with windows about two-thirds of the way up. The windows were higher than my head so I could not see out and it was rounded at the top. The ship was circular and on one side there was what looked like three large panels. There was a large screen above the center panel that looked like a T. V. screen, and on it I could see trees, roads and houses. I got a sense of feeling movement and could faintly see the lights of a city. Then I could see sky and stars so I knew that we were moving higher and higher.

There was a total of four beings on the craft. There were two types of beings on the ship, I could tell by the shape of their bodies. Most had broad shoulders, but one had small breasts and a smaller waist although they were about the same height. If only I could have seen the faces; it was impossible to do that with the type of visor they had on their helmets. One of the aliens came and stood just to my left and a little behind me. The top of his head was about shoulder height on me, which made him about five feet tall. I felt as if he were giving me permission to sit in the chair that was in front of the center panel from which they could fly the craft. As I sat in the chair I looked at the panels. Some had what looked like clear round plastic buttons with different symbols on them. I knew that these symbols were written in an interplanetary sign language that could be understood by different beings, you know, just like the signs that are on the bathroom doors with a drawing of a man or woman on them. Another of the panels had different colored buttons that flashed at intervals. I got the feeling that the aliens wanted me to steer the ship, and I hesitated for a moment before I touched anything. I didn't want to get myself in trouble. I knew that I should not touch the red button, so I pushed down on the green button and the ship dipped down. I couldn't feel much movement, but on the screen in front of me I could see the dark night sky, and then I could see the trees and ground coming up very fast. My stomach lurched or fluttered as it often does when you are in a car and it goes over a bump fast. As I looked at the alien for help; I got the feeling that they were amused at what I had done. The ship seemed to have its own gravity as the aliens and I had no trouble standing upright as the ship pitched back towards Earth. The ship seemed to level off by its self, so I left the driver's seat and started to investigate the rest of the craft.

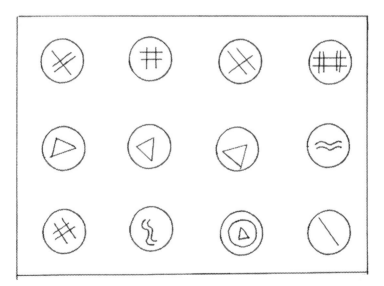

These are the button-like controls seen on one of the panels in the craft..

As I looked behind me at the symbols on the wall, I seemed to know what they stood for but didn't understand how I knew. The alien who was in charge started talking to me using telepathy. These were not words but pictures in my head. He told me that.

These are some of the symbols I saw on the craft.

1. **sign for maps**
2. **tracking device symbol**
3. **precision symbol**
4. **power source symbol**
5. **symbol for a planet**

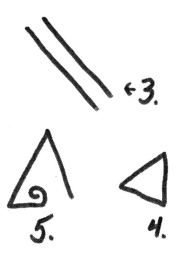

- We should be learning to be more understanding of our own people on Earth

- We should be more compassionate and keep an open mind at all times.

- We should learn all that we can and be willing to teach others what we know.

- We should be psychic explorers.

- He explained that I should be a teacher and teach the knowledge. (I had no idea what he was talking about.)

- Earthlings have a lot to learn before they can travel in space. (This was explained further in a channeling session years later.)

- There are many different types of species in space; not all of them look like what I had been taught. (This was different than what I had been learning at the UFO meeting place in Appleton.)

Then I saw the trees and lights and houses on the screen again. My thoughts returned to my family and I wanted to go home. I wondered what had happened with Edna because I had not seen her since I entered the craft. As the ship got closer to the ground I could see my car sitting in the road with the lights still on. I wondered if the car would start after all this time. All of a sudden I was back in the car with Edna and the car suddenly started, so I knew that the battery was not dead. Years later during a channeling session I learned the car had been taken along with us by the mushroom shaped craft through the use of something like magnets. As we looked around, I realized that we were not where we belonged. I had to drive around for quite some time to figure out were we were. We were on Highway 54, which is on the opposite side of New London from where we should have been.

After the session Hank asked what everything looked like when we went through the door. I told him that as I went through the door everything changed from cartoon to normal looking. Hank told me that I was the one who decided to go with the experience and that I was much stronger emotionally than I gave myself credit for.

Years later I went back and retraced the drive we had taken that night trying to figure out how long it should take to make the trip. It took 32 minutes for the ride from Appleton to the campground. There was also a problem with the amount of gas left in the tank. It was impossible to drive around for that amount of time, let alone drive to the campground from home, then to Appleton and back, and still have that much gas left. Maybe the aliens thought that we would eventually come to the conclusion that something did happen and could search out the answers, which is what we did.

At this session Hank gave us the suggestion to remember more of our experiences and this I did. As a matter of fact it was as if a floodgate had been opened. I now have many memories of what happens when I go to the spacecraft. I have not shared many of these memories with anyone because I can hardly believe what is happening. I am always hoping someone will share their experience with me that will validate what has happened to me.

Many strange things and sounds have showed up on the tapes of our hypnosis sessions. On one of the tapes we could hear the secretary typing in the outer office and the door bell jingling as someone came in, but we could not hear our voices that were in the same room with the tape recorder. Many times I would tell Hank what I was remembering; he would always ask questions about the memories and would reassure me that I was not crazy. One time I was listening to one of the tapes of our sessions and all of a sudden I could hear what sounded like a helicopter. I could hear the whoop, whoop of the blades and then I could hear a click like someone keyed a mike and said "that's right, we have it all on tape." I could hear the mike key again and then heard the whoop, whoop of the blades as it seemed to move away. Then I could hear the office noises again. The next time I played the tape, the noise of the helicopter was not there. I lent the tape to Edna and she heard it only one time. Her daughter also heard it, but the next time it was played the noise wasn't there. I played the tape four times and then heard the noise and someone speaking a second time, my daughter was there and also heard it. Then I knew that we were not crazy and what we heard was not our imagination.

We explained to Hank what we had heard on the tapes, and he had a hard time believing it. I told Hank that my house was entered and searched; we always locked the doors whenever we went away so I guess technically it was not broken into. They must have had some way of entering without forcing their way in. It always seemed to happen when I was out of town and meeting him. I guess it was the only time they knew I would be away most of the day. I got so paranoid that I even left a string in the door and when I came home it was lying on the floor. Another time I came home and found a man's Gray short sleeve work shirt with a J.C. Penney's label in the back. Later a pair of small brown cotton garden gloves was left on the bed; it was strange because we did not have any gloves like that and both the gloves and the shirt were too small to fit anyone in the house. My office looks like a cyclone hit it all the time, but the tapes of the sessions are always stowed and rewound to the beginning of the tapes. Many times I would find them in the wrong order and not at the beginning of the tape as they should have been. It made me feel as if someone was entering my home and using or listening to the material that I was collecting. The funny thing is I have always said if anyone wants to know anything, all they have to do is come to my door and ask questions. Dale and I have always been willing to share everything that we have. I believe that someone or something is keeping track of what is happening; it gives me the creeps, but what can I do?

On one occasion Hank asked if I would like to do a past life regression. He thought that if I knew who I was in a past life it might give me some insight into my life now. So we did a couple of sessions of past lives and were very surprised at what came up. When I was under hypnosis, he asked me to go to a past life. Then he asked me to look around and tell him what I was seeing. I saw three large pyramids in the distance. For some reason I knew that these pyramids were made with the help of aliens who had been present during the period of time they were built. (In a later channeling session this was verified.) The aliens had taught humans the art of levitation, which was using an instrument shaped like magician's wand. After the aliens left the process was somehow lost. He asked me to look at myself. To my surprise I was a dark-skinned Egyptian who had on the loose-fitting clothes of a slave. I was carrying a large leather pouch that contained water, which I was giving to the slave workers who were building a smaller pyramid. The men suffered to finish these monstrosities many were often crushed by the stones or were worked to death. While watching what was going on my heart felt very heavy. The slaves were nothing to these overseers and often died at a very young age. The taskmasters who were working for the king had their eyes set on the finished product, which was to be done as quickly as possible no matter what the cost, and nothing else mattered.

Another of the regressions took me to the time of Jesus the Christ. I was a woman who saw Jesus speak and followed Him from a distance. I remember how He spoke to each person in a manner that reached each individual in the way that was needed. Everyone felt that Jesus spoke to him and only him. He spoke with the authority of someone who believed totally in what He was saying. I saw Him heal many people who are not written about in the Bible. It also amazed me that there were many women following Christ and He accepted these women as equals to the men who were His disciples.

In February of 1987 I asked Hank to help me with a problem I was having with the channeling I was doing. There was some apprehension on my part. I told him I believed that as a channel I had the responsibility for the accuracy of what was said to the listener. Maybe I would not be held responsible in this lifetime but at some point in time I believed I would be. I also feel that if you cause people harm by your thoughts and actions you must take responsibility for that action. You cannot interfere in the path people have chosen for themselves.

Hank asked if I felt the messages were harmful to anyone or were the messages such as they could help spiritually. I answered the messages could help people spiritually and because I had a close relationship to Monn and the other aliens I felt that I could trust them. Hank said, "All I had to do was remember that I had control of the situation; I could stop at anytime I felt things were going to hurt anyone. He told me I had the strength and could stop at any time and I was much stronger that I gave myself credit for." He said that if I felt the messages did not seem right I did not have to pass on the message. Hank stated I was like a flower opening up. I had sat in the background and let other people lead and the time would come when I would probably take the lead. So I must stay strong and keep God as the pilot in my life's endeavors and then I could never go wrong. My only thought was, "why me, why did this happen to me?" It was time for me to accept the fact that I had volunteered for more than I realized.

One day Hank asked if he could bring his son to join in a session and speak with Monn. To my surprise I said yes; sometimes answers just pop into my head and come out of my mouth before I even think about it. The next time we met Monn spoke to them. I don't know everything that was said during the session because Monn requested that it not be taped. Hank told me later that Monn had asked his son to stay in school and learn all that he could because he would be using the knowledge he learned in the future.

The channeling has continued. One of the things that I have learned is that when I channel, my soul moves over and the aliens soul comes in, uses my voice box and any part of my body that they need to get their points across. I leave my body and fly anyplace I want to go in the universe. Because my consciousness leaves my body I seldom remember what is said during a channeling session. I seem to like visiting warm places but sometimes visit cold places and come back feeling very chilled. One time they told me not to eat food before a session as it was hard for my body to digest the food, so now I try not to eat before the channeling happens. There have been times when a session was cut short because the aliens said that my body needed to use the bathroom. Now I make sure that I use the bathroom before I start the session. When I listen to the tapes I am surprised at some of the answers to the questions that are asked, because I certainly would not have answered the questions the way they did.

I would like to get back to the story of Tina. She continued to come to our meetings for some time and often brought her son along. Tina went to an old theater that had just been remodeled in Oshkosh and was in use again. Many people claim the theater is haunted, and some say they have seen ghosts in it. Tina told us that when she was there she felt an evil presence and felt it had followed her home. She did not like the feeling and it was definitely bothering her. At one of our meetings Monn came through and told Tina that she should take some time to be with her son. Shortly after that Monn said she should tell her son how much she loved him, more often than she normally did and also suggested that she go to a doctor and have her health checked. Tina did not go to the doctor and within two weeks she was dead. She was only thirty-seven years old when she had a heart attack. No one in our group knew that she had a heart condition; could Monn see something in the future that we did not? Sometimes I ask myself if one of Tina's commitments in this lifetime was to introduce me to Hank the hypnotist and once that was accomplished she was free to go on to another exist-ence elsewhere. At other times I can only conclude that Tina's soul knew her body needed medical attention and tried to warn her. This has been a mystery for me and I often wonder if Monn will ever give anyone else such a message.

Fire Walking

One day I received a telephone call from Hank. He asked me if I were sitting down and I said no. Hank said, "Please do." After I sat down he asked, "Have you ever thought of doing a fire walk?" I told him that I had watched people doing fire walks on the television program, "In Search Of" and wondered if it were possible or maybe it was just some kind of a trick. He said he was going to have a fire walk and wanted me to participate. I said I had to think about it, we talked a little more, and I hung up. As I started to walk away from the telephone I asked myself, "Why are you hesitating?" It was something I often thought about doing, so I went back to the phone, called him, and said, "Count me in!"

Creating a firewalk is an all-day process. First you start by building a large bonfire using about two cords of firewood, leaving the wood to burn until there is nothing but hot embers left. While the fire is burning you dig a pit six inches deep, four feet wide and twelve feet long. After that is done you get a pep talk. You are taught to call upon a higher source to help you on your mission. Hank asked us to call upon whomever we knew the best. Some people called on God or Jesus. I asked my alien friends to help me get through this tough test. Hank gave us a lecture to encourage us to trust our inner strength. He explained how we each have everything we need to accomplish whatever is needed because we have everything inside of us. We only need to learn how to tap into our resources.

When the coals are ready they are placed in a pit and patted down smoothly so that no one stumbles and gets hurt. You stand at one end of the pit with Hank, who helps you prepare for your walk. As I stood at the head of the coals I had some fear that my feet would be burned but I knew in my heart I could accom-plish the fire walking. Let me tell you, you don't stand at the beginning of the coals with bare feet feeling the heat slowly drifting towards you without first tell-ing your body that it can do anything that it needs to do to protect itself. When I was ready Hank sent me on my way to the most powerful, exhilarating experience I have ever had: the realization that I had the power to take any action that I needed to protect myself. Wow! What a high to realize that I had the power to control my life.

As you finish the fire walk you are stopped by a person at the end of the pit because you are so focused on the walk that you don't realize it is over. Then another person sprays your feet with water making sure there are no embers sticking to them. Then you jump for joy after you have made the trip down that long, long twelve feet of coals without a burn or scratch. Some people would run down the bed of red-hot coals, some walked slowly. I always walked with a big smile on my face. Each person walked in his or her own manner and each person had a personal reason for walking, which we did not necessarily share. In the fire walks that I participated in not one person was burned or injured. The first time I fire walked I took a friend with me. We did this walk in November. After Beverly and I finished our walk we went to her car and took of our shoes and socks to make sure our feet weren't blistered or burned.

Hank did a good job of getting us all to visualize how we had that power within us to accomplish anything we needed to do. You can use a fire walk to help with any part of your life. If your life needs help with drinking, drugs, an abusive relationship, or whatever, you can do it. We all have that power within us. The moment you finish, you capture the power and want to share it with your friends. I persuaded some of my friends into doing fire walks, hoping that it would help them in their lives. I am sad to say that they didn't have the same experience that I did. They continued to have the same things happen over and over in their lives.

From different people I have heard some very unusual stories of why I did the fire walks. Now I have a chance to tell the real reason I did them. Fire walking is a metaphor of life's fire walks of fears, habits, etc…it is a wonderful exercise of self-discipline and commitment to beat your fears and get more out of your life. Fire walking is your ability to face the problems that you have and your ability to learn how to overcome them. When you fire walk you learn to trust your body to do anything it needs to do to survive, without harming itself; but, more importantly, to learn to survive without damaging your soul. Mind over matter really works, so you have a choice of letting fear control your destiny or you can be the driver in your life and feel alive.

Hank and I kept in touch over the years. One day he called and told me he was getting married again. We had lunch together and I congratulated him. He explained how he had met Harriet and after only a short period of time they decided to get married. Sadly, the marriage did not last long and after the breakup he left the area. We kept in touch for a short period of time with Christmas cards, notes and phone calls as to what was going on in our lives. One day I got a call from Hank, and he said that he was having problems. I told him that if he was ever in the area he had a place to stay but I never heard from him again.

It is very hard when someone comes into your life and holds a special place in your heart and then leaves. I realize now that sometimes this is the way things are meant to be. Hank is always in my thoughts; my only wish is that some day I will receive a phone call from saying he's okay. So now another part of my life ended, and I wondered what my next adventure in learning would be.

A friend of mine was over after I had written this chapter and I told her I was thinking of including a picture taken during one of the fire walks. I explained how I could not use a picture with anyone else on it because I would need their permission. She agreed with me, so we picked one of me crossing the fire pit by myself. It just so happens that the very next week I ran into Beverly who had taken the photo and I asked her if I could use the picture. She agreed to let me use it, so I went home to retrieve the picture from the photo album but it was not there. How could it disappear from a photo album in such a short period of time? I hope that before this book is completed the photo shows up again so it can be used. Similar things have happened to me ever since I got into this field. Someone or something always seems to interfere with the process of getting this information out.

My Introduction to Eric, On a Large Space Ship

I often go in the back yard to look at the stars on nights when sleep is just beyond my reach. One night unable to sleep, I stepped out the back door and stood on the porch. It was a cool evening with the smell of fall in the air. The stars twinkled in the almost black sky. The moon was only a sliver so there was not much light in the night sky. As I stood looking at the sky, the hair on the back of my neck stood straight up. It was as if someone was watching me. I looked around but the street was empty with no cars in sight. Seeing no one there convinced me there was no one watching. As I turned quickly to go back into the house, my whole body shivered as if the temperature was below zero. Once back inside I locked the door, quietly trying to convince myself that I was just being paranoid. My husband had to work the next day and I did not want to wake him, so I decided to try sleeping on the couch in the living room. Getting the yellow fuzzy thermal blanket out of the closet, I happened to look at the clock, and it was 11:47 p.m. I lied down on the couch and covered myself with the blanket. Resting very quietly with my eyes closed, I could hear the quietness of the night, but the feeling of being watched still persisted.

Suddenly I realized there was a brilliant bright light in the room; it looked like a very bright spotlight. My eyes were closed, but I still could see what the room looked like during the daylight through my eyelids. It was like going to the beach on a hot sunny summer day and looking at the sun, then closing your eyes and seeing the sun shining brightly through closed eyelids.

I tried to open my eyes; I tried to move but couldn't. I was paralyzed and agitated at the same time! My muscles would not answer the commands my brain was sending them. I tried to call for help; nothing came out of my mouth. Taking deep breaths and trying to calm myself down, I realized that I could breathe. Maybe I was having a heart attack? Did I have pain radiating down my left arm? Was I sweating profusely? No, I guess I was not having a heart attack.

All of a sudden, I could see three beings in the living room with me. Looking through my closed eyelids I could see what looked like the outlines of three beings with no shape except what looked like a head with a neck and shoulders. They seemed to be radiating the bright light. My heart was pounding; what are they doing in my house? How did they get in; aren't the doors and windows locked? How could this be happening? Then in my mind I heard them speak, "Have no fear, we will not harm you."

This represents what the alien beings looked like who appeared in my living room.

As I calmed down, I realized that I could move and my eyelids would open. The beings looked like what people are now calling light beings. They stood in a golden light so bright that all I could see was an outline of a figure inside this bright light. My yellow fuzzy blanket was no longer on me. I couldn't see it…where did it go? They said, "Follow us." My heart stopped beating fast and I felt love and compassion coming from these beings. I could feel that they meant me no harm. So I got up and stood between them, two in front of me and one behind. We moved single file through the front door, our feet never touching the floor. I thought to myself, who are they, where did they come from and how could this possibly be happening? I could feel in my mind their amusement at my reaction of doing such an improbable thing. My mind was racing, why was I calmly following them? How did they know what I was thinking and how did I know what they were thinking?

After going through the front door of the living room, my mind demanded clarification. Wait just one minute, how could we go through the door without opening it? I could feel them smiling at my questioning mind. We crossed the street in front of my house. There was an open field and in the middle of it was a small ship on the ground. It was round, saucer shaped, about 30 feet in diameter, silver in color, and standing on three legs. On the other side of this open field is Highway 41, which is one of the main north and south highways in Wisconsin. I was thinking, it is late, there are only a few cars on the highway, but no one seemed to see this unusual sight. None were stopping to look at us or the craft. Why weren't the cars stopping? How could they not see what was going on? The beings answered in my head, "We have a force field up, so they cannot see the ship. We can do this anytime we wish; that is why we are only seen when we want people to see the ships."

I don't remember how I got into the small craft…just all of a sudden I was inside. It looked larger from the inside than it looked on the outside. The three beings who escorted me to the craft were the only ones on board. But wait a minute, now that we were inside of the craft they did not look like light beings anymore. Could this be because of the difference in the earth's atmosphere or vibrations to what was inside the ship? I didn't know, but it seemed reasonable to me. They looked almost human now that it was easier to see them. They had small eyes and a round mouth and wore an olive green two piece suit. I looked around the craft, being very careful not to touch anything. Surprisingly, they allowed me to do so and seemed happy that I was so interested in how it worked; the interior looked very much like the craft in my Cleveland encounter.

We traveled for what seemed like a few minutes. I could see on a screen that we were approaching a ship about the size of a large city and it had an opening on the underside where smaller ships could enter. The small craft I was on entered the larger ship and the door hatch closed behind us. What I saw inside reminded me of a marina with lots of places for boats to dock. Instead of boats at the docks there were airships of different sizes, suspended in the air, somehow connected to the docks.

I became excited again and had to talk myself into being calm once more. The beings said, "You should leave the craft now as someone wants to talk to you." As I got out of the small ship and started walking down the dock, I noticed four very human-looking beings who seemed to be waiting to escort me out of the docking area. As we left the docking area we walked down something that looked like piers. That is when I noticed a man with dark sandy hair sitting behind what looked like a desk. He seemed to be questioning those coming off the ships before they were allowed to go through a door that I assumed to be the entrance to the ship itself. As we approached, he motioned us to go straight through. That seemed strange to me…why was I not stopped and questioned like everyone else? Were the aliens expecting me, if so why?

After going through the door, I was escorted down a long corridor by the same four beings. The ceiling and walls appeared to be concave although the floor was flat. The halls were very well lit; the light seemed to be generating from the ceiling and walls with the same intensity. I could see no light bulbs, panels, or fluorescent lights. Every so often there was what looked like panels that I assumed were doorways. There were no handles on these openings and I learned later that the openings were doors that slid into the wall like pocket doors. I took a deep breath and smelled what seemed like clean fresh air. It was very refreshing and invigorating. The four beings were keeping their eyes on me as we were moving through the ship.

When we came to a solid wall, it slid to one side, and upon entering I could see a small circular room and realized I was in a lift or elevator of some sort.

We got off the lift and proceeded down the hallway to another doorway. I looked around and saw a small room with chairs and a couch. The beings that had escorted me to this room suggested that I go into the next area because someone there was waiting for me. I tried three times before my feet would carry me into the next area. It was almost as if I knew that upon entering the room, my whole life would change. I knew instinctively my life would never be the same because of whatever or whoever was waiting for me.

Taking a deep breath and walking through the opening, I encountered a being that was hard for my brain to accept. At the same time, a feeling of great attraction entered my body, almost as if I were seeing a very dear friend whom I had been separated from for a very long time. He held himself with great dignity and was so sure of himself I just knew that everyone had a great respect for this being. Much later I learned that he was the captain of this ship. There he stood: I knew he was male, all seven feet plus of him. His skin was blue and did not look like ours. He had soft down like feathers on his body, and I could not see any clothes.

His head had a strange shape, almost like an eagle's head. He had a mouth that was shaped like a beak. He had an abnormally long thin neck. He had two arms which were longer than normal for his height. At the end of his arms were hands which had five appendages. At the ends of his fingers were things that looked like talons. His torso was quite thick but thin, he had no waist definition. His legs had no feathers or down on them and were short for his torso size; they were thin without any shape except for his knobby knees. At the end of his legs were circles where feet normally would be. His eyes were most striking, they looked like pools of beautiful blue waters off the island of Aruba. His eyes were all blue with no white. Maybe the best way to describe him is that he looked like a thin Big Bird except he was blue. He called himself Eric.

He scared me because he was so big and so different from anything I had seen; but at the same time I knew he would not harm me. Eric told me my whole belief system was wrong. He said that not all aliens are blond, blue-eyed, neither looking male or female. The most important thing I had to learn was that in space not everyone looked alike, nor do they think alike. My whole perception of the Universe was changed in the blink of an eye.

This big blue being stretched out his arms towards me as if to give me a hug. I hesitated, not knowing if I wanted those arms and talons around me. When I looked into his eyes, I knew there was nothing to fear. Going into his arms I received and gave the best hug ever. At the instant of the hug, I knew I was home. This was where I belonged; I knew Earth is not my true home. He unfolded his arms from around me, and said, "There are some beings here that I wish you to meet and remember; this is one of the lessons that you must learn."

We went through another doorway that was on the other side of the room, and I saw sixteen different types of beings. All of them were so very different looking that I wondered how I could explain this to anyone. Some had what looked like long hair all over their bodies and were over six feet tall. Some were short in stature and looked somewhat like the Pillsbury Doughboy, white and almost as wide as they were tall. There was a rainbow of different colored skins. All of the aliens that I saw had one body, one head, two arms, and two legs but not necessarily in the proportions we are familiar with. It was then that I realized not all beings in the universe would look like us. Some of the beings looked somewhat human and they had on long brown robes with hoods. I suggest that you rent the first Star Wars movie produced and go to the barroom scene, inside the Mos Eisley Cantina, so you can get some idea of what the beings looked like.

The room had four large, kidney-shaped tables and each table had four chairs. At one end of the room was a large desk with one chair. I had the distinct feeling that this was a meeting room, almost like our government meeting rooms. There were four distinct groups of beings nonchalantly walking and visiting with each other. I had the feeling that I was expected to visit with the four groups. I don't remember much of the conversations that I had with each type of alien. The first group of four aliens that I spoke to was in charge of the evacuation of earth humans. Group two was in charge of plant life and making sure of their survival. The third group was in charge of the evacuation of the earth animals. The fourth group is still a mystery to me. The only thing I can remember is that these aliens are a lot like humans, not only in looks but actions. They were laughing and milling around and seemed to be having a good time. So this group I have named the goof-offs.

At each chair was a different type of being representative of his/her planet. Some looked almost human.

Many were drinking something out of a container that looked like glass but I don't think it was. I was offered a drink and, being a good guest, I accepted. It was blue in color and could be rolled around in the glass; some of it would stick to the sides of the container. This semisolid, blue-colored liquid looked and acted a lot like Jell-O just before it sets up. It was fun rolling the semi-solid liquid back and forth in the container, seeing how close I could get it to the rim of the container and not have it spill out. There did not seem to be a distinct taste to it. I asked what it was and the only answer I remember is "happy juice." It is something like our wine and is made from the extract of a fruit or vegetable type plant. This is a natural drink with no chemicals or coloring added, and it did not have alcohol like some of our drinks do. (See drawing below)

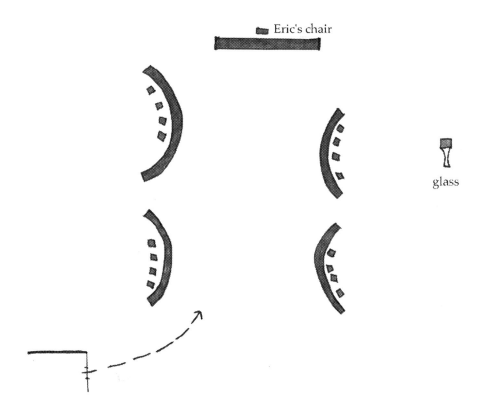

I was told it was time to leave, but I did not want to leave this place because it seemed as if I had finally found what I had been searching for my whole life. I felt as if this ship was where I belonged. One being then escorted me back to the small scout craft that I had arrived in. Back in the small craft were the three beings who had originally brought me to the ship. It seemed only minutes before we landed back in the field across from my house. Again no cars seemed to take notice of the craft on the ground. Again I floated back across the road and through the front door. I was then deposited back on the couch in a lying position, covered by my blanket. Again I was not able to move my muscles and the bright lights hurt my eyes, even with the lids tightly closed. The bright lights began to fade. By the time the lights were gone I could move my arms, legs and eyelids. With my body functional again, I got up and checked on my children and husband; they were still asleep. The clock said 12:35 a.m. How could all of this have happened in less than an hour? I checked all the doors and they were still locked. Did I fall asleep and dream this? No, impossible!

My husband is a really light sleeper but did not wake up as I climbed into bed with him. I tried shaking him but he did not stir. I looked at our dog Sandy, who was sleeping. This was very unusual as she usually barked at any movement in the house. Getting back out of bed, I again tried to wake the dog but had no luck. Becoming desperate, I gently nudged her with my foot, no use, she flopped around like a fish out of water. I crawled back into bed and started running everything over and over again in my head. I had to try one more time to wake my husband; again no luck. I started to shake uncontrollably and felt like I had been in a freezer for a long time.

It was about three months before I told anyone about this experience. How could anyone else believe me when it was unbelievable even to me? Much later the aliens explained how they had put my family in a deep sleep state. This was done because the aliens did not want my family to wake up and become frightened or agitated if they were to find me missing from the house.

So now my perception of the Universe, no, Universes, had changed. How big everything is, how different we all are but in some ways very much alike. I have been to this ship very often since then and learned that I have a room on board. It took a long time for me to accept this as fact; again I was not willing to accept things at face value. I had to have proof and it was not forthcoming. I had to learn that things could exist without having tangible proof.

Evacuation Ship and Planet with Housing

One night during my sleep the aliens took me to an unfamiliar ship where I was shown a huge square craft with rounded edges. It was shiny and silver in color and glowed with an unknown radiance. The aliens told me that this ship would be used for the evacuation of people from planet Earth.

As they showed me around the craft I saw individual cubicles. Some of them were small for only one person while some were large enough for the families that would be lifted off Earth when and if that is needed. The rooms were white in color and sterile looking. The aliens asked my opinion of the areas I had seen, I answered them as best I could. I explained that the rooms should not be so sterile looking, that they needed some color, plants, and pictures to make people feel more at home, maybe include something to remind people of Earth or they may get restless after a short period of time. There were sleeping bunks and storage areas built into the walls. I also saw a mirror over what looked somewhat like a sink. I don't remember seeing anything that looked like a bathroom, but that doesn't mean it wasn't there. I saw a large central cooking area where food would be prepared and a large dining area.

The common areas were beautiful. There were trees and grass that looked similar to ours, but they were not the same colors. There also was a small creek running through the area. They showed me shopping areas where you could stroll around and purchase things. I asked what kind of money people would be using for the purchase of necessities. Needless to say, I received some strange looks. They explained that they don't have anything like money, so I suggested humans would need some form of money to purchase items. This is a very important part of our lives; to some money is like a God. It was at this point I noticed that the being with me had what looked like our I-pods and was writing down what I was saying.

I knew the ship was big, so I asked what the size of the ship was. Instead of getting an answer, I was taken to a meeting or conference room where there was a large screen at one end. It looked like a movie theater on Earth. As I stood before the screen they showed me standing in the parking lot of a grocery store in Neenah where I often worked. From there I could see Highway 41, which had only four lanes wide at that time. A little to the right the highway rises over Highway 114 that is also four lanes wide. The alien told me to keep looking at the screen. Then I saw a craft rise from behind Highway 41; it was enormous. It went past Highway 150, which is about two miles to my right (north), to my left (south) and extending to the Breezewood Lane exit for a total of three miles. As it was rising the enormity of it hit me. It just kept rising. My neck was tipped so far back it was hurting and I still could not see the bottom of the ship.

I asked how they knew which people were to be picked up. They answered that everyone and everything puts out a vibration and by this they can tell whose vibration is at a level where they can survive being picked up. They also explained that vibrations of people often change and it was something that must be worked on all the time. This made me realize that no one has a guaranteed ticket off planet Earth. Many of the people I have had contact with over the years think that no matter what, they will be lifted off the planet when things get rough. The aliens explained that many people who are spiritual will stay on the planet to help those who are left behind. What they said was, "It is not important to save the physical body, it is important to save a person's soul."

It was also during this time period that they took me to a planet which was very similar to Earth. I remember being shown a row of homes that were two to three stories high but very narrow. They were blue in color and seemed to be set into the side of a very high, steep rock that was almost vertical. The houses were all connected but each had a walkway to the front door. The walkways looked as if they were made of crushed stone; it certainly did not look like concrete. There did not seem to be roads or anything that looked wide enough to be roadways. The finish on the houses was shiny, almost like plastic, it did not look like wood. There were curtains in the windows, and everything looked neat and clean as if no one were living there yet.

There were big structures similar to our enclosed football stadiums where masses of people could gather. There was no grass in the center of this area but there were many flowers and trees, almost like being inside a botanical garden or biosphere. The colors of the flowers were the most beautiful I have ever seen. Around the outside there was something very short green and lush. The next thing I knew I was back in my bed slowly waking up.

Over the years I have thought of this very often. They showed me a ship and a planet that was being prepared for humans if it was necessary. I find it very comforting that someone would take the time and trouble to prepare a place for us, if it were needed.

Good Friday, Who Is That?

I was working as a food demonstrator at a local grocery store on Good Friday, March 24, 1989. My job that week was to demonstrate Grammy Bears. This is a graham cracker product aimed at young children. I was working at the end of the middle frozen food isle, facing the checkouts and doorways. I was telling everyone how this product could be used in Easter baskets instead of candy.

Between one and three o'clock in the afternoon a man, or maybe I should say what looked like a man, walked past me. There was no noise as his heels touched the floor, which made it look like he was floating above the floor. He was not walking like a normal man. He moved with his face looking straight ahead, neither his shoulders nor his arms were moving. He seemed to be about a head taller than most men and walked as if he had a definite purpose. His hair was a sandy blond color, parted in the middle, wavy or draped off to the side and a little past his shoulders. The hair was very fine, soft and fluffy and bounced as he walked. Next I noticed his clothes. He had on a plaid shirt. His pants were made of jean material—they looked new and were dark blue in color. He had on a pair of boots; the toes were not pointed or squared. I felt they were boots but not cowboy boots as I could see the outline of the top of them through the legs of the jeans. The most unusual thing he had on was his coat. It was also made of denim-like material but looked new because it was also dark blue in color. The coat was floor length and quite full. There was a slit up the back that ended at his buttocks so that it looked like there were tails flowing behind. They seemed to bellow and flow behind him as he walked. There was not a wrinkle in that coat; I could not see how he could sit down and not get some wrinkles.

Another thing I noticed was that everyone was watching him just like I was; he was absolutely spellbinding. Even the men in the store turned around and watched him. This man had no grocery items in his hands and he was not pushing a cart. I never saw his face. The first time he walked past, I thought, boy this is strange. Seldom does a man get my attention! It was as if I knew the man but could not figure out how or where I met him.

He was walking from my left to right, and I kept my eyes on him until I couldn't see him anymore. After a few minutes he came from my right to the left. I had the strongest urge to look at his face. I just knew that if I could see his face I would know him. He stopped just across from my stand, but with his back toward me. I offered him some of my Grammy Bears, but he did not respond. I thought I would go over to him and offer him some bears, then he has to look at me even if only to say no. At that instant he took off walking toward the checkouts and the front doors. I wanted to follow him, but we could not leave our stands with food sitting out. He started to exit through the checkouts without stopping I could see him heading towards the front door of the building.

All of a sudden I had to see his face and did not care if I lost my job. I put the tray of food on the bottom shelf of my stand and carefully worked my way through the checkouts as fast as I could. By the time I was at the front door I was almost running. I went out the same door that he did, looked around and could not see him. He seemed to disappear—no one could move that fast!

Later during a channeling session we asked Monn who that person was. Monn answered that it was He, Jesus the Christ, who had come to Earth to check on humans. I know that answer seems far fetched, but it made sense. Why wouldn't Christ come to Earth to see how things were going? In the same channeling session we asked if He had visited anyone else during that particular Good Friday, and Monn said, "Yes. He made three stops." A priest in Pennsylvania was the answer. According to a report we saw in the newspaper, the priest was also visited on Good Friday. The aliens did not give us any information about the third person. We also asked Monn if anyone had recognized him and the answer was no. That was very hard to believe except that we all have a hard time just keeping our heads above water and don't seem to pay much attention to what is going on around us.

How did I get myself into this predicament? All I wanted to do was to study UFOs and try to figure out if they were real or not. Now here was this Jesus factor, and I started to wonder if God would be brought into the equation next. It was hard for me to accept the fact that maybe religion or spirituality had anything to do with UFOs. I had to put that knowledge in the back of my head and decided to wait for something else to occur that would prove or disprove what had happened.

Camping Again

A woman I'll call Annette joined the group. She is the most vibrant person I know. She has a ready laugh that can always bring a smile to my face.

Annette, Candy, and Krita decided to go camping for a couple of days. It was late fall with warm days but the nights were getting colder, and once the sun went down it got very damp. The dew made everything wet in the morning. We had to wear sweats, jackets, gloves and knit hats just to be comfortable once the sun went down. I am only a fair-weather camper, and it was definitely too cold for me to go camping. Dale, who had to work that day, and I decided to join the girls for a night around the campfire, but we were wise enough to go home and sleep in our own warm beds.

A woman named Betty from the southern part of the state came to our meetings once in a while. It was Saturday and Betty called and said she would like to join us. I explained that we were going to meet the girls at a campground and have our meeting around a campfire. Betty said she would love to join us; she drove as far as my house, and the three of us drove to the campground together.

To keep warm we built a big campfire and laughed at how hot it was so we moved our chairs away from the heat. We talked about UFOs, the Bible, and what it all meant to us. The stars were just beginning to peek out of a dark moonless sky. I had to go to the bathroom so I took my flashlight and walked down the road, which was ominously dark. Because of the darkness I decided not to walk all the way to the flush toilets, instead opting for the pit toilets which were fairly close. On my return trip I could see the blazing campfire and hear the laughter of my friends. The flames of the fire were reaching about three feet into the black night sky. In four chairs were my best friends; in the fifth chair was Betty. I had a hard time warming up to Betty, but I wanted to get to know her better because she claimed to have had some experiences with aliens.

As I sat down my friend Candy started telling a story she had heard about campfires. She said, "White men build big hot fires, then move away from the heat. Native Americans build small fires for warmth and move closer." Everyone laughed as we each placed another piece of wood on the fire and in unison moved our chairs away from the heat.

We talked about the aliens we were in contact with, and Betty shared a few stories about the aliens she had been in contact with for many years. She explained that they had been in her home many times and often made noises as if they were working or building something. She had one alien friend in particular that she called Teddy; she claimed he was her protector and would not let anything bad happen to her.

Betty explained that she could call him to her anytime she wanted and he would always respond to her call. We asked her how that could be, didn't he have anything else to do than be at her beck and call. She described how she would talk to him in her head and said she could call him down now. She asked if we wanted her to call him right then and there, she would have him land in the woods. We all sat with our mouths open; she became very quiet and looked as if she were concentrating. Then she pointed to the sky, saying something like "They are coming."

Everyone became very quiet, each of us deep in our own thoughts. I thought to myself, who does she think she is? Does she really believe she can do that? My heart started pumping faster and faster. Prayer was the only thing I could think of doing. I said, "Please, dear God, if these are not the good guys don't let this happen, don't let them come." All of a sudden there was a shuffling noise coming from the woods, it sounded like it was coming closer and closer, as if more than one person were walking. If only there were more light, so we could see better. I did not feel deep in my heart as if these were the good guys, so again I said, "Oh my God, is this really happening?" The shuffling in the dead leaves was coming closer, and whatever it was, was coming out of the woods. Oh my, raccoons! Only a family of raccoons in search of food, thank you, God. I was afraid it was aliens who abduct and experiment on humans. Betty laughed and said, "If we had been true believers, the aliens would have come."

As we were discussing the Bible and the churches that were mentioned in it, Betty was arguing with us about what it meant. She is very strong in her beliefs, and we knew instinctively not to disagree with her because we all have the right to our own opinions. I saw Annette whisper something to Krita and did not find out until later what the fuss was about. Annette whispered to Krita very quietly, asking her if she had hit her on the head. Krita said she didn't and asked if she really thought someone had hit her on the head. Annette said yes and wanted to know if she didn't hit her on the head, then who did. They both looked around and there was no one who could hit her on the head. Much later Annette explained to us that she should jump up and defend us but she didn't because someone had hit her on the side of her head. My guess is that someone had done that to prevent an altercation with Betty, as it would not have been beneficial to anyone.

Much later Betty came to another meeting at my house. She happened to come in as we were discussing a channeling session with some very personal information in it. She saw that we were reading something and demanded we share the information with her. She also said that if we did not share the information she would go up to the space ship and get the information herself. She felt she could get whatever information we had and threatened to go into our records and read everything in our files to find out about us. I was angry by this time. After all who did she think she was, coming into my home demanding information? I told her that if she thought she could get private information to give it a try because I knew in my heart that she could not get it. There was no way she was going to intimidate me or threaten my friends in my home and get away with it. The funny thing was we probably would have shared whatever was not of a personal nature with her, if she had asked nicely.

After that night I did not have a very good relationship with Betty for a long time. I am ashamed to admit that I was angry for a long time but eventually came to grips with the situation. Years later we met at the funeral of a mutual friend where we hugged and hopefully set the past behind us.

The Lightside Newsletter

In the fall of 1990 we decided we would print a newsletter to help bring people with like minds and ideas together. At that time there were quite a few members in the group, and it was agreed that if each of us wrote one article we could publish a good-sized newsletter. We had to come up with a name and one member suggested the Light Side. We decided it was a good name because it also described our desire to shine some light into the darkness on this planet. Our bimonthly, introductory issue came out in November of 1990. It was fun because each of us, by ourselves, would decide what our article would be about. When they were submitted at the meeting, we would discuss which order to put them in and thought it was funny because almost every time one article would lead nicely into the other. It seemed as if someone was directing each of us to write something that needed to be said and each newsletter had a central theme. Our first printing of fifty copies grew to over two hundred copies in September of 1992, when publication ceased. We were sending the newsletters out to anyone who requested a copy with some of them even going overseas. During this time we did not ask for any money because we felt just getting the information and material out was important.

If anyone wanted his or her meeting listed in the newsletter, we were willing to include that. We did some book and video reviews and also offered to print other people's thoughts. We also volunteered to answer any questions readers might have for the aliens if we could. Our main idea was to get people to openly discuss different topics and maybe get some conversation going.

Many of our articles included material that we had gotten from our alien contacts, although we did not say so. To our surprise not many people wrote with questions nor their own thoughts. On the plus side only two people over the years asked to be removed from our mailing list. I know that many people read the articles because I got feedback from them, although they did not want to write anything for the newsletter. I know for a fact that some people laughed at what we were saying and then asked their psychic friends if what we had said was for real. This was all right with us because they were talking even if it was not with us as we had hoped.

The cost of printing and postage became very expensive, and we explained the problem in a newsletter and said if anyone would like to continue receiving the newsletter, it would be appreciated if they could make a donation of five dollars for a year to help defray the cost. To our surprise not many people were interested in paying the small fee. It was a hard decision, but we decided to stop the newsletter and try other things.

Sometimes I like to go back and read those articles and remember where the group was at that point, as many people who wrote for the Light Side newsletter have left the group. I just hope they are still are on the spiritual path that we were all trying to find and have stayed the course.

This venture has taught me to be very supportive of anyone who tries this venue of sharing with people. It is hard to keep focused, always trying to keep an eye on what you want to accomplish. Working on the newsletter confirmed for me that anything you think you can accomplish needs a lot of hard work, patience, and faith.

Victor and Sarah

Monn had explained that each of us was special in our own way, yet we felt that as a group we were not complete. So we were searching for someone who shared many of our beliefs.

At first I thought Hank, the hypnotist who was working with me, was the person we were looking for, but he did not seem interested. It was Dale who came up with the probable person in a very strange way. One night he sat straight up in his bed, woke up, and spoke these words, "If Hank won't do it, then David can." Dale shared this with us the next time we were together. We were all surprised with that name, but who in the world was David? None of us knew anyone with that name who was interest in UFOs or aliens. A movie made for television was on TV. It was a true story that had a composite character in it with the name David. We felt that the actor who played the character wasn't the one we were to contact but maybe the real person. We certainly did not think that we would be able to find him, so we just forgot about it.

Then we got an invitation to a lecture and workshop in Milwaukee that was put on by a Reiki Master. The person who was doing the lecture had written a book about his close encounters with an extraterrestrial whom he also claimed to channel. Dale and I decided that we had to see, if this man believed the same way we did. The date was April 29 & 30, 1989; I utterly enjoyed his lecture as he talked about many of the things that his alien friend Sarah had shared with him. It was during the lecture that we learned that he was staying in Wisconsin with a girlfriend only about sixty miles from my home.

Victor was not happy with the arrangements that the Reiki Master had made for his sleeping facilities. Dale volunteered to share his hotel room with him because he had an extra bed in the room and to his surprise Victor accepted his offer. As they were sitting in the room talking, Dale mentioned that he also talked to an alien and how she had suggested that we would meet someone who was known as David. Victor seemed interested in learning more about us. He came to a meeting, and continued coming whenever he was in the area.

We were invited to a meeting in the town where he was staying. My husband did not want me driving there by myself; he decided to drive me but would not attend the meeting. As we were driving, my husband and I got into a terrible argument. It was one of the worst fights we had in a long time. It was so bad that I grabbed the crystal that I wore around my neck; to my surprise the crystal exploded in my hand. As I looked at the pieces in my hand, I was astonished that the negativity I was feeling could have destroyed such a beautiful flawless stone.

Later during a channeling session with Monn this was discussed and she explained that for every action there is a reaction. This has kept me very aware of my feelings, it made me realize what could happen if I went to the negative side with my feelings and actions.

When Victor shared what he knew we realized what we were missing, that being the spiritual connection to God. Victor also got me started reading the Bible and understanding what it meant.

Victor talked to Monn and got to ask questions about some of the things that his alien friend Sarah was not willing to answer. He also got to ask questions about himself. One in particular that I remember was he often dreamed about steam engine-type trains and the noise that they made. Monn laughed when she heard him tell the story and said, "You know, when you think you are dreaming it is not necessarily so. Sometimes when you go to visit the ships you bring back memories, and the memory relates to something you know on Earth that you understand." The train noise was actually a memory of the powerful sounding engines he heard on the spaceship, and the sound of locomotives was the only way he could bring back the memory and recall it.

We got to talk to his alien contact Sarah and learned more about her and the planet that she came from, which is within the Pleiades system. It was very interesting to hear another alien talk about God. She discussed what was in store for the human race. We also learned that both Monn and Sarah had volunteered to come to earth at this time. It seems that Sarah came to study the makeup of the planet and what is happening to it. Monn, on the other hand, is strictly here to interact with humans and help raise our consciousness and spirituality.

Victor and Sarah brought many other topics to our attention during the short time we were together. Sarah channeled through Victor that concentration camps were being built in the United States. The United States had underground bases; these were alien bases, alien and government bases. Victor had material that talked about MJ-12, which was set up as a government agency to handle the alien agenda. We often discussed the Illuminati, the Trilateral Commission, the secret or invisible government, and the 500 families. Since this was the first time we had heard of the Illuminati and the 500 families who control this planet, we had to go out and research these topics. We learned from several sources about 300 families involved, and much to our surprise, the information we found was almost word for word the same information that Sarah and Monn had given us. The aliens believe that there are at least 500 families involved in the conspiracy to control the planet.

Victor talked about the how the mastermind of deception is the one in charge of the planet right now. He explained how the dark side is full of deceit. When asked if they are of the light, they will answer, "I'm of the light." They also will disguise themselves as angels of light. These dark forces have deceived many people and aliens including a lot in the New Age community. The dark aliens and the Illuminati know us by the light that shines from within us. We were told to remember one thing: the dark forces cannot tolerate God's light; they will shy away from it, so use it everyday. If we as light workers don't want to be fooled by these beings, we must learn to use our instincts daily so that we know the difference between the truth and half-truth.

It was discussed that many of our religions and the New Age Community have been infiltrated by secret societies and much misinformation has been given to these groups. Not even the extraterrestrials know when things are going to take place; only God knows, so be careful of anyone giving dates.

Sarah told us during a channeling session that the Nazis and U.S. government had a spacecraft. The military knows that there are two distinct extraterrestrial groups here at this time. The government is working with the abducting extraterrestrial beings. Implanting of humans with small objects is being done by the government as well as aliens. Both are using these for mind control, behavior control, and keeping track of people. Sarah said that both are looking for people with certain brain wave patterns to implant. Many of the implants are inactive and inconspicuous, but if you have any orifices you can be implanted. Monn has said many times that the most important thing to remember is if you have the light of the Creator in you, you can literally melt these implants and they cannot be used to control you.

It was also discussed how the people who are really running this planet and the aliens are trying to clone people on Earth although it has not been perfected yet (Remember this is 1989). There is a life-producing element which is attacked by many kinds of unknown viruses, and that is why cloning has not been perfected on this planet yet. According to Sarah, the aliens can make a duplicate of humans on another planet and bring the duplicate down here.

Rejuvenation of the human body was also discussed and this topic was new to me. It was explained that it had been perfected and done to some important people on planet Earth. It is being done in underground laboratories and is part of a pact that gives us a false eternal life. It was explained that there are some complications such as not being able to keep the immune system clean because of synthetic blood and it cannot keep common viruses at bay by producing antibodies. We also learned that the secret government and the aliens have the knowledge of reincarnation and the power to transfer the soul from one body to another, over-coming the birthing process. These beings on our planet are called walk-ins. This got me to thinking maybe the swapping of the body and spirit could be used when the Antichrist is assassinated and then supposedly miraculously recovers as it is described in the Bible. This sounded unbelievable, but a couple of years later I met a man who told a story of how his soul was transferred from one body to another, so maybe this can be done.

Both Sarah and Monn discussed meditation often because we seemed to have a hard time with it. Sarah spoke about meditation and using it every moment of your life. It is not something to be used at specific times like when you are in trouble. It is just like prayer. It should be done every moment of your awake time, especially prior to going asleep. Why would God give you this ability and why would you use it only once in awhile? Meditation and prayer are a gift from God; it is not complicated but we seem to like to make it so. Remember prayer is talking to God, meditation is listening to God. Both aliens asked us to use meditation and prayer to make peoples lives more fulfilling.

We had previously heard of E.L.F. waves, but Victor and Sarah shared how the waves can give people mood swings, make them sick to their stomach, increase nervousness, make them belligerent, and give them the urge to fight. They both talked about how we don't have to accept these waves. The only thing that will work against us are our own doubt and fear—we must have 100% faith so that the waves cannot hurt us.

We talked often with Victor about the battle of Armageddon and how it will be fought on all levels between family members, countries, galaxies, and even the smallest microorganisms. He said it is a battle between good and evil within every living thing. Wow, that made us start thinking about how things around us seemed to be getting worse! People seemed to be getting kinder and gentler or they were getting more harsh and cruel, with the division between the two getting wider.

As light workers we were told we could help the planet and universe soften the impact of Lucifer, Satan and the evil forces. We asked Sarah where Lucifer was and were told he was being held prisoner on an asteroid in a neighboring galaxy while awaiting trial. He has never been to our planet. She also suggested that we could find some of this information in Native American Indian Incan mythology.

Sarah and Monn have suggested that we educate ourselves about spells, incantations, mind control, and subliminal manipulations. The only time these things work is when you have no control over your own thoughts. No one has the power to control you unless you allow that to happen. If you allow magic or manipulation to affect you, it can defeat you. We were warned that when we allow ourselves to go to the dark side of the force, we do it to ourselves. We were also reminded to remember that darkness can't live in God's light.

Victor told us to remember the mastermind of deception, Satan, is the one who is in charge of earth right now. His friends and followers are coming to the planet by the thousands every day. He is not in a reptilian form but many of his representatives are. We were told that only the good aliens, spiritual hierarchy and those who are very spiritual, work for God. Only they could step in and stop man or anyone else from destroying this planet.

Sarah said it is true people's hearts can be fed by ego, but consider yourself very privileged to be around at these troubled times. We are privileged that the Creator gave us the opportunity to be here at this time. Light workers are a group of many who are very special, because when you chose the heavenly force, what is called God you have every right to feel special and should take pride in doing the Creator's work. Light workers are very loving and compassionate, oftentimes too trusting for their own good. Many light workers are looking for answers, and they will find them as soon as they start working on their purpose. So now is the time for light workers to start spreading the message of Christianity, Buddhism, Islam, or whatever religion they are. The basic message is for us to be a example of being loving to everyone and living with our neighbors in peace. How can we go into space and interact with whatever we contact if we cannot do it on our planet?

One of the times Victor was in the area it was summer and we decided to go on a camping trip. Victor and I were lying next to each other on lounge chairs, taking turns channeling. Sarah and Monn got mixed up as to which person to channel through, and even the aliens joked about getting mixed up. Victor's dog would run into the woods, bark and make a fuss, and come out a short time later. This happened over and over again, making us aware that something unusual was happening in the woods that we couldn't see. Everyone had the feeling that we were being watched from the woods; it was such an eerie feeling that we were all on edge.

At night we sat under the stars and looked for UFOs. On one night in particular we saw thirty-two high flyers. Now these weren't just lights in the sky. There were sometimes six or seven lights at a time making X's in the sky, or they would zigzag across the sky, stop and change directions, sometimes looking as if they were going to bump into each other. That was the most UFOs I have ever seen in one night.

I have lost track of this gentleman since he left the area and miss him so much. Most light workers have a hard time adjusting to earth and everything on it. They are highly evolved souls who generally have a hard time understanding why people behave and think the way they do. If you think you are a light worker and have these feelings, there is a good possibility that you are one.

The Loss of William A Very Special Light Worker

One night after doing our television show a man called and explained that he had been having sightings and encounters. I will call him William. We were very interested in what he had to say, so I went to meet him. William was married and had a daughter. He had a lot of things happening at his house during the night. He remembered going on board a large ship and having a small craft at his disposal so that he could travel back and forth to a larger ship and do missions. William started coming to our meetings and added a lot to them.

It was amazing to me that William could have such good memories of not only seeing ships but of being on board. Every week he had new memories to share with us. He had the clearest recall of anyone as to the types of jobs he did for the aliens. He had almost nightly memories of what occurred including where he went and who he was with. William drove a space ship and went on many missions, helping aliens accomplish what needed to be done with someone in a human body, one time even freeing someone who had been captured by the government and many times delivering information from one group of aliens to another. He would describe what the ships looked like and what he did on board various crafts. One time he remembered going to an underground installation the Grays, Reptilians and the US government had control of. He even described rescuing children who were being held hostage by the aliens.

This was the hardest chapter to write because it was my first encounter with a light worker of seemingly high spirituality discontinuing his commitment to do a job for humanity and not realizing he was doing it. This was an eye opener for me as it made me aware that if this can happen to someone with such a high degree of spirituality, it can happen to anyone.

William remembered a previous life as a light being on another planet, which, according to my understanding, is a highly developed spiritual being. He also remembered doing battle with the bad Gray and reptilian aliens. (Remember that not all of these types of aliens are bad.) I remember his saying one day that the aliens should give him their best shot because he was confident he could handle anything that they could throw at him. He felt he was very powerful and they could not stop him. My stomach did a flip-flop because to me this was like waving a red flag at a bull and egging it on. I knew this was not good; I felt these aliens would try to affect him. He was so sure of himself that I just didn't know what to do or say.

A short time after William had said this he was contacted by a female from outside the area. The woman came to visit and they hit it off. She came to some of our meetings, and I am sad to say that William left the area with her. According to a couple that was in the group at the time, William talked as if he was leaving Earth and going back to his planet of origin. He used that idea to get the couple to help him abandon his family.

At the time that all this happened, I did not know William was in a troubled marriage because he never discussed the problem with me. After he left and was settled in a new area, we got a message explaining how he believed he had to go where all vibrations were tuned to the proper perspective so that he could do the job he was trained to do. The message went on and on about how he had no love and how he was very unhappy. He then explained how Monn had said that we might have to leave our family units and we should check with her about the decision he had made and Monn would agree with him. He also said his guide had told him that he deserved love and was happy he had found love. This was a lie, as no guide would tell you to walk away from your responsibility of a child or spouse. There are other ways of handling this type of situation.

It is true that Monn had said that we might be leaving our family units but then we would come back, meaning that we might be going to conferences or doing speaking engagements. We did speak to Monn about this, but she would not discuss it with us as a group. Later I got to talk to Monn on board her ship and she told me that William was fooled into believing what he did. The group of aliens that we were working with would never ask anyone to run away from their responsibilities on the planet. Monn explained that when we come down to earth we must live by the rules of the planet. If we make marriage commitments on Earth we should honor them; if we decide to have children we must honor the commitment to raise them. Children are one of the most precious things that we have on this planet. I feel William used Monn's statement to make it sound as if what he did was right.

After hearing William's message, we decided to respond. I personally told him that what he had with his girlfriend was not true love, it was a sexual attraction and it would not last a year. William had left his child in the care of his spouse but he had such terrible things to say about his spouse that I could not understand how he could leave a child in such a horrible situation. Getting a divorce was one thing, but running away from the child who needed him was another matter.

After a year and a month or so William and the woman he ran away with returned to the area. He told me, "See it did last longer than a year." I did not believe what he was saying because in my heart I felt that things were not going well for him. William wanted to rejoin the group, but he was not the same person; we could feel something different coming from him. He stayed for awhile, and then the woman he ran away with left the area. I never did hear the reason why she left. William drifted further and further away and believed that everything was all right with himself.

This was the first light worker we lost as a group. Looking back now, I did not see or did not want to see what was happening. This has made me very aware of my own attitudes and ego, to always look around and try to see what is going on.

Many of the dark aliens want us to fail in doing our jobs on Earth. Many people claim that the aliens make them do unusual things. The negative Grays and Reptilians don't have to make us fail at doing our jobs; all they need to know are our weaknesses and put those stumbling blocks in our path. Each of us must be aware of our weaknesses and make sure that we don't go there. We have choices to make each day. It is called free will, and we are responsible for each decision we make.

Monn warned us from the beginning that it would be hard to complete the mission we committed to do on Earth. When you get to Part Three you will see how she explained that love could be used against you to take you from your commitment. I personally believe that William fell for the oldest ploy in the Universe…being that love is important and we all deserve to love and be loved. After all, what could possibly be wrong with love? We all have weak spots in our makeup. The weaknesses many people have are drugs, alcohol, money, ego, and love. Could these addictions take over your life? When we let the addictions take over, the light dims and then the abducting non-spiritual aliens can come in and make contact with us. When you are one with the Creator, your light from inside is bright and the negative dark aliens can't come into your light. According to Monn, we are the lights that shine and help keep the planet balanced.

Part Two
Who Are These Aliens and What Do They Look Like

Over the years we have asked the aliens what they looked like, what their life is like and what they are doing here. We have asked a lot of questions about their ships and how they are driven. Sometimes the aliens amazed us with the responses to our questions, but sometimes the answers were very simple. They have talked to me extensively while we were face to face, but during sessions we often asked for details and verification of what I remembered of these contacts. Our questions and the channeled responses of the aliens are mainly given to you here in the third person. We felt that introducing many names could confuse the reader and make it harder to understand. We have also combined questions and alien answers in topic format for easier reading. These aliens don't generally volunteer information, if we don't know how to ask the questions, we don't get answers.

Monn

Monn is the name a female alien gave us to use for her because we needed a name to call her. Both Monn and I have Surak as our birth planet, and because of this closeness she was asked to volunteer and join this mission because it was felt that the channeling would be easier between the two of us. She looks relatively human and can pass for one. Monn has come to earth several times to walk among us. She explained that it is hard for her to lower her vibration level, thus limiting her visit to a short period of time.

Every time I think of Monn I can see her standing before me. She is approximately five feet four inches tall with blond hair and eyes that are a beautiful shade of blue; I cannot think of anything on Earth that is that color. She has a well-defined figure and could not be mistaken for a male. The first time I saw Monn she had a pageboy haircut that was about shoulder length, although one time I saw her with her hair cut short and curly. I guess she is like most female humans who like to change their hairstyles every so often. Monn looks to be about twenty-three years old, although she is older than that and her species lives to be about three hundred years in our time.

Monn had been trained in the military on her home planet and at first had a hard time with our language and had someone help her learn to speak it. However, now she likes to use our slang and is happy when she gets the words in the right place. One of the things I think is fascinating is her sense of humor. She loves to laugh even when she uses the wrong word and what she says comes out sounding funny. When Monn started speaking to us, she asked that it be recorded so that we could go back and look at what was said. The very first sessions were recorded by hand into notebooks, which, I am sad to say, were lost. We then switched to tape recording the sessions. Monn often teases us about our antiquated or primitive recording equipment. It seems no matter what we try, the tape recorders often don't work properly. She did not trust our memories and wanted us to share the messages and information that she gave us with anyone who wanted to know. Sadly I have to say that this sharing has not been one of the things we have done continually nor successfully.

Monn comes from the planet Surak, which is located in the Big Dipper at approximately 10 o'clock. This planet cannot be seen with any telescope that we have at this time because of the distance from us and being in a slightly different dimension. It takes Monn 93 minutes to get to Earth from Surak. It takes longer to get out of Earth's atmosphere and into Surak's atmosphere than it takes for the flight. Surak is a planet much like our own; however, they do not have as much water as we do although they do have enough for their needs. The temperature is more even than on planet Earth and they do have some mountains high enough to have snow on them.

Besides speaking through me, Monn is the shuttle pilot of a small craft, often shuttling dignitaries in need of a ride to meetings on board the Peace Ship. One of those dignitaries that she has given a ride to was the person we call Jesus the Christ. She said that He is the most wonderful person that she has ever met. It seems that He has the ability to make everyone feel as if he/she is the most important person to Him. He can speak to a great multitude of people and everyone can understand Him. She talked once about how she had sneaked into a meeting where He was speaking and everyone could understand Him without help from any translating equipment.

Monn has explained that her job is to work with us to expand our minds and raise our vibrations. This is not done with secrecy; it is accomplished with openness and love and by sending the light to all. She knew that for us to do our jobs and help mankind understand we must not have any doubt that the aliens exist. We must be bold, fully satisfied, and have full knowledge of what we are and why they are here, without any doubt. Monn says that is why she volunteered to have such close contact, so we would know that everything that we are experiencing is real.

Monn is a very loving person with a great sense of humor and enjoys laughing; I have heard her laugh and I have heard her cry. Humor is one of the things that most people who have had contact with aliens do not talk about. It seems that many of the abducting aliens do not have as many emotions as we do. Many people who have contact with the Grays say that they have a lack of emotions. The aliens that I have had contact with have compassion; they enjoy laughing, teasing, and expressing their feelings for mankind. I can only say my meeting with the aliens has made me a better person and I have come to think of them as friends.

On board her own ship Monn wears a form hugging, two-pieced, powder blue basic uniform with short boots ending just above the ankle that are usually the same color as the uniform. The belt around her waist is the same color as the uniform with an insignia where the belt slips together. The uniforms are made of a material that looks something like shimmering swim suit material. She has different colored uniforms, such as white, blue, silver-gold, and green, which are worn for different occasions. The dress uniform is usually white in color. It is form fitting and can have either a skirt or pants. When the aliens are off duty they can wear whatever they like such as the clothes they wear on their home planet. Her uniform has a six-sided star on a stand-up collar like the old Neru jackets had. This is the symbol for the System of Love and Light. The insignia means the Star of Light and it is used to recognize the bearer of light. This insignia has been used in space a very long time even before Israel came into being and adopted it as their national symbol.

Monn has had two ships during the time that I have known her, and her sister Melody was with her on both of them. When I first meet Monn she had a circular craft about thirty feet in diameter. In the fall of 1986 Monn, her sister Melody, her friend Derrick had a crash in a small craft that was attacked by a band of rogue beings while they were going home on leave. There were no weapons on Monn's craft so they had no way to defend themselves. During the crash Melody and Derrick were both injured. Melody left the service because of her injuries and returned to her home planet of Surak. Derrick was badly injured and at the time it was not known if he would be able to fly a craft again. I am glad to say that after his injuries healed he was able to rejoin the system of Love and Light.

Years later, while on another mission, Monn was again shot down and badly injured but had no permanent injures. After Monn healed she was issued a new triangular shaped ship, black in color. It can seat ten plus the pilot. It is entered from the right side of the right wing towards the bottom. When I first saw the ship I noticed that there were red lights around the outside and I wondered if the lights were permanently stationed in that position. I asked her about the lights and she said, "We can change the configuration and the color of lights to make us appear like an airplane or anything else that we might want people to think it could be. This is a better way of cloaking a ship than the old one." Her new ship has one of the newest computer systems on board. Now she could answer more of our questions asked during a channeling session without going to the main computer on board the Peace Ship. Monn is very proud of her new ship because it is driven by mind power, so it is important to be balanced mentally. If you are not mentally balanced you could get in a lot of trouble real fast trying to control one of their space ships.

We found out that Monn and Derrick liked each other a lot. We asked if they would be married and she answered that they did not know because there were so many items that had to be worked out before that could happen. They seem to think marriage is more important than a lot of people do on Earth. We then asked if her species married, and she answered that they did not marry as we do, they mate for life in the presence of God. Sometimes their jobs can separate them for long periods of time and this can be hard on their relationships. It is rare but sometimes a couple drifts apart and then they can and do separate.

Monn had this to say when asked what she would be doing after she completed her mission here. "Because I was originally trained in the military service on Surak, I have to make a decision if I will stay with the system of Love and Light or go back to my home planet. I love working for the betterment of mankind, but to do so I must give up my family and stay on board space ships. I would have a new home and a new family, but I can go home for visits. This is not an easy decision and must not be done lightly."

On Surak they have pets and there is an animal that is similar to our cats which has claws that can do damage to property, just as some of our cats do. They also have an animal that looks somewhat like a large but skinny cow. It has hair half way up its side that is like a lamb and on the top has curly fur about five to six inches long. The head is big and oblong, with a square chin area.

On Monn's home planet they sometimes have injuries that need treatment and even have parts of the body break down prematurely. They have something like our physicians and healers all rolled into one and these beings help when it is needed.

When Monn was asked about how they gather the information they share with us she explained that, "There is a large computer on the Peace Ship that keeps track of almost everything in this universe." She went on to say, "I have a small computer on board my shuttlecraft and when you ask questions during a channeling session we check with my computer first and if I cannot find the answer, I can link with the computer on the Peace Ship. There are always technicians there who can look up and find the information if it is available to you. If they cannot find out the information they go the head of the department. We are then told if we can tell you the information or not."

"Over the years there have been times when I should have not given you the answers and by doing so I have gotten in trouble. This generally happens when I use my own computer. So I would rather check and make sure before I answer, because you have gotten me to answer questions and I was not suppose to answer. Then I go on report and have to wait six months before it is erased off my record. Because of my wanting to give you all your answers I have been on report a number of times."

"In the 1990's we got a much better computer and can get almost any information I want, but I still have to be careful as to what I can tell you. Because I could give you answers that might affect your vulnerability or that may jeopardize some future actions.

That is why during some of the channeling sessions I have had to ask if I could give the information. There were times when I could answer and times when it would have been detrimental to you if I answered."

During 2003 Monn had this to say during a channeling session. "I'm glad that you all could be here at this time. I wanted to tell you a little bit more about my trip although I can't tell you a whole lot except that it lasted well over three weeks. I basically touched down on each continent on earth. I went down to listen to what the common people were saying. Because it is their thoughts and their ideas that Jesus wants to hear. So I was basically on a mission for Him. He also wanted the leaders that are highly agitated at this time to reckon to the fact that He is here. And that no matter what they do, He will win any battle or war they could start, because He has been commissioned to do so by God. And no matter who they work for, they cannot win and will not win the final battle on this planet. All they are going to do is cause misery and pain for a lot of the people of the planet. They are not listening, they think Jesus is not here at this time and they don't believe He is a messenger from God. So, we will have to wait and see what happens. But, I just wanted you to know that it is very serious at this time. So if we can get through March, we may be able to go off orange alert." (Again Monn said something that got by us, no one thought to ask more about the orange alert.) "So hopefully…say your prayers and don't let the negative side pull you off the course. We need everyone here. We need everyone who has started the mission and backed away. We need all these people to come back on to the course."

In January of 2005 Monn told us about another mission she went on, this was to our planet. She had this to say, "I visited some countries directly West of India but I cannot tell you where it was. I know what you are thinking and no I cannot give you two guesses. The countries I visited, shall we say, most of them normally dress in black flowing robes."

"I dressed also in black robes when it was necessary. I had some human looking male escorts with me for protection. My mission was to see some fairly large figureheads of these countries. In many of the countries we were not given permission to see these leaders. They did not believe who we were, so we did the only thing we could we do and walked through the solid walls. When they realized that even with all their military might they couldn't protect themselves they were ready to sit down and talk."

Eric and His Ship of Peace

If you remember, Eric is the being that I meet on board the Ship of Peace, which we decided to call The Peace Ship. Eric is very striking when first seen. He carries himself with great dignity and has an air of self-assurance; you cannot help but respect him. He is over seven feet tall; he is the color blue, the softest color of blue you can imagine. He has what looks somewhat like feathers on his body but it fells very soft, like down. His head has a beak instead of a mouth, which makes him look like he had an eagle's head. He has an extra long neck for the size of him, his body has no shape and there is no distinguishable waist. His arms are long for his body and at the end of his arms are hands with five appendages that have what look like talons on the tips of them. His legs are short and have no shape to them except for a bump where his knees are. He has round circles for feet and I still wonder how those small feet hold him up.

Eric is approximately 776 years of age in our years at the time of this writing, but because they have a long life span he is considered a young male in his species. His type of being don't normally wear clothes or shoes on their home planet, but sometimes they do wear coverings during space travel because of contamination. They feel that shoes and clothes separate them from nature and they don't like that.

When we asked what they eat, he said they do not eat of the flesh and seemed unable to understand how humans could eat the flesh of animals. We also asked if they have anything similar to our chicken. Eric answered, "We have nothing like your chickens and we do not eat the eggs of animals." They do eat something similar to our fruits and vegetables, including a lot of root-type plants.

We then asked if there is a male and female of their species and he answered that biologically they have a male and female of their species, who have a way of mating that is special for them.

Eric comes from the Dog Star System, which is beyond our scientists' realm of understanding at this time. In other words, we have not discovered the planet yet. Maybe it is in another dimension and our instruments are not advanced enough to detect the planet.

Eric told us that he loves to read but their books are like a small computer, something like our I-Pod's but about the size of our paperback books. You don't have to turn the pages you just push a button to get to the next page. He told us that he loves to get his hands on our books because he enjoys the smell of the paper and ink and says they are more fun to read.

The ship has been in service for approximately 2,743 of our years and has been observing Earth for approximately 72 years, actually since 1932. Eric is the 47th captain of the ship, but this does not include the first captain who launched the ship on a dry run. Captain C-Zog was the name of the being who took the Peace Ship on its maiden voyage. If you include him, Eric would be the 48th captain. You can continue to be Captain as long as you are mentally and physically able to handle any situation that may arise for a ship of that size and importance. One of Eric's jobs is to greet the dignitaries who come on board and to make sure they have everything they need. He often tells of how he tires of this pomp and circumstance but he would not trade the job for anything. He has worked long and hard to get this position and says it is very satisfying.

The ship is approximately 40 miles across and 38 miles high. Think of it as a balloon that has been squashed a little from the top and bottom. The speed of the ship is fantastic; it has a minimum speed of one mile per hour while the maximum speed is ten times the speed of light, which is almost the speed of thought.

Eric said, "The Peace Ship is maneuvered somewhat by the mind; however, it can't be done with mental strength of one person. So it has to be programmed to more than one person, as one person can't do it all with their mental strength. It is commanded with about 75% physical activity and about 25% mental. In other words, your brain waves have to match the pattern that is imprinted in the control system or you cannot take control of the ship. Everything has to match or you cannot get the control systems to work. The Peace Ship is manned continually for 24 hours a day. We have many crew members on board who can take over, although I am the only one who can override all systems and commands with my mind. I can override any system on this craft."

Because it is operated with mind control, mental and physical stability of the captain is important. If there is even a hint of instability, the captain can be removed by a board of fourteen or the captain can resign anytime he might feel he is no longer valuable to the ship or crew.

There are thirteen levels on the ship and over 1,200 rooms. At the top of the ship is the command center where there are three levels and each is about twenty feet in height. There is an average staff of seventeen people manning the computer boards in the command center at all times. When looking at the command center from the outside, it looks like a little bump on top because the craft is so large.

This drawing is of the second level where the officers have their private quarters.

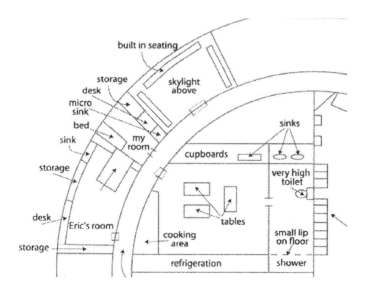

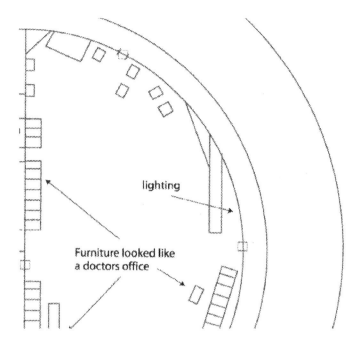

lighting

Furniture looked like
a doctors office

This drawing is also on the second level but on the opposite side of the ship. This is what I would call a small gathering place or lounge. It is a very informal area. I have attended informal meetings like our cocktail parties; except no one over indulges in drinks.

The next level is for those who have chosen to be on the path of spreading the word of the mission any place it is needed. Many of these people if they should die are reincarnated and do the same type of job again and again. This level has a total of 576 rooms, which has the capacity of housing 862 beings. Some of the crew also stays on this floor. The floors where the quarters are located are relatively short in height compared to some of the other areas.

The third level is the conference level where there are classrooms and meeting rooms. The Peace Ship was specifically made to accommodate a lot of people for meetings. There are many auditoriums on board ship. Some of these are very large and have stadium seating. A few of the rooms have tables where there are translating machines that can be put on the heads of those who cannot use telepathy. There is also something that goes to their breathing point so that they can have the correct mixture of whatever they need to breathe. I have even seen small meeting rooms where only a few people can converse in a very comfortable setting.

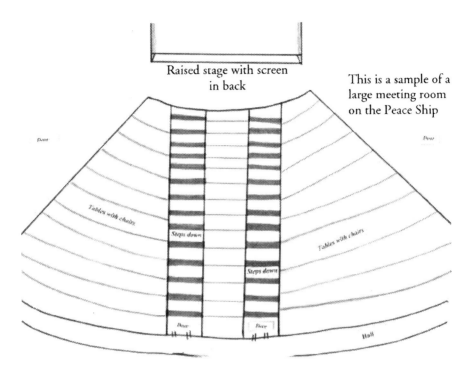

Raised stage with screen
in back

This is a sample of a
large meeting room
on the Peace Ship

This is one type of breathing apparatus that I
have seen on board the Peach Ship. I was
very surprised when I saw almost the same
thing on a television show.

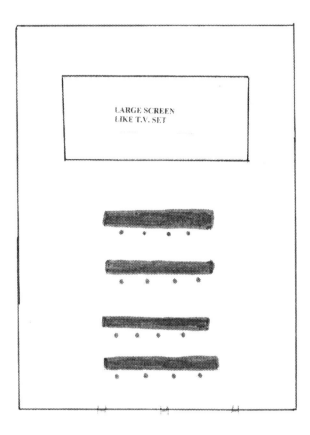

This drawing is of a small room 20 by 50 feet. This is used as a small class room or meeting room. There are table and chairs facing the front with a large screen that looks like our television sets.

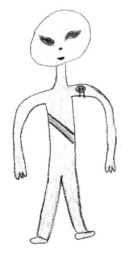

This little guy I met going into a lift on the Peace Ship. The hair on the back of my neck stood up and I had to back out of the lift. This was the only time that I sensed danger while on board the ship. His skin was kind of a pasty gray color. He had an insignia on his sleeve, with tassels hanging from it. There was banner across his chest. His uniform was one piece.

Alien that I saw on board craft about 4 1\2 feet tall

The goal of the Peace Ship is to produce a safe area where many different aliens and cultures can come together conformably and safely to work out any problems between races or planets. I remember going on the craft one night and realizing that the security was much greater than it had been. I asked why and got the answer that two beings made an attempt to get through the boarding area without the right paperwork. They were attempting to get to the computer area, which is located on the second level from the entry point of the ship. They wanted to cause trouble; luckily they were captured before any damage was done. Since that time security has been beefed up and now there are three types of security. There is an individual who scans a person mentally and physically, a non-invasive way of checking DNA. There also is a soul scanner. These are usually very accurate and since that time there has been no repeat of the incident.

The guest quarters are actually on one level because it is easier to keep an eye on these beings and it is easier to provide the atmosphere in the rooms that each individual might need. There are enough rooms for guests and their assistants in this area; they also can attain any food that they are accustomed to eating.

This ship belongs to no one and yet it belongs to everyone. The ship can travel to any area that is having trouble and supply help in any manner that is needed. Many planets represented on the ship do not always agree on how to solve problems but are willing to work out a compromise. Often you can hear voices rise in arguments and fists sometimes have been raised in anger. Still they work together for the betterment of everyone involved. That is why the ship is in our area now, because the planet is going through a natural process of raising its vibration level. This has happened before and will happen again. Many people believe that a pole shift or a planet coming close to earth will start this process but the aliens told us that this shift had already started in 1986. The problem is that we now have the ability to destroy the planet and ourselves. If we were to destroy the planet, it would affect everything in our Universe and the aliens do not what that to happen.

There is a large area where they make the atmosphere that is needed for all those who come on board as they don't all breathe the same mixture. Some of this equipment is miles high and wide. There are also levels for the repair and maintenance of equipment and shuttlecrafts. There are engine rooms for the movement of the ship, which also are several miles high and wide.

On one level there are streams that flow beside trees, grass, shrubs, bushes and flowers, although they don't look like ours. Very high up in that area one can actually see what looks like clouds, except the color is not the same. This actually produces what I would call rain which is then caught and used for drinking. There are small animals that run free in these areas and also some type of animals that are similar to our birds that fly. The reason for the plants and such is to help in the manufacture of oxygen and nitrogen and other compounds that I don't remember. This area also helps humans and extraterrestrial life forms to be calm and serene.

A separate level is dedicated to the growing of plants for the purpose of eating. The ship is self-contained, producing all its own food and energy needs without relying on any outside influence for its upkeep.

There is a level which we call the holo-deck because it is similar to what was on the Star Trek series. This is an area where we can go and create any situation we wish. Perhaps people/aliens are lonely for their home and family members and this area can be used to create a replica of their home world. There also is a recreation level where we can create an exercise in almost any form we wish. We can also have snow for skiing or ice-skating. This is a very popular area for the crew as they can create an area to exercise their brains.

On another level there is an area where we can shop and get supplies, however no money is exchanged as we receive credit for any work we do and then it is automatically removed from our account for any purchases that we make. In this area there are places where you can purchase food. I told the aliens about pizza and talked them into a little café where they make and serve pizza. Monn explained that Bonnie insisted on the pizza and we have learned to enjoy it. However they can and do replicate something that looks and tastes like pepperoni because they use no meat from animals.

At the bottom of the craft there is an opening approximately two to three miles wide where ships can enter and there are seven docking levels where ships can be docked. It looks a lot like our boat marinas where many ships of different sizes can tie up at one time. The larger crafts stay at the bottom because of their lack of ability to maneuver, the smaller ships go to the top levels and dock. The Peace Ship docking area holds 32 shuttlecrafts in the docking bay. Most small shuttle crafts hold twelve people, a crew of two plus ten guests.

The crew works three months on and then has three months off. During their time off they can return to their home planet if they wish. Officers and those on the first level of the ship are permanently stationed there, as this is a life-long commitment. The officers also have leaves any time it is needed and they can visit any place they wish.

Most of the cleaning is automatic and done by machines. An example of this is to your hang your dirty clothes in a closet and they are automatically cleaned by wave action. Boy would I like that in my home.

Eric told us that there is renovating of the ship going on all the time. It seems when we get one area done, another needs attention. The Peace Ship has a cloaking device that makes it impossible for us to see when it is in use. This is used only when necessary for the safety of everyone on board.

In 1991 an earth cat was taken to the Peace Ship and Eric explained, that "We are not allowed to keep pets, but we were allowed to keep the cat as a mascot, but can you imagine how it would be if everyone was allowed to have a pet on board a ship of this size. It would be like the "Tribbles" show from the original Star Trek series and that could happen here. Everyone would want a pet and pretty soon we'd be over run with them. We have a hard time the way it is with air supplies, the combination of oxygen, nitrogen that people need. And the different foods that are grown to serve these people. We just can't afford that on this type of operation.

Six years later we were surprised when Eric told us that the cat had kittens. Knowing that pets were not welcome on the Peace Ship we asked how that could happen. Eric responded with, "Somebody brought a cat with them and we had babies. All of the kittens have homes elsewhere as they cannot stay here."

In 1995 Eric said, "I have visited your planet many times but I did not have my blue feathers on as that would have made it very obvious that I did not belong there."

"If I walked on the planet in my bodily form it would frighten everyone. I do however come to the surface of your planet occasionally but not in my own bodily form. I don't rent one; maybe I could just hop in one that's in a closet and not being used and come on down. (Eric says this as a joke.) I can and do however give the illusion of looking differently but it takes so much concentration that you become weak very quickly."

"Yes we can give the illusion of us looking differently and so can the dark side. They use illusion very often to fool you into believing they are someone else, sometimes even a loved one. But you can break their concentration of giving you the illusion of who they are and you can see who they really are. You do that by confusing them with antics; either by making a face or giving them orders not to do what they are doing or maybe ask them to check with their leaders to see if what they are doing is all right. First you have to realize that they are different from you, and then you can realize that they don't understand your emotions. They cannot even understand your language real well, so it wouldn't take much to confuse them."

Lea

Lea is also an alien and at first she did not have much contact with us, however, as time went on we have had more and more contact with her. She is short in stature, about five feet in height. She has very, very black, shiny, straight hair that is cut short, all one length and she tucks it behind her ears. Lea's ears are more elongated and pointed than our ears; they look somewhat similar to Spock's on Star Trek. Her skin is olive color, which makes her Greek looking. The eyes are the same color as her hair but instead of round centers she has yellow pupils that go straight up and down. She is of average weight for her height. She has a nose that is quite long and narrow and full lips we would probably say are a little large for her face by Earth standards. There are four appendages on each hand that are finger like. Each is different in length, and one finger is a little off set and works much like our thumbs. Lea doesn't have fingernails and we told her how some people use them for screwdrivers, she laughed at the thought of that. She has had pizza because I suggested she try it. On board the ship she said there are more hot drinks than cold ones.

Lea's figure is straight up and down, not curvy like Monn's. For clothes she wears a robe with a hood and a sash at the waist. The robe is dark brown in color. The coverings for her feet look a lot like our summer sandals, but I don't know what material they are made of. Lea looks to be about 35 years old by our standards, although her species has an average life span of about 300 of our years. An accident can shorten their life span but they normally just go to another existence when their mission or life is over.

She does not have a home planet because she was born on board a ship in space. Right now she is stationed on a ship that is twenty-four miles across and about thirteen stories tall. This does not include the boarding and docking areas and the command center. It is smaller than the Peace Ship. This ship was constructed in space as it is easier to construct such a large object there.

The reason that she communicates with us is because Dale who is a member of our group, is on loan from the Christ Command, the same command that she is in. Lea explained that the ship's commander is the being we call Jesus. "He knows all and sees all that are under His command. Let me tell you that if you are a light worker, you are known to this being. He has compassion for everyone big and small. My immediate boss is third in command on this ship; she is the top female officer. I am between the officers and the personnel and have all the problems from both sides that have to be handled. All days on our ship start with meditation and end with meditation, no matter what shift you're on or what your job is. Right now there are many commands near earth working to help the planet and humanity."

Lea says they are here because of the evolution of the planet and to keep track of things as they progress. This includes raising the vibration level of the planet and hopefully raising the vibration level of humans. The group she is with has already prepared space ships for evacuation. The ships are ready and in place to do that job. Plants and animals are already on board and waiting so that earth can be replenished if necessary.

Her main job is what we would call a psychiatrist or psychologist. When she does her work, she blends with the patient's mind and soul so she knows exactly what the problem is. In other words, nothing can be hidden from her and the job of fixing the problem is accomplished very quickly. Lea readily admits that she does not get to work with humans as often as she would like to, so she does not know much about us.

For a long time Lea had the use of a small craft for shuttling dignitaries from her command. She explained that her small ship "has a crew of seven plus myself, it could be used for evacuation of ninety-two people for only a short distance because there would be a problem with the breathing of the air. It would only be used to get people to a larger craft. My ship is quite large. It is approximately three of your stories tall. It is 120 feet across and I think you would call it disc shaped. Some of the older ships were bell shaped but now they have a much sleeker style."

Lea's species do not marry as we do on Earth. They blend with each other because then they know everything about each other. (This is not a sex act.) When they do that they then decide if they want to spend a lifetime together. If they decide to stay together they go before God and make that commitment. They usually do not have children if they are on a mission or stationed in space because they feel it is irresponsible to have children only to go off and leave them.

She vibrates at a much faster speed than we do. That means that the pressures and gravitational pull on earth is greater than she is used to. It is very hard for her to operate on earth and she cannot stay on the planet for any length of time. Her oxygen mixture is different than ours and it is hard for her to breathe on planet earth.

Lea is a very serious person. She is all business and there is no playing around in her presence. Her job is very serious and her posture and nature reflects that. Lea has shared with us information about our Bible, their religious beliefs, our religious connection to the aliens and how these all fit together.

In 1990 Lea told us more about her job. "The job of our command is to make sure the planet gets back to the condition it was intended to be in. That is the good side of our job. The bad side is the waiting around up here in space. Part of my job is to move the dignitaries of our command safely to where ever they are needed."

Much later she got a new ship that will be used in the evacuation of humans from our planet. The new ship is seven stories high and approximately 2.4 miles across. The ship can house 1,700 people on board plus crew. Because there is not enough area for food growing or regenerating ability, these people cannot stay for an extended period of time. There are 73 shuttlecrafts on board which take only one pilot to run. With this ship she can come as close as 22.3 miles to the surface of our planet. As you can see the aliens have more than one job because in space you never know where or what skill will be needed.

In September of 2001 while talking to Lea she surprised us with these statements. "My new ship is the "Ship of Hope," that is what it translates into in your language." A short time later Lea quietly admitted, "I had a slight accident with the new ship I was commissioned to pilot. It wasn't a bad accident just a few bumps and bruises that's all. I bumped into the Christ Command's lead ship with my new Ship of Hope. I wasn't paying attention just thinking about how I would explain to all of you about Moses from your Bible."

"I do have to pay for the repairs on the ship out of my salary. I can pay for it because we don't have many expenses in space but I will be wearing my brown robe for some time now, no new ones for me. We don't have money like you do we are given something like credits for our service which we can then use to buy things that we need."

"I would like to explain to you that when Moses came down from the mount and he saw the people worshiping idols instead of God he became angry. Just as he is very angry with what's going on in the world today. He is in flesh form just as Jesus is and he has visited Earth on let's see…it was December 17, 2003. He actually came to the planet and he visited the Far East, because he can blend in with the people there quite nicely. He came back very angry and gave his report to Jesus and I have not seen Jesus cry in a long time. But there were tears in His eyes as He heard the report about all the atrocities that are happening on the planet."

Part Three

The channeling has been happening for almost thirty years. I would say that there have been one hundred sessions. With so much material to go through and sort it turned out to be a bigger project than I expected. By putting the material into topics and changing the question/answer format into a narrative I felt it would make the material easier to read. Some of the material had very personal information about specific individuals, this was purposely left out. The following are the answers to many of the questions we asked the aliens. Many times we asked the same questions of Monn, Eric and Lea and to our surprise most of the time we received the same answers from all of them almost word for word. I have not put in how each individual answered as that would have been repeating the answers but I have included all their answers by combining them.

So You Think You're a Light Worker

Following are many of the offerings that Monn, Eric and Lea had to say about light workers over the years. In 1989 Monn tried to explain to us about light workers. Her comment was, "A light worker is a group of beings whose sole mission in the Universe is to go wherever the force of good is needed. They travel many Universes to do their work. Light workers are schooled in a special school for their jobs on the planets that that need help.

Right now there are people here who have come from a higher vibration level and are commonly referred to as light workers. A light worker has a soul that is on a spiritual path; it is someone who believes that there is someone or something that is more powerful than they are. A light worker is one who carries the light of The Creator across the Universe and spreads it to many distant planets. It's the only name that many of the people on the planet recognize as someone who's in tune with the Creator.

There are masters (see masters heading for description of a master) who are on this planet right now and they are only what you consider normal humans. They do not have any great scientific knowledge at this time because they are here to help spiritually. When you attend conferences you will find a few masters speaking; but remember the person sitting next to you may is also a master therefore, he is equal to the speaker and could also know more than the speaker.

Light workers have a soul that is very balanced, kind and compassionate. It is someone who can love a person no matter if they agree with them or not. A light worker is one who very much understands the vibrations of those around them. They never try to control or judge anyone, nor should they allow anyone to use them like a doormat.

Many light workers have a hard time with love and sex and sometimes get the two mixed up. You get a very euphoric feeling from both love and sex; many believe this is the same feeling you have when you are spiritual. Many humans want this feeling and believe the sexual act gives them what they think is the same feeling, but it is not. Can you, as a light worker remember fully the life you came from? It was where love was given fully, not the sexual love. It was where compassion, understanding, and the willingness to give all that you can to others and then in return receiving more back than you gave. At this time at this level of vibration it will not happen, but once Earth evolves to a higher vibration it will happen here.

Many of the light workers are having an invisible mark placed on their dominant hand. It is a mark the dark forces can see. This is a mark that some will recognize and respect you for your work, but some will also try their best to take you off the path that you have chosen for yourself. This mark will also be visible to the third eye, and only if you have reached the right level will you be able to see it.

Many people feel that light workers are the chosen 144,000 people talked about in your Bible. But the light workers travel the Universe gathering people, holding them together, and taking them to the light for God. These beings are going to be teachers, the servants of the hierarchy. Besides the 144,000 there is going to be a great multitude which no one could number, and these beings will be evacuated from Earth if it need be. The 144,000 will be the teachers of the multitude."

In 1990 Monn explained, "If a light worker has one moment of doubt that the Creator exists, he could be lost. If the light workers doubt for one moment who they are and who they work for, they can be lost to darkness and then must start their way back to the light again. As a light worker you must find a solution to counteract the evil on this planet. I would like to say sometimes you are your own worst enemy. You can do more harm to yourselves than anyone else can."

1997 Eric told us. "If you search for the answers to your questions, you'll be directed to the right place and find them if you have the faith and trust. You don't even have to speak it out loud; sometimes you will get answers before you even realize you have a question.

As a light worker you can change the world by hooking up with like minds. Two minds and souls are stronger than one. In the same token everyone has the right and the power to accept or reject any negativity or deny any negativity that is sent their way.

Many light workers are infiltrating the government work force; the dark side is also infiltrating the government. The positive aliens are more open and honest and do not use the devious tactics that the dark side uses. It may take the positive aliens a little longer to get a job done, but they are stronger. They warned us to…be careful as this is a hard job and don't let yourselves be deceived by your own achievements. Do not let your ego take over or you shall not finish your job.

If you are a light worker, your reality is not on this planet; your reality is in the heavens. If you are searching for something but you don't know what it is, if you have a feeling that you are here for a purpose, you probably are a light worker.

At this time there are a little over 52,000 earth souls on the planet. An earth soul is a soul who has Earth as its first incarnation. You see, the rest of the souls here at this time are from somewhere else in these Universes, so chances are you were originally born on another planet, maybe in another system I guess that makes Earth the melting pot of souls. It is a good place for learning and that makes most humans aliens. This is a great time for any soul on Earth to make great strides in its spiritual growth, but be careful as your pride and ego can affect your spirituality in a negative way.

If you are a light worker, you may have a problem with drugs or alcohol or any other type of addiction that there is. Many light workers don't understand Earth and try to escape the trappings of the planet. If you are in this situation you may be in trouble. If you use drugs or alcohol, it opens something in the back of your head that allows negativity to enter. This means that you could do something that is not what you would normally do. Have you ever done something while under the influence of either one of these drugs or alcohol and after the affects wear off wonder what really happened because your memory is fuzzy? Or maybe your friends tell you that your personality changes while you are under the influence. If you believe you are a light worker, please change your habit as this is an open invitation to the dark side of the force to enter and influence you in a negative way. They are waiting for the opportunity to use you in a negative way.

You can recognize other light workers if you pay attention. Many times a person walks into your life and changes it for the better; that is a light worker's job.

These are the types of missions they can do although a light worker is usually here on Earth for an extended period of time.

Many light workers are getting confused and that is why we have been harping at you, to look at yourselves. If you don't like what you see, change because the battle starts from within. Light workers must have their own little soldiers in a row and have themselves together before they can help anyone else. When getting up in the morning, look at your eyes. Do you see bright shinning eyes looking back at you? Do you see the light of the Creator looking back at you? Many people can see the light; and if you don't have the light burning brightly inside of you, the darkness comes and there is no light in your eyes. Do your job by sharing the Creator with all, not by words or cramming it down their throats, just be it. People may not sense what they're seeing or feeling, they just know something is different.

For many years light workers have fooled themselves into believing they are doing your work. Now you must run quickly to catch up or you will fall by the wayside. Never giving up is a wonderful psychology but you have to take the first step. You have to take the first step yourself before I can help or your guides can help you, before Jesus Christ can help you, and before God will send the help to you. You must strip yourself naked and learn to love yourself before you can love anyone else. As you become more aware you will realize how devious this planet is and how you've deluded yourself. We are very worried about the situation that is going on with the progress of light workers and about what people are doing right now.

They, the aliens we work with, have said that they are very worried about the situation that is going on with light workers' progress. They need every light worker at their full potential. You need to keep in close contact with each other, be there for each other. Share problems with each other, recognize when light workers are in trouble, and go out of your way to help each other, in return they will help you. This is what a light worker needs to do.

Many light workers are not awakening on schedule. The negative is so strong that they are having a hard time waking up. The negative side is using mind control and they are using it effectively. Light workers can counteract this by using their light.

Unless we get our light workers doing their job, 72% of the population will fall to the dark side. That number can change hourly. Think of it like you're standing on a roadway and the center line is the 50% divide. To the left are the negative people and to the right are the positive. As you make your choices and change your thoughts and ideas, everything will change for the better or worse.

On Earth there are 664 light workers who are on the surface and do not leave the planet, but the number changes every day. Many other light workers are on the surface of Earth, and most regularly visit our ships that are circulating the planet.

Many heads of state know who the light workers are and yet some light workers themselves don't know who they are. A lot of information has leaked out about light workers. We had a book with the list of their names stolen, and many files have been opened that have gotten into the wrong hands, so we had to beef up the security on board our ships. We also had to retrieve from a crash site records that were kept in a book with names of the light workers who are on the planet at this time. Luckily, we did get the book back. Years later we were told that there had been another security leak: the negative aliens know who you are and they can come to you using our names. They can infiltrate your dreams and meditative states, and it is up to each individual to be discerning and know to whom you are talking.

There is a large concentration of light workers in the Pacific Northwest that also leads into north western Canada. Wisconsin also has a large concentration of light workers, but for every light worker the negative side has its workers.

If a light worker should fall away and then realize what's happened, they can work their way back again. The Creator is all-forgiving and does not hold a grudge like many of you do. I'm sorry but we also do that. We are not perfect. We aliens have much learning to do. We, too, are on that track back to The Source. We as aliens fail and fall then we pick ourselves up and try again. We are learning every day just as you are because we know that it is possible. We do not give up. Life is nothing but a learning school that never ends because your soul always continues into another lifetime. Once you no longer try to work your way back to God or grow spiritually the soul extinguishes. If you see those who have fallen away, remember they, too, have a spark of the Creator in them. Don't toss them away in the garbage. People's lights are one of the things that are holding Earth together at this time. This Earth is in its full cleansing cycle, and the only thing that is keeping the cleansing from becoming more disastrous is the light workers. You may not realize the job that you are doing and things do seem crazy on this planet, but they would be much worse without the lights of all that are here.

Many light workers are here and think they know who they are but not all are accepting their jobs. Many have accepted their jobs and then turned to the other path. It is the negativity on this Earth that causes a lot of the problems. So we must accept everyone for who and what they are as well as you must accept yourself for who and what you are. There have been many light workers who have accomplished their jobs and left the planet. The time has come for all the light workers to open up, to shine their lights, to shine the Creators' light and erase the darkness that is hovering over this planet.

If you become angry and go with that, you allow the negative side the opportunity to feed off your strength because they feed off the energy that it takes to be angry. Use love, compassion and forgiveness. I know this sounds very simple, but love is the basis of having everything that is needed for a good life.

The forces of dark are going to use a sinister plan to take over the planet in a peaceful way, using very old witchcraft techniques with very modern technology. This can be done with ELF waves (for further information look under the heading ELF) to the point where they are going to drive people mad.

Light workers often choose mates who are not as spiritually evolved, trying to help them, and sometimes karma calls for them to choose a real hard one for a mate. Oftentimes light workers have the habit of letting people walk all over them.

Psychic battles are on the rise. It's a battle of weapons and a battle of minds. Psychic battles can leave wounds and scars just the same as if you were battling with weapons.

The dark side is breaking protocol and they're at a level three. Remember that the best battle is to stand with love and compassion, not negativity. Send the love and light to those you cannot understand. Don't allow the negativity to feed on your thoughts as that draws the negative force to you.

Jesus always sends the negative His love and hopes that they to shall come back to His light. How many people do you know in your own families who are negative? Don't be negative to them, stand tall and shine your light to them. Share your light with them. If they cannot take it, that is up to them. I cannot tell you all things as I see them, but that is only because I must not interfere on your plane and level of existence. Where there is hope and faith, you can win. Just hang onto hope and faith.

Using your lights and asking God for protection is not enough; you need action. If you think you have blanket protection, you are deluding yourself. If you are not a living example, you can fool yourself, but you can't fool God. Try to model your life after Christ. He went out amongst people he knew despised him, who didn't agree with him, and did His work. You don't get brownie points for walking away from your fears. After all, if Jesus had given up, what would the world be like? We need all light workers working together, for where one is weak another one is strong. And as you link together, it can't be broken. Strengthen to the point where you would be willing to give a life for one another.

There are many small groups on the planet who are searching for the truth and they shall probably remain quite small. Many of these groups will eventually meet and will recognize each other as they have met on board spaceships.

Light workers have a universal family and many have chosen to live on board a spacecraft which they call home although they can go back to their home planets once in a while.

You don't always have the opportunity to step into the lion's den; sometimes the lions den comes to you. You must be prepared. The dark side wants everyone's soul. You won't even know when you have lost your soul, and that's the sad part. Just remember you won't always have the choice of picking when you will be faced with the adversity. It may come to you at any moment so be prepared. They are working on every crack you have; I want you to be aware of that. Handle the situations in your life that are causing you problems. All that you perceive as well and good in your lives is not. We cannot interfere, that isn't God's way of doing things. If you ask for help, we'll try to assist you if we can.

When you stretch out your lights as we have taught, you can connect your light with ours. I know when this is done because I can feel a special warm glow that comes with it.

As a light worker, you need to show people that there is something beyond the existence of this planet. Most people are so involved in survival that they can't look beyond their noses and that may be part of your job, showing them that there is something beyond this planet, this Universe.

The government knows that we are speaking to you, but we sometimes block their listening equipment. Our jamming system works efficiently, but sometimes we don't jam and let them have a little information to keep them happy.

All who are waking up or have awoken or even those who believe in UFOs without much knowledge have all chosen to be here at this time to help humanity in any way they can. I think it is time for the knowledge to come forward that there are people here to help the planet and its people. It can be done gently and easily without getting in people's faces. You must learn to respect those you are speaking to. If you see fear in their faces or you feel that they are fearful, you must learn to back away. We are here to help, we are not here to hinder or frighten anyone. That is why we do not come and join the meetings because even with the knowledge that most of you have joining a session would be frightening to you. So be aware of who you're speaking to and how much you're speaking to them about, give them only what they can handle.

It's all right to give people a little bit of this information, but let people come to you. Most people know that you believe in UFOs, and a lot of people make fun of it; but if they or anyone in their family should have an experience, they know who they can speak to.

The path for each light worker is an individual path, you must search for yourself. You will know when you have your breakthrough if you have learned to meditate and have the balance and compassion you need; then you will know when things are right for you. Each of you has your own job to do and it is up to each individual to realize what it is. It's going to be a long hard soul searching process and progress. Survival of Earth is important, and the humans on Earth are going to have to do it. Some light workers work very closely with Christ and go with Him wherever He goes.

As a light worker, when you go someplace you don't have to expound your own ideas or good points. Sometimes your just being in a room makes the negativity subside and you can counter-balance the negativity. Don't look for a great revelation in people. That's kind of how the dark side works.

Keep your faith and believe that any seed you plant will grow where God wants it to grow. There might be lessons to be learned from everyone you meet.

Share ideas with one another; sort out which is right for you as an individual. We all have different missions and reasons for being here; I feel I also have an important job to do for your planet. Many light workers have made decisions along these same lines. Touch those around you with love, compassion and understanding and you shall receive ten-fold back. To give out negative thoughts is to receive negativity back. If you believe that you are low and you deserve no better; that is what you shall have. You are the maker of your own future, make it for yourselves. If you wish to travel the stars or be one with God you must have the things that I have mentioned or you shall never get past your atmosphere.

Many people have chosen the road away from God. We must stand strong and firm and face those people without fear because they live and they grow upon fear. They cannot survive against the strength of God. Keep Him in your heart and have no fear, for He is the strength of the Universe. Love one another, be honest, do not be afraid to share your feelings with each other and expand with this love and compassion. Do not accept the negativity of the people that are in your lives or that walk through your lives in your everyday jobs, your everyday living. Don't allow them to pull you down to their levels, instead reach out with love and compassion.

People see what you are not so much by your words but by what's in your heart as it radiates from within you. So many people talk a good life but it's not in their heart. You should live and radiate Gods' laws. You should not only talk the talk but walk the walk. He did not give you ten suggestions, he gave you ten laws to follow. He also expects everyone to follow and respect the laws of the planet you are on. How many people do you know who do not follow the laws of the road? How many people do not follow the civil laws? If you think you are a light worker, religious or spiritual, and do not follow these laws, then you are not who you think you are.

Let me explain it this way, if it is raining on one side of the street and not on the other and you cross from the raining side to the dry side of the street, you do not quickly dry off. This is how it is if you don't follow the laws of the land or God's law. It takes some time to work your way back to the Creator of all."

Giving Up the Life of a Light Worker

While discussing how light workers get to Earth, a method was explained how, "One light worker chose to come to Earth whose species had an average life span of 389 years on the planet she came from. On her planet she worked with plant life. When she found out that the planet Earth needed help she decided to terminate her life to come to Earth and help out. She chose to do that because she felt she had something to offer the planet.

This is not considered suicide because it is the giving of your life to help many others. She did this without the consequences of suicide that you have on your planet. This is not giving up and wanting to just get out of life, this is being in service to others.

This person was then born on Earth; she is not a walk-in. This means that she had to overcome all the negativity and the problems that face the people of Earth before she could do the job she came to do."

Groups of Light Workers on the Planet

In1997 during a discussion about light workers this came up about how a light worker got to certain areas. It was explained: "Originally people volunteered to come down here into the areas that were going to be most diluted on the dark side. That is where the original people went to, and now there are not many left. Most people have bought into the earthly wants and needs, so there are very few left. There are approximately thirty-five of those groups left. I cannot tell you where they are as it would not be wise for you to know or for the information to be out there. These thirty-five groups have not fallen into earth thoughts and ideas and have stayed true to why they are here. There are people coming into awareness every day but at what level? You can't throw someone in off the street and expect them to have the faith and the knowledge and everything at this late date. There used to be a group for each continent, but now there isn't a group for each one."

Hub of a Wheel

"This area has many light workers; it is like a hub of the wheel. Many light workers will move around, go places and come back. These moves will not be a permanent one. They are like spokes on a wheel going out from the hub. These light workers will be reaching other people or will be moving out trying to connect with other light workers, and this will be happening all over the planet."

Temple of Love, Wisdom, Knowledge

"There are many temples where you can go and be taught. They are located in different parts of the Universes. I don't know if you would call these places a spacecraft or not but they are whole unto themselves. These are physical places that are solid; you walk on solid material. You touch it, you feel it, it's a real place, and at every temple you learn something different. Many people remember going to these places, sometimes having picnics or sitting by a bubbling brook and reading or listening to a lecture. If you are a light worker you have been there.

Of course you must practice love and compassion each day. What would a light worker be if they did not use prayer for their fellow man everyday? These things are hard to keep going, but with practice you will become the balanced person that all humans were meant to be."

Balance

"Balance is one of the most important things in your life. It is very important to stay balanced and keep on an even keel. To keep balanced you should remember that everyone is a teacher and a student. This is where the balance is; no one knows everything and everyone has something to learn. Remember the Creator; remember that He is the force within you and that you are never alone. He always stands with you, but He does give you power, and it is your choice to use it in whatever manner you wish. The most important thing is to keep on an even keel and try to keep balanced.

The best way you can protect each other is to stay balanced. Send your love and energy to each other all day. You are only as strong together as the weakest link. So keep balanced. Keep in touch with your Creator. Realize that no one can stand by himself. Positives and negatives blended together as one are stronger. It's like the strong screen which will keep bugs out of your room. One strand won't do it, but many together do a wonderful job. So work together. Share your love, share your problems, and be stronger.

Satan is stretching his hold on this planet. Balance, God, faith, and love need to be introduced into your lives. The law we all should live by is to be an example so the children can see how it is done. One little doubt is like a pinprick in a filled balloon. When you have children, you have a responsibility to share the knowledge of being balanced so that the negative cannot influence the children. Just because a child is grown up does not mean that you cannot still help them to learn to become balanced because then Satan has a hard time influencing them. That's why the dark side is afraid of meditation.

Those who are not meeting the changes in the vibrations in this planet are becoming more psychotic, very emotionally, physically and mentally unbalanced. You must share your strength with this planet. You can have a stabilizing influence to help the planet just with your thoughts and your deeds.

If you are in a state of imbalance, then the aliens can come and take you against your will. If you do not keep your balance, they will keep after you. The longer you are off balance the easier it is for them to infiltrate you. If you get unbalanced enough, they could implant you and get you on the wrong path. The aliens can get into your head and put bad thoughts there if you allow yourselves to get unbalanced. Remember, there is strength in numbers, call for help from your guardian angels, Jesus, or God. They are there to help but you must ask.

Many light workers think that they live in balance, but almost every day they become unbalanced by thinking negative thoughts or talking about those around them negatively. How can they help anyone to be balanced when they cannot balance themselves? Are you allowing your anger to take control of your lives? Are you trying to control someone else's life? If you are honest with yourself, then do something about it. We talk about the camps dividing but you divide yourselves.

Without balance you have absolutely nothing, nothing. Those that are balanced and have their instincts honed very fine will know where to go during the end times. They will know where it's safe. Not all will survive, but it's not important. What is important is your soul's survival. You give up this body and your soul returns to the Creator, when you've done all that you can do to go back to Him.

Most humans feel that brain activity is intelligence. Earth wants to teach your brain only things that you can see touch and feel, but your heart can teach you how to live in complete harmony with the Universe. So you must learn to listen to your heart more. Your brain teaching is what is getting this planet in trouble.

The Grays and Reptilians have tried to brain scan you, but your balance and your strength in your faith make it inoperable. But they can still get you to do their bidding by hiding a message in music or any sound. This is only a temporary because once you understand what is going on and you can counteract it. This sound activation is audible but can be covered up by other noises. Your ears would pick them up if it is directed at you. This sound can very easily be hidden in music. So it is very easy to get young people who like to listen to heavy metal to do things they normally would not do. This is one of the reasons we harp so much on balance. It is a big defensive tool for your survival."

Your lights

"There is a light inside of you that the Creator has given to everyone. It is your connection to Him and can be used as a protection from aliens or humans who are on the negative side of the Source." Eric explained, "As you learn to stretch your lights and you send them out, they will reach as far as your thoughts. The lights that each of you have are holding the Earth together. This Earth is in its cleansing cycle, and the only thing that is keeping this from becoming more disastrous than it is right now is the light worker. So you may not realize the job that you are doing. Things do seem crazy on this planet, but they would be much worse without all those lights shinning."

There have been planets where they have actually disintegrated because of the disasters and the calamities that have happened. The time left for the planet depends upon how much negativity people are giving off and how bright our light workers are.

Many who are here on Earth refuse to open their minds and see what is going on. Those people are becoming more confused and more negative, and that negativity is what is hurting this planet right now.

Some people are saying that those "not of the light" cannot enter Earth but they can leave. How can this be? Haven't you noticed the horrendous thing that is happening on this planet? Read your newspapers. Just the sexual crimes alone should give you a clue that negativity is increasing.

If you could light a few candles/people in this world, you are doing well. For every candle/person that you light, they will light ten and each one of those ten will light ten and soon there will be no darkness. Minds and souls will open up to the real world, the real Universe."

Meditate

"Many earthlings do not know how to meditate. To meditate is to concentrate your mind power. It's just like a child learning to read or write you have to keep trying, practice and practice. I would suggest that every day you try to meditate to clear your mind of anything negative. And while you're meditating, try to get your mind to concentrate on one thing and one thing at a time. A mind is a very strong instrument, but you have to learn how to use it.

When you meditate you let go of everything. It is letting go of anger and fear and letting compassion come forward, loving unconditionally.

Learn to meditate and you can stand in front of His throne anytime you wish. People even during Biblical time meditated, Christ even talked about meditating. They used to meditate and during the meditative state they would send their mind and their soul out and see things. You are definitely able to do that now in your time period, and as you become more spiritual you will probably succeed in that yourself.

You have to keep yourself balanced all day long or it's going to take you hours to get your body down so that you can meditate. If you allow yourself to become stressed out during the day, you cannot meditate as easily as it should be.

During the day there are so many busy thoughts running around and so many people thinking, and not necessarily good thoughts either, but just clutter. At night the clutter is stilled because most of the brain's thoughts go to rest. This is also a good time to meditate because there aren't so many of these thoughts bouncing around. If you can learn to relax, sometimes the guard goes down, so don't pick up all these things bumping into your territory. You should practice balance all day long as it prepares you for meditation at night.

When I sit down to meditate and things that happened to me during the day run through my head, then I must stop, take some deep breaths, and tell that part to shut down so that I may become one with the Universe and flow with it. You have to balance, to shut out the problems, to center yourself so that the peace and calm enter your body. It can rejuvenate your body, and that is one of the reasons that we can live longer than you on the planet Earth. These pressures, the negativity, help to destroy the body but when you meditate you can keep your body healthy. As you meditate it rejuvenates and restores what your body needs to work properly. To meditate is to learn how to center yourself and then you can meditate anywhere, anyplace, anytime.

If you do not properly meditate every day your atoms, every atom and cell in your body becomes disoriented. It does not vibrate at an even pace so it does not work in harmony, as it should. That's when diseases set in like cancer, heart and blood diseases. If you don't meditate you will not be balanced enough for your body to survive for a long time. So if you meditate, it can help fight illnesses, it can give your body the energy it needs to heal itself because then the body doesn't have to fight your unbalance.

There are so many ways to meditate. Many people think to meditate you must sit very quietly and blank your mind. Some people meditate when they're very busy with their bodies but their minds feel like wandering. Some people still their minds and bodies, but please don't empty it out too much as humans don't have too much in there to begin with, so don't blank out your mind completely. Just try to focus on seeing color and hearing pretty music. Try many different ways to meditate as there is no correct way or wrong way. There is only the way that works for you. Sharing how you meditate might help someone else in their quest for getting in touch with their teachers or their guides.

The negative beings, be they alien or human, are increasing their power, and it will be harder to meditate. It's your responsibility to keep your mind, heart, and soul focused. It's your responsibility to keep your eyes on where you want to be; it can be done. It's going to get worse, as in time they will be dispersing a gas to try to hold you back. This gas is dispersed by plane. So you're going to have to try harder and harder and harder. The more you meditate the easier it will be for you to keep meditating.

When you meditate properly you can take your soul to any place you wish to go, like to a space ship. It is not important to do this everyday at the same time but it is important to stop each and every day to do it. True meditation can stand you right before God, and you can stand in front of his throne anytime you wish. You can meditate while taking a walk; once you learn how to get yourself into a meditative state quickly you can do it even when you go to the bathroom at work. It can rejuvenate yourself quickly so things don't upset you as much as they did before.

Some people say, "I'm gonna meditate tomorrow, I'm gonna do it tomorrow." But if you meditate to turn inside yourself, you will find your own answers. You will see God. You will talk to Him directly; you won't need a third person. You won't need channelers; you won't need preachers and you won't need someone to tell you how to pray.

While you meditate request more memory of why you are here and what your job is, keep requesting until you're blue in the face. It will slowly come to you. Keep your eyes on those around you because many times your answers come from people who interact with you already. Remember that when you allow and ask for the spirit, the light of God and Christ to enter you while you meditate, you do then become peaceful, you become more knowledgeable. And if you keep that in your heart you can stay on the path, it's His gift to you."

"My definition of meditation might be a little different than earth's idea of meditation. To me meditation is going within and quieting the mind so that the heart can become one with the Universe, become one with God. Meditating is going home to God, being with Him as one, soaring through the Universe as one. He is part of you. Understand it all, love and embrace it all. Love should be part of you; it is being in oneness with everything. You can feel love, strength, power and contentment in meditation. In those few moments everything would be perfect and nothing would matter because you would be home.

Praying is talking to God and meditating is listening. If you are balanced, if you do it regularly, if you trust, if you have the faith, if you allow yourself to step into a deep meditation, you will hear in your mind the answers you need. Remember you can go to God's feet and you can be with Him, to blend with that light.

During meditation some of you could use soft music in the background. But this could distract others so it depends upon the individual person; use whichever is best for each individual. However, in a group effort maybe something very soft in the distance could be used, but it is not necessary. On average it is better to have less sound around you, less chattering all the time as this allows you to be better balanced.

At first meditation often ends in a sleep mode, and while you are sleeping your conscious mind goes to sleep but your subconscious mind opens up. But you want to get beyond this point. You should not try to empty your mind but try to focus your mind on one thing. Some people see colors or light in their meditation. Try to focus on a certain color and step into the color, let it surround you, and then try to learn from that color. Try that. Everyone is different. There are many ways of meditating, and you must find the one that's right for you. During meditation ask for knowledge to come to you.

It takes practice to quiet your mind as it is busy with daily activities. Once you learn how to center yourself during the meditation you can meditate anywhere, any place, any time. It is best to set aside the same time everyday to learn meditation. To meditate easier you should be balanced in your daily life. You should be practicing balance all day long because then you can go quickly into the meditative state.

If you are a spiritual person, a balanced person, you are not in danger during meditation and the other side cannot enter your body nor do you any harm. If you are unbalanced you can be interfered with more and more often. Remember, don't use drugs or drink alcohol. Be kind to each other, plants, animals and everything that is on Earth. Wish everything well.

Meditation is one way to talk to your guides or alien friends. My thoughts are sent out and who picks them up, I do not know. During meditation your thoughts are sent out and anyone can pick up on them, so be careful not to send out negative thoughts. Once a thought is thought, it is forever.

During meditation you could also see into the future but most people do not get into a deep enough meditation to accomplish it. You can use meditation to make implants inoperable; you don't need someone else to do it for you. Sometimes we are our own worst enemy. You've got to let go and give yourself to God. Relax, by giving up control; you'll actually be receiving more. Try giving up a little control, and you will find that you have more control in your life than you've ever had before. That is why the dark side is so afraid of meditation.

When you are ill or are recovering from an accident and you do meditating during this time, you can speed up the healing process. This gives your body the energy it needs to heal itself because the body doesn't have to fight the imbalance before it can start to heal.

There are thousands of ways of reaching the Creator, and meditation is one way of doing it. We think that praying is asking God to hear us and meditation is a way of listening for His answer. Remember, during a meditative state you may not get the answers you want. Accept the answers, because we don't always know what is best for us.

You each have your own way of reaching the source; there are thousands of ways to reach the Creator. God doesn't care how you do it; He only cares that you try.

God is not going to save someone who goes to church and goes home and is rotten to his family. He is not going to save that person any quicker than the person in a jungle who believes there is someone who is greater than he and lives with kindness in his heart. It's what inside you that count's in His eyes."

Compassion

"Compassion and the understanding of each individual in their own right is very important. Remember don't look only at the body, look at the soul. The body is something that is deposited at the end of this life and a new one taken at the next, but the soul goes on and on.

You will never leave your planet without the compassion that God intended you to have. I think that those who love with no strings, those who allow people to grow and have their own area of life, are the most compassionate people in the Universe.

Compassion is something that Earthlings have a very hard time with. Without compassion you cannot love, for love is not something that you can hold in your hand and hold over someone's head. Love is allowing people to grow, to move away from you, to have time of their own and they in turn give the same to you. Without compassion you have no love, you see they are almost the same. There have been people who have shown your population what compassion is, a good example is Mother Theresa.

You are going to have to be comfortable with yourself, understand yourself fully 100%, and not have any negative thoughts about who you are, where you are, or what you're doing before you can stand up in this world and say why you're here. We are all going to have to learn to be very, very strong. I feel that if I can save one person, one soul, it's worth every bit of effort that I make. I feel that one person's soul is more precious than anything in this Universe and most people on earth do not feel this way. Earth is me society, an I—Me society, but once you have the compassion that you need you are no longer an "I or Me" person. You realize that the greatest gift you can give during your lifetime is to share your love with other people. The compassion that you can show other people is trying to understand people and being there when they're in trouble, not condoning, nor condemning, but just to stand there and be the hand that reaches out, or maybe just give a hug to someone who is feeling low. That is the greatest gift that you can give yourself, the other person, and the Creator.

To us a child is someone who has not yet reached his or her full potential of understanding, love and compassion. A child is not judged by years but by their capacities to understand and be compassionate. Some of your very young people are much more compassionate and have lived many more lifetimes than people in their fifties and sixties. When a child has reached a level of choice and the flip comes, some will not survive. Death does not mean their soul dies; it only means they discard the covering for their soul. They go on to another existence and receive a new body.

Life is a learning experience and has to be lived. And each individual has to deal with it their way so they can learn. You are here to do a job, as I'm also here to do a job. I know I could walk away, you could walk away, no big deal, but then we must repeat our lifetimes and take care of the karmic debts that we have incurred. I have too much compassion to walk away. My life is not that important. I am willing to give my life because this life is nothing. Our souls go on forever, so what is this covering of the soul but a piece of clothing to be shed. Life is everlasting and as we live our lives and learn, we become closer to God. I love all souls; even those who try to hurt me, even my enemies. Learn forgiveness, learn compassion, be understanding. You need compassion to understand when you do something to hurt another.

How many of your family unites are being torn apart by thoughts and words, instead of trying to understand each other. Go out and try to touch all the people you can with the idea of compassion. Living together in this Universe takes a lot of giving and taking, you must do both. It's a sharing of ideas and emotions. When the person next to you needs that, do that for him, because when you need it, he also shall share that with you. If you are negative, you are drawing that force to you. Don't allow the negativity to feed on your thoughts.

You can tell if someone is speaking the truth by looking into their eyes when they're speaking. Through the eyes you may see the soul. You must follow your instinct, your feelings and impressions. Listen, ask questions and file it away, in time your mind and your soul together will make the decision if this is the truth or not. You must learn to rely on yourself for the truth, because inside of you, you have all the knowledge. God gives you the knowledge and the understanding of how to get it. You have all the answers for yourself inside. It is not important that the answers for yourself are the same as someone else's. A truth that you hear now you may not understand; you may not realize it is the truth until many years down the line. Do not close your mind; keep it open and receptive, understanding and compassionate. Compassion is something that earthlings have a very hard time with. All you need to do is be a good listener and understand. Many humans believe they are the center of the Universe, but may I say that each person is important but God is the center of the Universe and all that is.

All light workers at sometime will go through survival training so that they have the skills and the knowledge needed for their survival, if that is what they plan to do. They have to go to the classroom so that it can be brought up into the subconscious on this level. Then everything they've learned in their other lifetimes in the Universe can come forward. Some even have to go to classes to learn how to remember what they've learned in-between lifetimes. They are from different places and are uniquely different, as different as night and day, but they all have the same inner compassion that was needed for these jobs. Sometimes it is better not to remember too much on the earth plane. You must survive on this planet, and if you know too much it would be hard to speak and not frighten people. Everyone, please have more compassion for your fellow beings, give more to others, they need your strength and your love. But also remember not to allow anyone who is only a "taker" to take from you because you are not helping them in this process. Like when talking to a child, you must be understanding and firm, not allowing them to take more than they need or can use, without becoming weak yourself.

It is important that each one of you realize that to become one with God, you must become one with the Universe. You must be in tune with even the smallest things on your planet and you should be able to feel the emotions of everything and everyone around you. It is possible to do this with practice, but it's going to take a lot of work to become compassionate with everything in your life. Even with what you think has no feelings, such as a piece of furniture, new carpeting, or the animals in your life. They all have their own auras. After all, a piece of furniture once was a tree that breathed, it was one with the Universe. It may now not be a living thing as you assume life is, but if you can tune into its vibrations, you can also tune in to God. Practice, practice, practice!

A truth that you hear now you may not understand and you may not realize it is the truth until many years down the line. Do not let your mind close, keep it open, try being receptive, understanding, and compassionate. If someone should try to hurt you physically or emotionally they would not be compassionate. Why would someone you know try to hurt you? That is not a true compassionate friend or being. People can send out bad vibrations to you but it is your choice to accept them or not. If you're silly and stupid enough to accept them, that is your problem; we all have the ability not to allow it to happen.

Many light workers are here at this time because they carry the strength of love and compassion. You can be compassionate for those who do not believe as you do, but do not be afraid to speak about what your truths and your understandings are. You are supposedly living in a free country. It is your right and privilege and your job to speak the truth as you know it. In no way is your job to harm anyone. Light workers do their job with kindness and compassion but are firm in their commitment, and this can radiate from their inner body.

You are not here only to procreate although sex happens to be a part of life. Sex is not an important part of your lives or mine, but it is a good part. You are here to have spiritual growth and have the soul progress back to God. The important thing about life is to mingle with people. The hug when someone is feeling low, the touch of the hand when we feel the other person needs it. The important thing is the melding of the souls to each other, the ability to be able to interact with compassion and understanding with those around you. God wanted people to live together in peace and harmony. Compassion and understanding of each other, being able to interact with each other that is what life is all about.

We of the love and light system do not abduct because of our compassion; we would not take anyone if they show fear. The aliens that are abducting and hurting people have no compassion, and these terrible atrocities are happening across the world. It is not love or compassion to say, "Oh sweetheart, I really feel sorry for you." Never a word should have to be spoken for this to come through. Have you ever seen a kid that instantly recognized another child, a child that they've never seen before, go right up to that child and give them a hug? That's because they can feel the inner love the inner radiance that is the creator's light from within. In the same token, a child can feel when a soul does not sing with the love of the Creator and they back away.

Compassion is not just having sympathy for someone; compassion is the trying to understand each individual in their own right. This is very important, try to understand the soul. Remember, don't look only at the body; look at the soul. The body is something that is deposited at the end of this life and a new one is taken at the next, but the soul goes on and on. When you look into someone's eyes, you can see the soul, and by placing their fingerprints with yours, finger to finger and thumb to thumb you can feel the soul. Show compassion and understanding to all. If you look into the soul you can tell when someone is suffering be it a physical ailment or loneliness. By showing compassion you can make the suffering better.

You will never leave your planet without the compassion that the Creator intended you to have. You will not be welcomed into the galactic family without compassion. I think those who love with no strings, those who allow people to grow and have their own area of life, are the most compassionate people in the Universe.

Monn explained that she had too much compassion to walk away from her job. "I am willing to give my life for this mission because this life is nothing; our souls go on forever, so what is this covering of the soul but a piece of clothing to be shed. I try to love all souls, even those who try to hurt me, even my enemies. After all, you need compassion to understand when you do something to hurt another.

How many of your families are being torn apart by thoughts and words instead of trying to understand each other? Go out and try to touch all the people you can with the idea of compassion. Living together in this Universe takes a lot of giving and taking. You must do both. It's a sharing of ideas and emotions. When the person next to you needs ideas or emotional support, do it for him/her, and when you need the same he/she may share with you. If you are negative, you are drawing that force to you. Don't allow the negativity to feed on your thoughts.

What you put out in the world is what you get back. So do you want people not to like you, do you want people to be angry with you? Do you want people to distrust you? Why not send out loving thoughts, loving ideas, compassion and understanding The choice is yours.

Show everyone the positive side of life. Bring them into the good side. Help them walk into the sunshine of life. Life is laughter, life is love, life is giving to other people and being compassionate to one another. No one can ever have enough compassion.

Addictions

"There is a slight problem here on this planet. Many of our light workers are choosing, different paths which is very hard for us to accept, but everyone has a choice.

It is very important that if you wish to raise your levels to step into our light, our vibration level and higher, you are going to have to learn that there are steps to be taken first. Here on this planet people become very self oriented, very much self-gratifying. I must have more money. I must have more jewelry. I must have more hours to work so I can afford to give my family a nicer place to live. And you must realize that this is only a temporary high when you receive these things. And then both your body, and mind like that high and it demands more, so that they can feel this high again. You can get yourself into this vicious cycle and it is not the way to go. You see, you already have everything that you need to be comfortable any place in this Universe. You have it all inside of you. If you have the capacity to love yourself, the capacity to accept yourself, for who and what you are and you are willing to forgive yourself for your shortcomings, you then break this addiction. It is important to realize and remember that if you carry the light of God in you, it is all you really need. For God does provide for His people. God will always make sure that you are taken care of. When you are not taken care of, then you are putting yourself in that situation for a learning process. It is your own decisions and your own choices. That is why so many of you people of Earth find yourself constantly in the same types of situations with the same types of problems such as always being short of money or always falling in love with the wrong type of person. It is because you need to learn something from the situation. You will constantly put yourself in the same situation until you learn from that. So if you want to get out of this addiction you seem to have, you must stop and look into yourself.

Don't judge yourself. Just say, OK, this seems to be my problem, what can I do about it? What can I learn about it? How can I change myself? Monn didn't say change other people, she said to change yourself. You cannot ever be happy by control, by trying to control other people. Happiness comes from within. Happiness is being willing to allow other people their own freedom and their own choices. It's a very, very hard thing to do. There are many people who like to control their husbands, their wives, their children, their jobs, especially the people who work underneath them. And you know it lasts only for a certain time and then the people rebel. And these types of people never, ever ask themselves why. They always blame everyone else. And they are going to have to do the same thing over and over and over until they learn what they are here to learn. Love and compassion is all that we need. *Remember* the light of *God* and the light of *Christ* is in you and around you. Love yourself. You love God. Do you love Him unconditionally? Think about it. Do you love and accept yourself for who you are? Can you accept yourself for who you are? Can you accept the people closest to you? Do you ever try to control them? All of these questions are hard ones to answer. But learning these lessons means that you have risen to another vibration level, and there are many levels that must be met. You cannot send a child to kindergarten and expect them to know the multiplication table. They must start at the beginning and go step by step. So, too, must man and woman. Sometimes it takes many lifetimes to accomplish this. And you are going to have to teach many people where to start it's not going to be easy. People seem to learn better when they see those around them doing it. Remember that almost every person has an addiction, whether it is love, money, wanting a fancy home, jewelry, or whatever. And this addiction is actually costing them their happiness because their mind tells them I have this, now I want more. So their level of happiness goes down until they have to fight and claw to get more. And then they're up high again. This addiction is a big problem. Remember that the only happiness and the only things that you need to survive are inside of you. Show this to people by your actions. Show them by your willingness to accept them for who and what they are. Show them by the love in your heart and the love in your eyes. Let them see that soul that shines so brightly within you. Yes, there will be some that will try to stop or harm you but you have the strength to accomplish it. You are strong at this time and you can stand alone in front of whomever and send your love to them. We stand here and send our love to all, those who have chosen our path and those who have not. It does not matter. Just because it is not your path it does not mean it is not the right path for them. Send your love. They may need it at some point in their lives.

Just fill the heart with love. Throw out all those bad things. Accept yourself for who and what you are. Love yourself in spite of it. Love those around you for who and what they are. Don't try to control them. Take care of yourself. They shall see the strength in your convictions and whether they wish to accept them or not is up to them. Throw out your addictions it is a hard thing to do sometimes, but it is possible and you wouldn't do it overnight. But that is the first step to the next level and the first step is the hardest."

Ego and Controlling Others

Monn had this to say about ego and the controlling of others, "Many times you can have a problem from the past that has to be faced before you can become a more spiritual person. Ego can make you jump to conclusions by thinking you can teach everyone the thoughts that you have because you are right. First think what you want to say and mull it around before you speak. The best way to teach someone is not to let him or her realize that you are teaching. Just suggest, give ideas, and let them see the love that is in your heart, and that will allow them to accept what you are saying as the truth.

Sometimes when you see someone, it is like looking in a mirror because they are so much like you and you both have the same types of ego problems. Most of the time you do not recognize this in yourself but you can see it in someone else. Often what you dislike in someone else is that which you possess yourself. If you have problems with someone else, it's best to check yourself for the same problem. If you wish to control or change someone, it doesn't work; change yourself as that may help to change him or her. Remember, they may be far more spiritually advanced than you are and if you pay attention, they may have something to teach you."

You May Have Talked To an Alien

"Many light workers have spoken with beings from space, be it on the surface of the planet or on a space ship. You have met them face to face and did not even recognize them. We are not so different from you. We are not gods. We are not superior beings. We are not angels. We are a race that was created by God just like you but in a different time and place."

Suggested Exercises for a Light Worker

"Use your light of protect," Monn said, "You must always remember to strengthen your light of protection a few times a day. Imagine you're inside a balloon of your protective light and surround yourself with it. Take your arms and your legs and stretch it out away from you, stretch it and reach out as far as you can. Pull those that you love inside your light/balloon. Stretch that light beyond them to include those that they love too. Do this every day so that you can do this automatically. When you get into your car, put the bubble of protection around the car and everyone in it. The more you use it the stronger it becomes. When you feel that you can protect yourself, do those closest to you. Stretch your balloon of protection to those in your city, then your state and then your country. The most important thing is to realize that you can put this bubble or balloon of protection around the planet. You have the ability and the strength you need to do this; reach inside yourself, it's there. All you have to do is remember that this is a God-given ability. Use it, strengthen it, and nothing in this Universe can penetrate it.

Don't get me wrong, negative beings do try to penetrate the protection. They just seem to sit around and wait for you to drop your light. Practice, stretch it out. I don't think any of you realize the strength of your lights. The only time that these negative thoughts, these negative beings can invade your space is when you allow this to happen. It's your choice. This is a good exercise for you to realize the strength of your light. Your light and God's light are one. I hope you will keep stretching your balloons of protection."

Changing the Flame on a Candle

"Try to raise and lower the flame on a candle. This is a good exercise to learn how to use your mind because someday you may be called upon to use that mind to move the Earth! At this time I run my ship by mind power. It can be done. For a long time the people of Earth have felt that if you can't touch, see, or smell something, it does not exist. Wrong, very wrong!"

Moving a Paperclip

Monn gave us this suggestion, "I wish you to try to use your mind because it is very powerful and you don't know it. Try moving a paperclip with your mind. You must believe that you can do it. All things are possible. You must realize that you are part of God. God can do anything He so desires, so can you. But please remember to use it for good or you will have a karmic debt.

You can move a physical object by thought, but remember you are trying to use a part of your brain that you have not used in this lifetime. Just like a baby learns, you must start by practicing, you must practice and practice. Deep relaxation and intense concentration are needed at the same time to be successful. You want to try to put all other thoughts away when you do this. You must be in a relaxed, balanced, calm state and not think about anything else but what you wish to do."

Blending Of Souls and Telepathy

"Blending of souls is done to be able to understand another person's every thought, action and deed. This is not a sexual act though many Earthlings get a very euphoric feeling when it happens, just as when they experience the sex act. Many of you have blended souls with your teachers before you were born, and that is why they can connect into your memory banks. This blending was done before you came down here so you can have contact with them, so you can learn from them, and this is also one of the ways that channeling can be accomplished.

Most aliens communicate with an Earthling by speaking into the mind, as that is a much simpler way of communicating. You are capable of doing this, don't be afraid of making mistakes, be adventuresome, go out and reach for that goal. It takes a lot of personal will power to step forward and take the chance. I am here to say step forward and take that chance, it's time to step forward and seek. It is like hearing a voice in your head; it is a feeling of something being instantly in your head without any thought. It is being able to touch other people without trying to tune in. It is a type of blending with another soul.

To be telepathic, you must also allow people to step into your space so that they may read your messages and you must be willing to step into them so that you may read their thoughts and ideas. Actually, it is a blending of two thoughts. You must be willing to do this, and too many people of Earth are unwilling or unable to allow other people to touch that part of them."

About The Soul

Many of the souls on Earth are becoming more spiritual, but along with that some are more negative. Many who are coming have chosen to be born here so they can advance with a leap in their spirituality. Many souls have chosen to be born on Earth to experience what is going to happen to this planet. Souls have levels of spirituality, and the more spiritual you are the faster you vibrate. Sometimes a highly advanced soul vibrates so fast that it cannot be seen by those beings that vibrate at a slower rate.

We don't consider this to be a dimension; some people talk about being in different dimensions or places and refer to themselves as having seven bodies at the same time, with a part of their soul in each one. That's absolutely false. You have one soul, you are one entity and you are at one place at one time. The rate of vibration of that soul affects where you are…so I…I don't know how to say it any differently."

Soul Recognition

"You have lived many lifetimes and you generally do recognize a soul that you have spent time with or have been very close to in another lifetime. As you become more aware of what's going on around you, you will probably start recognizing more people in that way. This is a feeling of being connected to the person but most of the time you do not understand what you are feeling. Sometimes it feels like a telepathic communication is going on between two people, this is what we call soul recognition. It's fun to watch two souls who recognize each other but don't realize what is going on. Often times each one is trying to remember where they met before.

This can also occur when you meet someone, who you have seen on board a space ship, you don't remember seeing him or her on board but you know the person is familiar."

What Is A Soul and When Does It Enter the Human or Alien Body

"Everything has a soul, be it a plant, animal, or stone. The human body is the vessel that you carry the spark of light that is shared with you by God. If you should lose your body, your soul goes on to another existence. You won't necessarily be born on Earth; you may be born on another planet far across the solar system. The soul goes where it can to learn a lesson. The objective of a soul is to work its way back to God. Again I say God because that is what you call Him; to us we are talking about the creator of all.

A soul does not die. When the body dies the soul goes to a place where it looks at what it had done during its previous lifetime. How long it must stay there depends upon how quickly the soul learns its lessons. Then the soul and the Creator make the decision as to when and where it will be reborn or where it could be used as a walk-in. Many walk-ins on Earth at this time will decide to let the body perish so they may go immediately to another planet for another mission. There are almost as many choices and decisions to be made as there are people.

If you were created as a thinking, sensuous, compassionate soul, you will always be that type of soul. Now if you go to another planet you may not look the same but your soul would be the same. You would be the sum of all that you had experienced. A lot of people joke that maybe someone like Hitler should be a rock and maybe he should be stamped on for a million years so that he would understand what he had caused. It doesn't work that way! If you are an inanimate object, you will always be one, once an animal it would always be one, etc.

It is important to remember every rock, stone, and drop of water is part of the Creator, it has a soul. The power of the Universe is in it. A crystal has a soul and accepts energy from the Universe and can pass that energy onto people. The important thing to remember is you don't need power from crystals or anything else. You are a thinking, reasoning being, so don't pray to one of God's creations; go to the source for help. You don't need to go to a middleman to speak to God or Jesus, you already have that power.

All souls can be called a light source. If a soul could be captured on your film, which it can't because your film is so primitive, it would register more like a light on the film than anything else.

There are some differences in species as to when the soul enters the body. For earthlings, it is near birth or at the actual birth. The soul departs the body as well when near death or at the actual death. The body can function for a while after the soul leaves, which could cause many of your doctors to say the patient is in a coma. That's why sometimes keeping people on life support machines is not good. You see, the soul has departed and only a shell is left.

Your soul radiates a golden light and your soul is separate from you body. Without the soul the body is nothing but an empty shell. The soul can travel the Universe anytime you so wish and desire it, if your vibrations are right. I think you call it astral travel on your planet. That is not really how it works, the way you think on your planet, but it is close. Many in your medical profession have seen this light move on at death, and there is a difference in the weight of the body when it does. There have been articles written about this happening and you can find them if you look.

When you astral travel, the soul keeps in touch with the body; you are connected by thoughts not silver cords. When you astral travel the soul leaves and your body runs automatically on very low power. This means the body slows down very much, body temperature drops, breathing rate slows, and the blood pressure drops. The longer your soul stays away from the body the greater the risk of something happening to the shell.

A walk-in can stay away from their bodies longer than someone who is born on Earth only because their soul has the memory that it can be accomplished. Earthlings can teach themselves to do the same thing but it takes a lot of practice, good balance in the body and the ability to reach deep meditation.

There is only one person who can destroy the soul and that is the Creator. A nuclear explosion or a nuclear reactor melt down could alter a soul. A possible painful death could cause the soul to have fear, and it could take the fear along with it into the next lifetime. You see if you are not at ground zero you can have a long and lingering death, and the trauma could be carried into another lifetime. This fear would have to be dealt with over the next several lifetimes. Even those people at ground zero do not have their souls destroyed."

Soul Computer

"Instead of using implants we now use a soul computer. Each soul has a different vibration, and once we have made physical contact with you we can enter your soul's pattern in the soul computer. With that we can tell what you are doing, what you are feeling, or where you are at any point in time.

I have to go to school all the time. My latest schooling had to do with evacuation training and the setting up of a special soul computer for evacuation of the planet. We are taking the light workers soul imprints and then putting them on this special computer so we can contact them easier in case something happens very fast."

Soul Mate

"A soul mate is someone who has been together in many lifetimes, and they can recognize each other when they meet them in their current lives. Soul mates are not necessarily husband and wife. This time around you may be mother/daughter, father/son, father—daughter, next time you may be brother/sister, but it is a closeness that you feel for a person. Your souls seem to reach out to each other and know each other instantly. A soul mate is someone that you can relate to, you can understand each other; they don't question what you do, you don't question what they do. It is understandable that as an individual each one has their own thing that they must do. You allow each other to do these things but you still have this attachment; they just seem to recognize each other and blend together in harmony. This could also be two very close friends and you love each other for doing these special things."

Twin Flame

Monn had this to say about twin flames. "Many people believe and feel they have a twin flame and it is very important then to find their other half. Actually, some of the light workers separated from their twin flames for this job. Sometimes a separation of beings that are meant to be together has to be done for the sake of a job. This separation has occurred with many people who are here on Earth working at a great cost to those they leave behind, often feeling a great sadness with the separation, and yet they know the work must be done. Twin flames are not always like each other; it is a fact that many are the opposite of each other. When you think of twin flames you think of your spouse, your mates and that is not how it is. Many times your twin flame can be your parent, your child or brother/sister

Not all entities have twin flames; there are some who are created without a twin flame but not many. Christ is the closest description to one who is a single flame, one who is created whole unto himself; you see, God created him that way. Jesus did not have to work His way to perfection because God created him that way.

Many twin flames have worked very hard on Earth to create a successful relationship. You see, when you are on Earth with a twin flame, you have a lot of strength together. Having a good relationship with anyone takes a lot of work, a lot of giving and taking. Being with a twin flame can also be a problem because sometimes one lets the other half do all the work.

Many people talk of twin flames being one male and one female essence, thus making a balance. Many believe when a certain male or female essence is needed on a planet that half comes to it; this is not fact because the soul does not change or have a male or female essence. The only change that occurs is the vehicle that the soul rides in.

If half of a twin flame falls to the dark side of the force, the other one does not wait for that person to come back into the light because it may take many lifetimes for that to happen. They are then assigned to work with other beings because missions must be completed no matter what. Often those that fall away believe that their twin flame is still with them; generally this is someone in disguise trying to get them to believe their twin flame is still by their side."

Eric had this to say about twin flames in 1990. "Twin flames many times separate to do their jobs, which are in service to humanity. When we separate, we are always reunited with our other half in another time and space. Sometimes separations are necessary for jobs; many halves are here on Earth at this time and many halves are in space. A separation like this is not as long as it seems for in the span of the Universe a lifetime on Earth is but a blink of the eye. Most of the aliens working here at this time have someone on Earth you would call a twin flame. They are just two souls who blend and unite for eternity. Although many separations do occur, they always return to each other unless one decides to go to the dark side of the force.

If you are working with your twin flame and then you somehow slip up and don't do your job, I am sad to say they do not wait for you to decide to continue your job. They are reassigned to others who are not their twin flames. The pain of losing you goes with them, but the job must be completed even with another being.

Often those who fall away believe that their twin flame is still with them although it is generally someone is disguise trying to make the person believe that they are their twin flame. That is why you must always pay attention to your heart; it will tell you the truth. Many entities in the Universe can change their appearance and deceive you but the soul is always recognizable. It is up to you to recognize the beings for what they really are and not as they want you to see them."

Sisterhood and Brotherhood

One of the persons attending a session in 1989 remembered something about a sisterhood and asked if each planet has a sisterhood.

Monn was speaking at the time and said, "Each group of planets has their own sisterhood or brotherhood. Some systems have many planets that are inhabited and some systems only one, so representatives are from quite a few planets but not all.

You earn the right to join a sisterhood or brotherhood and you must be asked to join. Many light workers are from different sisterhoods or brotherhoods, but not all are joined. Let's put it like this. In a Universe that has many planets with beings on it, one being earns the right to become the representative of each planet for that section. Then they join together and they send one to a larger section of planets who have all sent representatives to do the Father's bidding.

Each command that is here at this time has a sisterhood and a brotherhood representative. These sisterhoods and brotherhoods of light have names, but I cannot tell you what they are.

Many of these beings wear cloaks, and the color of the lining is the degree of the height you have attained in that order. Gold is the lining color of the highest you can become."

Masters

"When you become a full master, you are allowed to wear a dark brown robe. You on Earth are not all masters, so don't get a big head. On a scale of one to ten with ten being an ascended master, let's just say that you're all above one. There are different degrees of masters, too you know. Light workers are higher than your normal working forces in our command."

The Difference Between Master and Avatar

"If I can compare one who is in high school to one who has is graduated from college and gone on to their master's. That is about the difference between a master and avatar. The master compares to one who is in high school."

When asked what the rank is from master to avatar Monn answered, "Not yet, you are not ready." When asked if maybe those at the meeting were elders, Monn replied, "I cannot answer that at this time." (This took place in 1989)

"When answering your questions, before I can give you an answer, I check with my computer, and if that is not up to date on the level that you are learning, then I must call on each teacher and see what each of you can handle. Then and only then can the question be answered, although at times I blurt out the answer and get myself into trouble for giving you more information than I should!"

Battle for Earth, Good Versus Evil

God

"You on Earth call the Creator of all God and, I want you to know He is real and it does not matter what you call Him. Different names are given to Him in different parts of creation. God has given you the gift of instinct, be cautious and follow your instincts; you must believe that you have it. Realize you are part of God and He can do anything He so desires, and you can also. We are all individuals and yet we are all in God's image.

God is the spark of life, the light that is in you. You can use God's light to protect yourself, surrounding yourself both inside and out with this light. There is nothing that can penetrate the light if you believe. You may also use the light of Jesus Christ as a double protection. But God is in every individual person. You are His seed. You are part of Him. When this is done correctly, you will feel an inner peace and warmth; that tells you, you are cradled in Gods hands. If you have a little bit of doubt, this protection will not work.

I would like to say that only God creates a soul and He is the only one who can un-create a soul. He does not do that very often. If you learn from the mistakes you make and go on to better things, you have improved your stand with God. He has given us choices and understands that we do make mistakes. As long as we learn from them and acknowledge that we have made mistakes and try not to do them again, He understands. But even He, like parents, tire of the repeated mistakes without accepting the responsibilities for the errors, for not accepting the things we do wrong to other people, and not trying to make amends. These souls when they die go to classes. We are not allowed to make errors, and we must forever try to learn from our errors and are not reborn until we learn. At some point if we do repent enough, God may give us a chance to try again. He looks at each individual and then makes the choice. God has changed His mind and allowed people to be born again, but there are some that He hasn't allowed to be born again.

I would also like to say that God gives everyone a spiritual name that usually follows you through all your lifetimes."

In 1991 we were told, "God loves all of creation, all things. Even if you get a little ticked at Him, even if you do evil, He loves you. If you realize you made an error, He will accept you back with all the love He has. I want you to know what seems like a thousand years to us is but a moment to God.

God has a law which is that all things have a growing period, a dying period, and a rebirth. That is God's law and God's law cannot be changed. But we can change the courses of people, their attitudes, and their karmic debts by our own positive attitudes. Remember all your thoughts, once they are thought, are sent through this great Universe of ours, so think a thought and it shall be sent and received. That's why negative thoughts are not the best thing to have. May I say this, evil or bad entities feed on negativity, yet they whither and shrink from love. You have a very old saying on your planet; kill with kindness. You can change people; you can change the course of this Earth. But I say that you cannot change the natural course of evolution of Earth.

God has sent many beings to the planet to represent Him and many of them have been called Christ just as Jesus was. Some of these beings started different religions on the planet which have continued to this day. There is not one religion on Earth that has all the correct knowledge; they all have a piece of it. It is important to find the pearls in all religions as it will be your salvation."

Colors And Rays What Do They Mean?

In 1989 before a channeling session we were discussing colors and if each one had a meaning, so we asked if they would share the meanings and spiritual connotations of colors. Monn answered with, "Each part of the Universe has a color code. We all accept the white light of Jesus and the light of God as being a gold-silver color. But each sector of the Universe has its own ray of colors and meanings, so that is a hard question to answer.

A ray is a pure light and is usually an offshoot of a color from God himself. That is the purest form of energy and light. In the center of all is the gold/silver light of God. Then there is the light of Jesus, which is the white light. Then from there God sends out His rays of light, be it blue, violet, green or yellow, and these lights then send out their own light. The blue light sends out many shades of blue. The green light sends out many shades of green. Not quite as strong and not quite as pure, but they are still lights, because all are still part of The Creator. Each of you has your own color of light depending upon where your spirituality and vibration level is. Every being has the white light of Jesus Christ and golden/silver light of God in you and you also have your own light."

Jesus

"All of us respect and love Jesus; He has a very special quality. He has so much love for all. You too, can give and have that type of love. I try to show my love to you through this work that I have chosen, and each of you should be doing this.

Jesus was nothing more than a physical being while on Earth in a human body, because He had an Earth mother and had to contend with everything that is on the planet. It took Him time to, how do you say it, for the veil to be lifted so He could remember why He was here and what His mission was. His soul is the creation of God, and He carries the remembrance of that with Him just as you do. Jesus really is the Son of God as it's taught in your Bible although some people believe that His father was an alien from another planet. His father…is God…who has the highest spirituality and highest vibration level in the Universe. Jesus was born here because He wanted to help mankind.

Jesus can and has walked on Earth many times, sometimes without being recognized. When He returns to be the leader of the planet, He will be coming as a lion and He will at first not be recognized by most people. In the time that Jesus has been away from Earth He has gone to other planets to work and has been called by other names. Once this planet is back on the right track, He will go on to another job, another mission. The book, "He Walked the Americas" refers to

Jesus but the stories are not all correct, just as your Bible is not one hundred percent correct. They are stories that have been told and retold, and some of them have been changed here and there. Jesus the Christ did come and walk these lands on this continent (North, Central and South America) as well as the Holy Land. He walked through Asia and the lands that you consider Europe. He has visited many people and walked on Earth after His resurrection trying to understand people but has not stayed for any length of time.

The day that Bonnie saw Jesus, He made three stops on Earth but did not speak. He comes only to those who believe He is the messenger of the Heavenly Father. So remember the person standing next to you could be Him. You will know when you see Him; you will see God in Him if you allow your instincts to come forward. There will be no mistaking who He, is and He needs no name because He radiates the image of God.

There are many people on Earth who have claimed or will claim to be Christ or Jesus. You will have to make the decision for yourself if it is the truth or not. Hopefully, you will make the correct choices and decisions. But don't make the decision on what other people say, make it with your own feelings your own emotions. Make a judgment only when you can meet the person face to face so that your eyes can meet and you can look into his soul, and then you will know the truth. You will be able to recognize whether he is lying or telling the truth. Don't forget the eyes are the passage to the soul. Just as you can see evil in the eyes you can also see goodness in the eyes.

Satan has the same capabilities as Jesus. Remember, Jesus had said that, "False prophets and a false Christ shall come in my name and shall deceive the elect if possible; we can all be deceived if we don't pay attention and learn to use our instincts."

Monn said, "I have shuttled Jesus back and forth to the Peace Ship quite a few times. Jesus is approximately five feet eight inches tall with blond/brown hair and the most beautiful eyes that you'd ever want to see. To different people He appears slightly different, but if you ever come face to face with Him, there is no question of who He is.

Most of the time Jesus is so busy that I know I can't speak to Him, but there have been times when I have been able to speak with Him, and He is the most loving, compassionate, understanding person that I've ever met. He makes you feel like you are the most important being to Him. Even when He's busy I just love to watch Him do His work. I just kind of sit in awe of Him because you can you feel the peacefulness and contentment radiate from Him. Jesus makes you feel like all the cares you have in the Universe are taken care of with love, compassion and forgiveness.

I have sneaked in and watched Jesus lecturing in a hall with many people present. Now most people when they lecture in these halls use machines to interpret what the speaker is saying, but with Jesus it's not needed as He speaks in a language that everyone can understand. When He speaks in front of an audience, each individual knows that Jesus is speaking to them personally. It's like you're the only person in the room and it's like Jesus knows exactly what you're feeling, what you're thinking and what your beliefs are. He seems to know whatever you need to hear at that moment. When He speaks a room just becomes radiant and quiet. He seems to speak to your heart, not to your mind so there is no misunderstanding or any doubt about what He is saying. You know that no matter what you do, He will always love you."

Eric explained, "Jesus can take the meanest cat or being and can make it purr like a little kitten, just by saying, hello. When the different cultures meet on board it is very hard as they each have different ways of handling situations and these have to be worked out, ironed out. He has a way of listening to two sides of the story and saying, "Is it important?" His remark takes the wind out of everyone's sail. These systems have to work together for the good of all. If the walls on the Peace Ship could talk, there would be many stories to tell."

In 2001 the question was asked if there were other names for Jesus and it was answered this way. "He has worked on many planets, and each one has called Him by a different name. We call him Jesus because that is the name you recognize Him by. If we were speaking to someone who does not recognize that name we, would call Him by the name they can recognize the Son of God by. No matter what species, everyone seems to recognize Him when they see Him in person. By the way, Jesus does not eat meat. It's very hard not to eat meat in the third dimension, but once you get into the fourth dimension, it is a rarity to eat meat."

"Jesus is very special. You see, He is whole unto Himself, a single flame, but most are separated and are part of a twin flame."

"Jesus often said that His words were not his own and they came from the Father. Many people today would call this a form of channeling. Jesus was a man and he only spoke the words that were given to Him when they were needed. There were times in Jesus' life when He lived just like any other person; it was only when He started His job/mission that He actually spoke the words directly from God.

What Jesus did we don't like to call channeling as that is a word that Earth beings have used; we like to use or call it a form of communication. It is the way that we can accomplish talking to you without the face to face contact. Jesus and God can speak directly into the human mind but are you ready to listen? In your situation where you are now, you don't want to speak to God face to face. I know that a face-to-face contact with Jesus or an alien would be more convincing to people, but even if that happened there would always be someone who did not believe that it happened."

Christ

"Christ is a title that is earned by what you have done in the past and what you do in this lifetime. It is a title given to anyone who does God's work. A Christ can hear God's words and follow His direction. Then and only then you may speak for Him. Only a few people on Earth at this time have earned the title of Christ."

In 1995 we asked about the possibility of there being more than one Christ on the planet. To our surprise the answer was, "There have been many Christs who have walked on Earth. Melchizedek has been there three times. In all probability he will be on your planet shortly. I don't know if you'll meet him face to face as it depends on how things go."

Christ Command

"Jesus Christ is the Supreme Commander of the Christ Command. They have approximately 1000 ships in the area near Earth. I think calling what they do a military action is the wrong word because on your planet military means killing, shooting. Our military service is only for protection; it is only meeting force with equal force. It's not a first-strike force it is only for defense."

Lea, who you met earlier in this book, has shared this information about the command she works for. "Jesus who is the Commander has made four trips to your planet and no one recognized Him. He did this so He would know the pressures of the planet and could understand what light workers are going through. He wanted to understand their feelings and emotions and what problems they are running into.

The Christ Command is here to keep track of things as they progress. They are and have been specifically chosen to coordinate space ships for the evacuation of earthlings, plants, and animals so that this Earth can be replenished when the time is right. It is a large task to gather all the flowers, blades of grass, and animals to the smallest bug. They wish to preserve all that the Creator has created, to put this planet back in the order that God had intended it to be; then the beauty shall show forth like at no other time. Our ships are quite large and at this time are gathering many, many more ships in the hope that more people will be joining them. It is the light workers job to make sure more people will be coming with us.

Over the years some of the people of Earth have taken our messages and ideas and used them for their own end, but so be it. That is why there is confusion between us and the Ashtar command. Many people claim to be with the Ashtar command and work with Jesus. But many of them have been infiltrated with the dark side of the force. You see we are those that work in the light. Our supreme commander has the same soul that was on your planet and was called Jesus the Christ. Our mission, when it is needed, is not only for the evacuation of Earth but to bring Christ back to this planet so that Earth can be brought back to what it was intended to be.

The leader of the Christ Command has been on board Eric's ship. They are part of the whole that is here at this time with many other groups. There have been meetings for evacuation of planet Earth, and they are trying to make a connection so people can raise their vibration level. There are so many people out there who need a light bulb to go off in their head, and some need a little kick in the butt to get them started. So many systems are working together for planet Earth trying to save as many people as possible. All systems do not agree fully on the best procedures or best practices, but they still work together hand in hand for one single goal and purpose.

"There are three hundred thirty six beings that are attached to the Christ Command on the planet at this time. That number is always changing as people are always accepting or rejecting the light of the Creator. May the light of Christ shine on all!"

Christ Consciousness

Many people talk and write about the Christ Consciousness, but what is it, really? I have never heard a good explanation of what it is. This topic came up during a channeling session, and I have to admit I still don't understand exactly what it is. Everyone talks about it but no one has clearly defined what it is so that I can understand it. Here is what the aliens said about Christ Consciousness.

"When you are confronted with someone not of the light, send them your love and light because they cannot accept the love because the love is sent in the light. And negativity cannot survive with that. So by sending your love and light it will bother them unless they're willing to accept the Christ consciousness and light. If you send negativity, fear or anger to them, they feed off that and become stronger and can use it against you. Negative emotions are like a mirror reflecting back but if you send love it can have the same effect. Like if you send your love, it will reflect back upon you. This is the law of Karma. Karma is, what you sow, you will reap.

You have the choice of allowing the negativity around you to affect you and to draw you down. It is your choice. Be aware of it and don't allow it to happen. At some point in all lives you must take full responsibilities for yourself and your actions. You must be able to forgive yourself for your past actions. You must be able to forgive yourself and ask for God's help to go on. We all make mistakes. Anything that has happened in the past is not an error if you accept your responsibility in it and you are willing to learn from it."

Angels

"Angels, like God, are neither male nor female. An Arch-angel is neither male nor female although they can incarnate on a planet. When this happens, they usually divide into a male or a female or whatever way the beings were created on the planet they are entering. Once an Arch-angel incarnates on a planet it has to work its way to back to becoming an Angel again."

Lights of Protection

"Each of you has the white light of Jesus Christ in you and you also have the golden/silver light of God and you have your light, which has color. As you become more aware you will see the light more and it will be there whenever you need it. All are offered the light, it is up to each individual to accept it or go on without it.

You can use this light to get rid of bad aliens or spirits. With aliens you must consciously tell them to leave, let them know you will not accept their mentality. Don't allow them in your space.

If you are bothered by spirits or feel some evil in your home, use your light of protection. You may also use holy water to bless it if it makes you feel better. Any time you use anything in the Lords name it helps. It is a ritual that is not needed but it makes you stop and think about calling Him to cleanse your home, your body and to chase out all that is evil. It is something that should be done more often, especially when you feel there's a lot of negativity around you. You don't need to use holy water to do this. You can use anything that is natural anything close to nature while using God's name, the Lords name or both. You can use anything from nature that has not been disturbed from its natural way of being or harmed by any chemicals.

There is evil lurking in the Universe and the white light of Christ will protect you. If you are bothered even with the light, consciously tell that force to leave.

Tell them that you will not allow them in your space. They're little tricksters and will try to fool you into believing that they have left.

I have talked to you before about God being in all of you, but you are not God. God's light is in you and with God's light you are protected. You may also use the light of Jesus the Christ as a double protection. Surround yourself inside and out with this light. There is nothing that can penetrate it if you believe 100%.

Let me put it this way to all of you. Our jobs are to get you to stand in your own light, in the light of God, and in the light of Christ. We want you to be able to stand by yourself alone and to survive; when that is done we must back away and allow you the opportunity to experience it. If we did not back away you would continue to try to lean on us and expect us to be there to support you. We shall all stand together as friends again when this work is done. I promise that, for it was the agreement we all had and that shall be.

You can protect your family by using your light but remember they also have free will and they can accept that protection or reject it. Remember this light can be used in two ways, negatively or positively. It is your choice and you must live with the reactions to your use of that light positively or negatively. You can use your light to hurt people, if you use the negative side of the force. Many negative things are going to be thrown against light workers, so protect yourselves at all times with your light and use it wisely.

Once you learn exactly who you are and are willing to accept it in your heart, you shall stand strong in your convictions and take the message to all who come in contact with you. Sometimes the biggest messenger is one who does not speak but one who stands in the light and shines for everyone to see.

When you walk into the lion's den you want to shine your light, and those that will see it will see it. No one is meant to save the world, but you were meant to put a little light here and there. The most important thing to remember is that if you walk in the light, the darkness has a hard time in your presence."

Light Worker

Many light workers are here, but not all are accepting their jobs. Some light workers have accepted their jobs and then turned to the other path. It is the negativity of this Earth that causes a lot of the problems. So we must accept everyone for who and what they are, you also must accept yourself for who and what you are. There have been many light workers who have accomplished their jobs and left the planet by disappearing or death. The time has come for all the light workers to open up, shine their lights, and shine the Creators' light to erase the darkness that is looming on this planet.

The path for each of you is an individual path; neither we aliens nor anyone can feed you your answers. You must search for yourself, so you will know when you have a breakthrough. You have to learn to meditate, be balanced and compassionate, so you will know when things are right for you. This is going to be a long, hard, soul-searching process and progress. Survival of Earth is important and humans on Earth are going to have to do it. Some of the light workers work very closely with Christ and go with him wherever He goes."

Born-ins And Walk-ins

"A born-in has the soul of beings who decided to come to Earth for a specific purpose. These souls have decided to come the hardest way possible. They have chosen the birthing process on the planet's surface. These souls have to grow up with all the negativity of the planet. These are souls who have risked the most, but if they can succeed they can reach a greater level of spirituality. Don't be awed by talk about walk-ins being so great and special because they have chosen a much easier route to become an earthling.

Walk-ins are beings that have come to this planet not by birth but by entering a body that is already here, usually at a severe traumatic time or near death. This is always done with the full consent of the soul that was originally occupying the body.

A body is a group of atoms with a nucleus of a soul. When the soul leaves a body to become a walk-in, the body is disassembled but not destroyed and the soul moves on to another body or form. Some walk-ins will finish out their physical life in the earth body and some won't. In other words some walk-ins will stay here on the planet and the body that they are in will be destroyed, but their soul will survive. Some aliens/walk-ins who are here in human form will leave in their earth bodies, others will go aboard ship in their earth form and help the people of Earth. This will be done so humans won't be terrified or frightened. Some will work on board a craft and the body will die of natural means. Some of the aliens/walk-ins will come back to this planet in human form to help get the people started again. Hopefully, humans will not make the same mistakes that were made before.

All of this was agreed upon before they walked into their bodies. All the decisions were made and agreed upon fully and were fully understood before they ever came to this planet. Many don't remember or understand at this point but will later on at some point as they become more aware of who they are and where they came from.

A walk-in can stay away longer from their bodies when astral traveling than someone born on Earth only because their soul has the memory that it can be accomplished. Earthlings can teach themselves to do the same thing but it takes a lot of practice, good balance in the body and the ability to reach deep meditation."

Seven Systems Working On the Light Side of the Force

"All told there are seven commands working to evacuate Earth, when the transition of the planet happens, be it natural or manmade. They are here to try to help the people of Earth if they ask. A command is a group of people working together; it doesn't matter what the name is as long as you're working for the same goal and the same Supreme Being. Along with the evacuation we also must prepare to repopulate the planet, so it is not just the evacuation. It is the keeping of the people and the animals and it could be for up to three years. We then have the problem of trying to relocate the people and return them to their rightful place in the Universe. We all hope that that is possible and we all need to be able to understand what each one is doing."

The Christ Command

"The Christ Command is headed by Jesus Christ, He is their supreme commander. They are here waiting for the right time to let themselves be seen."

Love and Light System

Eric informed us that, "The Love and Light system is working with The Christ Command. We all have differences, but we all work for the salvation of the human race. As you are our descendants, so you are part of us. Light workers need to work with this command because we aliens need to understand human behavior. The System of Love and Light is a group of humanitarians who are not as well known as the Christ Command because we do not speak out as much or are as forward.

Those that are connected to the Love and Light system have come from many parts of the Universe. They have given up their families and home planets to spend their lives on ships in space for the betterment of other beings. Those within this system have come from many different backgrounds, some from the military on their home worlds and others come strictly from the spiritual realm. But they have worked for Jesus the Christ right along, even when He was born on your planet. There are many children here of Earth who are light workers for Jesus, and many have been imprisoned by the dark forces, but they are coming into the light because of our strength and our compassion and are surviving and becoming stronger. The time is coming when they shall step forward and be acknowledged.

The members of the system of Love and Light have made a commitment to work for the advancement of beings on planets that are in trouble. They travel from place to place, system to system, and universe to universe on board space ships, helping those who need assistance. This assistance is offered out of love and compassion and is done so that everyone on the planet and the planet itself can raise their vibration level and recognize that there is something greater than they are.

The system of love and light has a panel of twelve that they report to, but the ultimate leader is Jesus the Christ. He is the one who is coordinating this effort for planet Earth."

In 2001 Monn told us, "The love and light system also reports to a council of sixteen. Each member is from a different area in the Universe. Each member of the council is a different species and each member has in-put into the council. They meet in a room something like the circular room in "The Phantom Menace. Each species would be equal and decisions are made for the good of all. Many of these meeting have been held on The Peace Ship.

There are many council's which sit and make decisions for the good of all. There is a council of Elders who are advanced beings that oversee a percentage of what is happening, but there is also a council that sits over the Earth. Each planet has a representative on some of the councils, and there's even a council that sits over the angels and then there is a council that sits in the heavens."

Summarian System

"The Summarians come from the planet Summari. This is an ancient civilization that mostly destroyed themselves by not being kind to their own planet. They trashed it so badly they had to leave.

They came to Earth approximately 12,000 years ago and proceeded to destroy themselves here, but a few did escape back out into space. At the time many of them believed they were doing the will of God, but many people are fooled in this manner. They, like all of us are trying to learn from past mistakes."

Sirus System

"The Sirus System has thousands dedicated to making sure that the habitats for humans are done correctly. These living quarters must be adequate and supplies such as food for humans must also be there.

These habitats are on other planets and large ships. Some of these planets are mobile. Earth is a ship, it's mobile and it's moving but in a single orbit. There are some that look like a planet but it can alter its own course and move through space. This can be done by building your own atmosphere around the object. You can keep air, oxygen or gasses whatever the inhabitants of the planet needs, to survive, during its flight."

Orion System

"The Orion System has many planets, and they are not all good. It is like night and day between beings on the different planets. Many Orion aliens are abducting humans and experimenting on them. Other beings from that system are here to help counteract what these negative beings are doing.

These Orions who are here to help will be handling most of the food preparation. That's why the animals being collected are very important. You can't have beef without cows. Everything has to work in harmony. After you leave Earth you will become more vegetarians. You shall learn that you can survive without the flesh of animals. That is very hard to accomplish when you are in the third dimension."

Two Distant Systems

Near the end of 1995 we were told of these two systems for the first time. We were not told what they did, where they came from, or who they were. We were informed they came from so far out that we could say that they reach the heavens. From this comment we questioned if they could be powerful beings yet distinctly different species similar to the Cherubim, Seraphim or Archangels mentioned in the Bible, and we were told they are something like that.

We were also told that five of these systems have panels that they report to, but the other two don't because many of your people call them angels. These beings are the second and third level below God, so they actually answer to God. We asked but were never told about the level directly below God.

Those Working On the Dark Side of the Force

Antichrist

"The Antichrist will probably be a charismatic young man with a lot of passion who has some European background. He could also claim Jewish heritage, but then that could almost be anyone. There are actually five who are now living on Earth who could become the Antichrist. Which of the five will be strong enough to come forward is not known by us, two are in the Trilateral and the MJ-12. There is a good possibility that he could come from the United States or from the European Union. The sad thing is that they don't even know who they are, and the only thing these people have in common is their desire for power. Who they are I cannot say, only that he is part of the "now" generation. This guy, more than likely, will be the New World Order leader, the one who will head the whole thing.

Once the Antichrist knows who he is and steps forward he will be doing miracles. He will have quite a following and they will worship him. He will enjoy the power trip. The anti-christ thinks of himself as good as God, therefore he thinks he can control anything and everyone, just like God does. But he's forgetting one thing, God does not control, He allows His creations free will.

There are some very evil people on Earth at this time, but the one who is really evil will probably be followed by people who will think he is wonderful. There are many on Earth right now who could be fooled, but those that are of a higher vibration level will not be misled. You will see through this man, and I mean the word man literally.

Remember the Antichrist, bad or evil, whatever you want to call him, will at first have a good message, and when you start believing everything he says will be the time when he will turn and let the truth come out.

I know you want to know what the ranking of these negative leaders are; so the head is Lucifer, then Satan, the Antichrist, and the false prophets. Each of these has many beings working under them. The top three like to present themselves as a trinity, just as God is presented in your churches as a trinity.

There are many foot soldiers of the Antichrist on the planet at this time; they are the forerunners of the Antichrist just as light workers are the forerunners of Jesus The Christ. These beings are like lieutenants and they take orders very well and can execute orders to perfection. There are two false prophets already working on the planet.

When the Antichrist receives a fatal wound, it will probably be to the head and he will make a miraculous recovery. I know, in the Bible that it says he will suffer a "head wound." This could mean a gunshot or maybe it could be a blow to the head that would normally result in the death of the human body. He could be resurrected by using a cloned body of himself, and even a soul-transference could be done. Wouldn't that be a miraculous resurrection? All you need is a hair or a piece of skin to get the DNA to produce a cloned body. Most humans have already been tagged and bagged by the negative aliens.

The Reptilians and Grays are very close to making themselves known to the people of Earth, and with the work and implantations they have done on humans it will help make them part of the Antichrist's army. The bad aliens, who live underground on Earth, are planning a take over on the planet, and they may do it for a short period of time, but the Antichrist will snap it out of their hands.

One of the scenarios of the end times is that the battle of Armageddon could be fought between Christ and the Antichrist in the fourth dimension and Christ would be victorious. I would like to say that no one knows for sure what the future holds. I do not know. This battle of Armageddon will happen, but when and where it will take place is beyond my knowledge. I think and I hope you understand that it is the Antichrist's decision when he is going to step forward. Just how long God and Jesus would allow this to go on…I do not have any knowledge, it is their decision when this will all end.

During the flip there will be so much commotion, there will be so much pain and suffering, there will be a lot of fear, and everything will be negative. The Antichrist feeds and survives on this pain and suffering. One good thing is that they cannot survive at a higher vibration level.

Many stories have been told about Jesus that are somewhat like the ancient stories of non-Christian entities. This was done so people would not believe in the story of Christ. If you are lazy when it comes to looking at these negative things, if you don't open your eyes, you will fall for what the negative side will say. Remember the truth shall set you free. The good news is there will be those who resist the Antichrist and I know for a fact that Christ and spiritual beings will win."

Satan

"Satan is in control of Earth at this time. God has given this planet to Satan. Remember in your Bible, God sent him to Earth. He may be controlling this planet but God is in control of the Universe. God will let Satan work his wiles only so far and then He will stop it because He will never let this planet be destroyed or blown into a million pieces. In the meantime it's up to the light workers to counteract his negativity. You are God's foot soldiers; you are to prepare the way for his Son.

Satan is using the powers that God has given him in his own way, but remember everyone has these powers. If you have faith without doubt, you can stand, nose to nose with Satan and have the know-how not to let him exercise his power over you. You have the power of any incantation that he or any of him followers can conjure up. You may not realize that yet. The amount of faith or lack of it that you have will determine the amount of power Satan will have over you.

Satan was loved by almost everyone in heaven until his fall, and he still has a legion of followers. He does not go through the Universes picking up followers; he only puts things in their paths that could trip them up. Satan sends out his troops to tempt people and pull light workers off the path. These types of battles between good and evil happen on almost all inhabited planets at some point in their evolution.

Satan plans to turn brother against brother until man no longer exists; do you see this happening right now? There is a fine line between good and evil. Most people step over the line before they know what they have done. Both those that work on Satan's side and those that work on Jesus Christ's side are on the planet at this time.

Be careful, Satan can come as a ghost or as a loved one. He can whisper in your ear, and if you listen you are in trouble. Listen to your instincts that warn you if something is wrong. Your mind and heart should tell you, 'My loved one would not say or do that; what I am hearing is not right.' Then you must send that voice or ghost on their way and tell them you will not accept what they have to say. For if you accept what is being said you will fall.

Satan can and would pose as an entity that claims to be working with the light, in the light and of the light, but actually he is not. Don't forget that he was an angel when he fell. He took a lot of the powers with him because God gave him the chance and the opportunity to come back into the light, which so far he has declined to do.

Satan's followers believe that he is God, and he has a panel of twelve who oversee the Earth situation. They keep track of all the humans who are working on his team. The not so good Grays and Reptilians have a lot of technology but are not very spiritual, and some of them have teamed up with Satan and his group.

If you feel that there is some place or someone you should avoid because they make you uncomfortable, that is probably where you should be as a light worker.

Don't go there with a chip on your shoulder, show confidence that they have no power over you. They have no power to destroy you; it is only your own lack of faith that can destroy you.

During the final days Satan and his foot soldiers will be doing miracles. If he succeeds in fooling enough people, Lucifer will come here personally to take the planet."

Lucifer

"Lucifer is top dog and then there is Satan. They are not the same being as many faiths believe, just as many don't understand that Jesus Christ and God are not one. Lucifer is the main man, Satan and his legions are below him. Lucifer is being detained, and if Satan succeeds in taking over the planet, Lucifer will get his freedom and come here personally to take over the planet. If Satan does not succeed or does not succeed in fooling this planet, then there will not be as much destruction as if Lucifer comes under full power. Although the battle of Armageddon will still probably take place, the battle will not be as large. There would not be as many lives lost and not as much of the planet would be destroyed if the people are not swayed by the Antichrist, Satan and then Lucifer. Revelations in your Bible will be played out but to what extent depends on the people of this planet.

God gave this planet to Lucifer because He hoped that His angel would prove that he could become a hierarchy angel again. Instead he made himself a God and allowed his power and his ego to step in the way. We don't understand why anyone would accept Lucifer as a substitute for the Lord and I want to say that he is not a good one.

In the past Lucifer has not come to the planet, but Satan and his legions of fallen angels did and mated with the higher animal form on Earth, thus changing the direction of their evolution. This higher animal was only one genetic code away from them, and that was the only way the reproduction could have taken place. The genetic code has to be very close in order for a reproduction to occur. This was not acceptable to God and He was angry.

You call these angels who rebelled in heaven fallen angels. We prefer not to call them angels, we call them Satan and his legion of followers. I know you want to know how these names fall according to your military standards, so I will try my best. First there is Lucifer, then Satan and then the Antichrist. Each one would have what you would call captains, and then I think what you will call your lieutenants and, of course, the foot soldiers. I think that is how it relates the best.

This planet is very beautiful, and Lucifer's crew is hard at work here. They want Earth as their own. We of the Love and Light system have lost about 5,000 workers who came to the planet to work at this time to the dark side of the force."

False Prophet

"The false prophet will do a lot of preliminary work for Satan. This will be an ego person who loves power. He will be kept in the dark until the Antichrist lets it be known who he is. Satan and Lucifer will share their power with him, and he will more than likely enjoy the power. The false prophet also shall be fooled with this power at first and yet he will not realize until too late that he actually has no power.

I cannot give you a name of this person. You are going to have to recognize him for yourself or you will be taken in by his actions. This person probably will not be a walk-in although there is a very low possibility that it could happen that way."

Bad Aliens

"Bad aliens are the ones who abduct humans for their own use, and these beings have no love or compassion for anyone. They only have what is best for them on their agenda. These negative aliens bother a lot of light workers because there is information stored in their brain that they are not aware of. You are most vulnerable when you go into the sleep mode. So during the night is when they will bother you the most. When you realize that you are strong enough not to allow them to get to you, they will then leave you alone. If that memory of yours starts to come forward and you are not balanced and strong enough, they could get the information from you. We also have these negative types of beings out here amongst the stars.

There are many alien species in the Universe whose DNA is very close to yours. One of the major reasons the Grays (bad aliens) are abducting humans (against their will) is to make hybrids. They are trying to make an army that has the physical power that they do not have. These negative aliens cannot transfer their soul into a human body because genetically they cannot take their soul and put it into a human body as the crossover puts too much of a strain on the soul.

Some of the larger countries on the planet have gained technology from these bad aliens when they signed a pact with them. The aliens gave them the technology to produce AIDS and Ebola, which they introduced into the population to get rid of what they consider the unwanted useless eaters. These bad negative aliens and the military both have a scanner that allows them to understand and know your thoughts. They are also trying to figure out how far to turn up their instruments so they can affect your mind. They want to get into your head and put bad thoughts there. The bad aliens can take you against your will and put thoughts into your head or implant you if you are unbalanced.

Many of these bad aliens live underground here on Earth and are planning to take over the planet for themselves. We fear that if a war is started in the Middle East it will send ripples like a chain reaction, much like a nuclear fission, throughout the whole world. If this happens the bad aliens have a plan to step in and try to stop the war. Their plan is to fool earthlings into believing they are your saviors. They may take over the planet by force for a short period of time, but the Antichrist will snap the power out of their hands. So just be aware and don't be fooled by what you might hear or see in the sky.

Some of the negative aliens torment people to keep them off balance because then you cannot be the balance for the planet. Some people have a natural way of handling this by following their instincts. If you have not learned to follow your instincts and are just waking up, it is hard. But each and every one has the ability not to allow them to torment you. Don't think you're going to fail and don't give in because then you are opening yourself to them. Think positive, believe that you're on the right side, and put the negative thoughts out of your head that are giving them the room and power to move in. Don't do that. Use the positive."

Monn explained that, "The Russians, the Chinese and many other earth governments are working with the bad aliens to some extent. The aliens want all their bases covered, so they have contacted the major governments on your planet. That is how some of these countries have come up so fast. The bad aliens shared some of their technology with them just as they did with your government."

Shadows

"Shadows can take on many forms, and they will take on any form they feel is necessary to fool you. These have very dark souls. I have heard them described as a wispy, smoky, cold feeling in a room. Some are seen as a shadow of a cat or a person; many have big black hats on. Before they fell to the dark side of the force many were beautiful in form. These beings could have walked on your planet without cloaking themselves and not be discovered.

Evil is darkness, and that is why they are often seen as black shadows. These being will be given a chance to repent and be welcomed back into the light side of the force."

Contrast between the Forces of Light and Dark

"Both sides of the force are working on the planet at this time. It is very hard for those in the light because we work under stricter laws and regulation than the dark side does. We play by the rules; they don't have to. We are more open and honest and do not have the devious tactics that the dark side uses.

Their supreme leader, Lucifer, is in captivity right now so the dark side on Earth reports to Satan. They have two people right now on Earth that are preparing the way for him and most people don't even realize that they're working for him. You see, if you are not working for Christ and you don't make a choice to do good things, you automatically work for the dark side of the force. Being a fence sitter and not choosing a side means you are not making a choice and you are automatically drawn to the negative side.

The dark side does not have a council, but they have a panel of twelve who oversee Earth's situation. They keep track of all the humans who are working for him just as we keep track of our workers. No one knows if or when Lucifer will be released, but when or if he gets here almost everyone and everything will be fooled. The dark side has reinforcements coming to join them and they are traveling by spaceships. These aliens are very cunning. This is one of the reasons we are here at this time to help the planet in this transition, although we have the law of noninterference that we must adhere to.

The dark side, which includes the bad aliens, is interfering with earthlings, so be wary if you have full memory of going on board a craft because this is usually a screen memory so you don't remember what really happened. They give you enough to let you feel comfortable. Many times these negative beings let you have some memory or give you a little information that you can prove is correct. The object is to make people feel comfortable and then they start to take a positive message and put a little twist on it to maneuver a person to the darker side of the force. I have one thing to say about the dark force, they will always speak the truth and have a positive message with wonderful flowery things to say at first until they have you believing anything they say, and then they bring in the twist, just a half notch off center so that they can manipulate people into believing whatever they say. When you are not in a mental state of well being, you can be deceived very easily.

The dark side of the force, which the negative aliens are working for, is hoping they can take over 42% of the population as it would be as the hundredth monkey, turning this planet to their dark side of the force. The Grays that are working with the dark side are stepping up abductions, and your government has a pact with them so this means the government is involved.

Right now, 72% of the population is teetering and might fall to the dark side of the force. The time has come for all light workers to open up, to shine their lights, to shine the Creators' light, and to erase the darkness that is looming on this planet. As more people are waking up, the light workers are getting stronger and gaining strength while the knowledge and vibrations are starting to change. More of our cosmic friends are coming to help you, but we cannot do it for you. We have light on our side and we have the right leader, but you must do the work. Survival of this planet is important, and the people on the planet are going to have to do it.

It feels like this part of the Universe has taken three whole steps backwards. Things are stepping up, shall we say. They know which button to push, they know where to hurt you; it could be family or even an addiction like drugs or alcohol. The dark side uses what works best on your weaknesses or what some people on this planet think are not weaknesses. Some people on your planet think that getting money and power any way they can is not a weakness. Those who wish to see this section of the Universe go to the negative side of the force are stepping forward. They are using all the powers of the Creator on the dark side of the force. But do not be afraid for they only have power over you if you allow it. You can use all the power of the Creator to be the light that shines in this world; you are of equal force as long as you stand within the light.

When you experience death, the dark side can come to you and try to deceive you as your soul is passing over. At that time your soul could be snatched and used for their evil purpose, even cloning. However, children are protected until their age of reason. You should prepare yourself before death for this crossing over so that you will not be deceived. Many people who do not believe in the Creator or a supreme being could be deceived as they have not learned to judge for themselves if good or bad is showing themselves to them.

Be wary of those who claim to be from Atlantis and Lemuria. They were destroyed because they started to play God, just as your scientists are starting to play God now by cloning and genetic altering. There were some good people in Atlantis and Lemuria who were spiritual, but the majority of the priests and scientists of the time were not spiritual. They were working on the dark side of the force.

The dark side has now diluted approximately thirty-five groups of beings which volunteered to come to Earth, and many have bought into the Earth and the earthly wants and needs. If you have a mustard seed size of doubt about who you are and why you are here that doubt will control you and take you to the dark side, and it will be hard getting back. After all, all they have to do is put doubt in you to get you a little bit off the track. Those of the light side of the force have been having trouble and their lights are dimming. Many beings, be they human or alien, have come to the light and many have gone to the darkness. Many lights have been extinguished. Many lights have shown much brighter. Many light workers have fallen. Many people have been waking up to their mission and their job.

We cannot allow the people not of the light to get the best of us who are in the light because our jobs are very important. Remember that nothing is one hundred percent evil, for in them there is still a spark of the Creator, some place. It may be a little spark, but like an ember in a fire it can ignite and keep the world warm. Put your light out, surround yourself with it as the dark side cannot survive in that light. Share your light with everyone and if they are of the light they will join their light with yours, and you shall both become stronger."

You Won't Find These Faces on the Post Office Wall

Types of Aliens Visiting Earth
Pink Alien Being

"There are many species in the Universe, and some are close to your DNA but not quite the same. There is an alien species that is short in stature and has pink colored skin with little body hair. This is a species who like to collect smells. Their sense of smell is very advanced; actually, it is much better than their sense of sight. They enjoy repugnant smells and trade smells much in the same fashion you collect and trade sports cards. They do not like wearing clothing but do wear them when attending social events or interspecies functions."

Preying Mantis

"This being looks like a preying mantis and are visiting the planet. They are here mostly to observe because they have not had that much contact with humans. They have been involved in some experimentation while checking out humans but have not been involved in producing hybrids or anything like that. You see, your species is a wonder to almost everyone in the Universe. You have the free will choice but what you do with it is interesting."

Translucent Being with Wings

"There is also a species that is almost transparent, almost translucent-like; many earthlings call them light beings, but they are actually a species.

There are beings that fly but not in this Universe. They have a wingspread of approximately eight feet, their bodies are very strong, and they walk upright. But, unlike your birds eyes their eyes are placed on the head more like a humans. In other words, they don't see to the side like your birds do, they see forward. There is also a group of beings that have something like a translucent fold under their arms that they did use to fly but not anymore."

Nordics

"Another species in the Universe looks very close to what you do. These beings visit, but to my knowledge none are living on Earth. You call them Nordic, that is your name for them not ours." (Nordic looking aliens are said to have blond hair, blue eyes and are very good looking.)

Grays

"All of the Grays are from the Orion solar system. There are good and bad beings there; it depends upon which part of the system they are from. About 70% of the beings from this system are on what we call the negative side of the force. Most of the Grays that are on your planet at this time have destroyed their home planet by mismanagement. The Grays are very technological advanced but with very little spirituality; they enjoy playing God and do so by creating and destroying at will.

We do not fear the Grays, but respect them because of the power and the technology they have. These are the ones making hybrids, they have not perfected the process yet, so these hybrids cannot pass for humans physically at this time. With all of their abductions they are in the process of trying to perfect that flaw. These hybrids are hard to control because of the human part in them. The Grays don't have much strength or the physical stamina needed to fight and make war; therefore, one of the reasons for producing hybrids is to produce an army. The Grays came to Earth 176 years ago for the first time under the influence of the Reptilians although they had visited the planet earlier. One of the most frightening things is that the Grays believe the Earth is their planet and they want to take it over."

Reptilians

"The Reptilians are more powerful than the Grays although they do not have a great force on Earth. The Grays work for the Reptilians because 2,700 years ago an alliance was formed between the Grays and Reptilians with a contract that was signed on the Gray's home planet.

The Reptilians have been on Earth many times. About 110,000 years ago your time was the first contact. They left and came back about 27,000 years ago your time but left again because there was nothing they could use. About 10,000 years ago they became interested in what was on Earth and stayed for some time. They introduced their genes into your gene pool because they thought it would make a difference. This mixing of genes resulted in humans having negative tendencies.

There were basically four species of aliens that came to Earth and changed the course of the planet by leaving colonies or settlers. There was interbreeding of the species and that caused the difference in sizes and colors of humans you have on Earth today. In your part of the solar system there is life but not as you know it.

You should realize that there are many different forms of life and different dimensions and all exist together in one Universe under God."

Light Beings

"Light beings do not have a physical body like humans do; they come in a body of light. It is a soul without a body, in other words, not like you or I are.

Most of these beings have worked their way up to this level of existence. They are closer to God than most of us will ever reach. The next time around these souls could be born on a planet to learn something or to do a job. When you are born on a planet then the body takes on the characteristics of that planet.

A light being can exist for as long as they desire in that form as they do not have to go through the birthing process. There are many planets in this Universe that are very behind planet Earth in their spiritual evolution. And, of course, there are some rotten people out in space, as some people do choose a less spiritual path. Little do they realize that one way or another we must all pay for our wrongdoing's whether it is this lifetime another lifetime or maybe even never being allowed another lifetime.

When a light being travels in space to the best of my knowledge they do not use a physical craft. They have the ability to travel without one. A light being can appear even to a blind person. They can make themselves be seen through the mind's eye or they can be visible to your eyes. You could become a light being; remember, it is your soul that evolves; some people even call them angels. This is the name that your Earth people placed on these beings. I would like to say that angels do not have wings as your paintings show."

Bug People

"There is a species that looks like a bug and has a shell which is removable. This species originally needed the shell for protection but is no longer needed. They have round feet and have no need to wear shoes. They are biped, stand upright, and are quite tall and thin. I believe they have seven fingers. Their planet is in the federation system."

Ant like Type of Alien Being

"There are a group of aliens that looks somewhat like your ants but much larger. They are superior in intelligence to humans."

Ant Eater Type of Alien

I had a memory from September 7th of 2003. I saw a very strange animal with a long snout and body with short fat legs, which looked similar to the anteater type mentioned above. It was eating popcorn off of my bedroom floor. Now I know I did not have a single piece of popcorn in my house anywhere, and yet when I woke up there it was a piece of popcorn. This is all I remembered of what had happened on September 7th. I found out later that this was a type of being I had had contact with on board a ship.

"There is a species that looks a little like your anteater with a large trunk like your elephants have. The body is long and slender with very short, stocky legs. They have come on board the Peace Ship to meetings and have learned to love your earth popcorn."

Monn explained that the alien and myself, had talked and he expressed an interest in visiting Earth. I asked him if he would like to go home with me and see how Earth people live. He agreed to come along with me. These being love popcorn and took it from the ship to Earth with him. He stayed for only a few minutes; looked around and left. They are kind of cute and have only been in this system for a short period of time.

I vacuumed up the single piece of popcorn from my bedroom floor. I knew that it would not provide proof of where it had come from because the popcorn on board ship is grown from corn just as ours is grown on Earth.

Grasshopper Type

"There is a group of aliens which resemble your grasshoppers. They stand five to six feet tall and have the same-shaped head with antennas on top. Their eyes are large and look like they are going to pop out. The arms and legs are thin."

Another Alien Life Form

"There is an alien life form that is sending radio waves and they have been doing this for quite awhile. Your people are finally admitting that they are picking it up. The signal you're getting now was sent out before they started their space travel.

They are jointed in the same manner that the aliens were in the movie 'Arrival.' We don't call them insectoid but you probably would. Their legs look a little like a grasshopper or praying mantis because of the way their legs are jointed. Their heads are a little larger and they do have larger eyes. When you talk about insectoid you usually assume they are not as mentally on par with humans, but these beings are very advanced mentally.

We say that they are more like a neutral race; they are neither good nor bad. They're explorers who have been exploring approximately ten thousand of your years. So they are relatively new to space travel. They live four hundred to four hundred fifty years. Your life span is relatively short because of the negativity on your planet and the closeness to the sun. You must learn to expand your minds and be kinder to each other so that you can be kinder to those that you meet in your space travels."

Urak

"This species is generally between four foot six and maybe five two. They have a very deep brown skin but their hair is white and their eyes are a pale green color. Their planet is very dry but is not hot. The temperature is like what you would have at about 10,000 feet above sea level. So it's not hot and it's not cold but is sandy because of the lack of moisture. They don't need as much water as humans do to survive and their bodies have very low water content. To get water they have to dig very deep into the surface of their planet to receive any water at all. They have three moons above their planet.

Their system is 12.72 light years away. It is at the very edge of this Universe. Five of us met with them on board their ship. They are searching this part of the Universe and we were trying to give them a little insight into what they will find here."

Things the Negative Aliens Are Doing

Implanting

Over the years we received the following information on implants. "Implants are a small device that is put in the body normally behind an ear or inserted between the skin and the skull. They are usually used to keep track of someone or something. These implants are so far advanced that your x-ray machines will not pick them up. I know this is going to be hard to believe, but between the aliens and government doing implanting, 67.2% of the population has been implanted. You see, these can also work very well on some people who are very balanced if they have one seed of doubt. You see, if you have no doubt or fear you can make them inactive, or shall we say, fry them. Beware, many people are being told they are special and have a special mission so they need the implants.

The Grays, Reptilians, and a few other races use implants to keep track of humans so that they can abduct them. Many of the more sophisticated implants can affect your mental stability such as "Son-of-Sam" who hears voices. With an implant they can feed you all kinds of information and get you to do things that you would not normally do. It can control the human spirit but only if you allow it. With an implant you can lose clarity of thought especially if it is negative. It is very hard to stay balanced twenty-four hours a day. Ultimately, the chip that's being implanted by the negative aliens can interfere with your choice to stay in the light.

Only 13% of the implants are ours. Years ago we needed to know how the human mind works and the capacity of your intelligence so we used some implants. We needed to know how you received and stored information. You don't have the same reasoning process or mental capacities that we do, and we don't understand how you think and how you process your thinking. You do not react to the same thing the same way every time.

We no longer need implants because we now keep track of people by their soul patterns. When something goes wrong or if you should get in trouble, it's like an alarm goes off; it is the emotional panic that sets off a warning, and then we know there is trouble. We try to keep track of all light workers, but with all the pressures that are on Earth, it was impossible to keep track of everyone.

The difference between the Grays, Reptilians and us is great. You see we believe it is everyone's individual right to back off and not be involved with aliens. We allow that to happen but the Grays and Reptilians don't.

Even if you are a balanced person, implants can work well on you as they can create a virtual reality and the person will believe what is fed to them. If they have any doubt in their ability to stop it. Not all of mental patients, prisoners, police, or military personal are being implanted but there is a bit of brain washing going on."

In 1990 Monn had this to say about implants, "Implants can control people's minds, but with some people their egos control them. How many people do you know that are proud of how many implants they have? They have to have more than the next person does. How many people have paid to have implants removed but never had one in the first place? Many who do the removal claim that the implants are in another dimension and therefore cannot be seen. These people are…how do you say it…taken to the cleaners by these charlatans."

Again in 1997 we talked about implants and it was explained, "Some of these implants could control your mind. Look how negative the people are becoming. They are opening themselves up to be implanted. They let their guard down and entertain stinking thinking, which lets you wide open, and then you can be implanted. It's not just one thing that lets the implanting happen, it's the combination of everything. Your ego and I wants can also put you in danger. Don't think or let anyone talk you into thinking that you are negative for then you could become so. Remember once a thought is thought it is forever.

Inoculations have also been used to implant people but you can protect yourself and your children from these implants. If you teach your children about spirituality and teach them about God the Creator, when they accept the light in them, the implant shall not survive. This goes without saying that this also includes adults. If you don't want implants, you don't have to accept them because you can make them inoperable or even expel them if you wish. But you must have 100% faith that you can do it, then the implants will not survive."

Implant Found in a Child's Ear

One of the people who came to our meetings found a device in a child's ear and gave it to us. It was round and very small. It looked as if it was made of metal. Actually, it looked like a miniature sewing machine bobbin. We asked about the implant, and this is what Monn had to say:

"The spiritual aliens did not implant the device. There is a group of Gray beings who are here not to harm or kill anyone but are strictly on a scientific mission and don't realize that they are frightening humans. These are the ones who did the implantation.

If you are balanced around the people you love you can influence them by your spirituality and then they have the power to expel or destroy anything that is not good in the body. This child is quite spiritual and expelled the device; it came out the same way and shape as it went in. I suggest that you keep this in a safe place and hope that in the future it can be used to help other people."

Removal and Deactivation of an Implant

"If you have an implant, you don't need anyone to remove them for you because you have the ability to make them inactive. All you need is to share your light and love with the implants and they will become inoperable. But if you have one seed of doubt, it will not work since one seed of doubt is like a pinprick in a balloon filled with air."

Number of People Abducted By 2001

Monn had this to say; "The total number of people on Earth abducted at least once is 47%. That is the number that we know; this includes government, Grays, Reptilians and everyone else we know who are abducting humans."

Hybrids

In 2003 Monn explained that, "There is now a generation of hybrids that has grown. The ones that look more human are being used in abductions to try to make the abductees feel calmer. In some cases this is working very well. They're at the forefront and are the ones who decide if the abductees are calm enough for the Grays to come in and do their work.

I have to look on the computer to find out how many of them are living underground. Just a moment please. Okay, there are 5,652 hybrids that are living in underground bases at this time. They haven't mastered the hybrids enough so that they can be on the surface without people wondering about them. They don't have it quite right enough yet to be able to walk among humans. Close, but they must use wigs and contact lenses to walk among man.

Most of these hybrids are not able to have children. That is one of the things they are trying to fix, but, as with cross breeding in the animal kingdom, God has the plan of cross breeds not reproducing. They are trying to fix it but so far have not been able to produce a hybrid that can reproduce, and that is why the hybrid program is still going on."

Where Are These Aliens And What About Their Ships?

Underground Bases and Tunnels in December of 1988

"The underground bases are both alien and alien government-type bases. These are connected with massive tunnel networks that go across country and out of country. There are also submarine entrances to these facilities. There are some entrances in your area in Wisconsin. Some ships go into the water and bury themselves in the silt so they can meet and exchange information there. These are preplanned meeting places. These beings you would classify as Reptilian types.

Your lake Butte des Morts and Lake Winnebago are very shallow, and they meet there quite often. These lakes are connected to the tunnels and are used by the Reptilians and Grays. They don't seem to be very interested in having contact with us. We have tried three times to meet with them at their convenience, and they have not been interested in doing so. I think they are interested in your planet because it is such an interesting place. You people don't seem to understand how beautiful it is.

There are three different groups of Reptilians here at this time. One seems to be interested in figuring out the technology that you have. They are very elusive, but seeing as long as they are not involving themselves in the planet's progress, we won't get in their faces. So they are keeping an eye on us and we're keeping an eye on them. One group of Reptilians is working with the Grays and they are interfering with earth's progress. We are keeping an eye on all of them."

Alien Nation That Lives Underground

In December of 1988 Eric had this to say when asked about the underground alien nation: "The negative beings that are underground would submit to the Antichrist because they know his power and would take humans for slaves. Even the elite who think they are in power will have a big surprise in store for them, because these bad aliens have more power than the humans do on this planet. What is going on is much bigger than even your elite can come to terms with.

These Grays are able to shape shift but not quite shape shifting like I think you believe. They cannot physically change from one form into another. They can make you think that what you are seeing is different than what you really are. They do this through thought, not physically. It is an illusion of what you see. I want you to know that the Reptilians can also make you think they are someone who they are not."

In 1993 and 1995 the topic of shape shifting came up again. This is what was said almost word for word each time. "These Grays are able to shape shift but not quite shape shifting like I think you believe in. They cannot physically change from one form into another. They can make you think that what you are seeing is different than what you really are. They do this through thought, not physically. It is an illusion of what you see. I want you to know that the Reptilians can also make you believe they are not what they really are."

Underwater Alien Bases

In the spring of 1997 there were many reports in the news of animals beaching themselves. We decided to ask if there was anything unusual going on. Their answer was, "There have been three new underwater bases built in the past five years. These are alien bases and they are huge. It's like the size of a city underwater. Two of the bases are completely occupied and one is just about ready.

These are not for stockpiling craft and fighters so the aliens can take control of the planet, think more futuristic. Actually they don't need many ships to take over the planet nor do they need much firepower. This is why they have been implanting humans to control your mind. It has been working. Look how negative some people are becoming. They are opening themselves by stinking thinking, and that brings people down very fast. It not just one thing that brings people down, it's the, I wants and the ego's. Many humans want to be normal, wanting a perfect life, which seems to be just out of reach.

Most governments know about most of the underwater and underground bases. They know about two of the new underwater ones, but I'm not sure about the third one. It is not the underwater bases that are disorientating the animals, such as whales beaching themselves. But the ELF and HAARP waves are causing earthquakes and volcanoes under the water and these are affecting the animals."

Cheyenne Mountain Rescue Mission

In September of 2002 a friend of ours told us of a memory she had about being on a rescue mission with aliens at an underground base at Cheyenne Mountain. She remembers the rescue but did not know the reason for the rescue. She only remembered that it was scary and very dangerous. We discussed this rescue during two channeling sessions.

We were told that, "The beings had been sent on a mission to scout out a minute amoeba they felt might have been missed when trying to locate and save all the creatures on Earth in case of total destruction. The beings were captured and held at an underground base seventeen miles down under Cheyenne Mountain. These being are highly evolved and cannot be destroyed but they could and were being held captive. The aliens gave them a lot of pain, especially in their heads.

Our mission was to get as many out as we could; our only regret was that we could not get all of them out because some were so far entrenched in the underground base. Hopefully, we can in the future go back and rescue more of them. We think it will be harder now because they know that we can get in and out, but if the opportunity arises we shall try again. We were and are not comfortable with the situation, but we felt if they were in danger of being extinguished, we would try to get them out no matter what the consequences would be. We were at what you call a Mexican-stand off.

We wanted to get the rest of our friends out, but we had to do it carefully because we did not want to start a war with the Grays that could consume most of the planet. The aliens were drugging the beings with something that wouldn't harm them but does stop their telepathic abilities."

In December of 2002 we were given the message that, "We have been very busy recapturing the remaining beings from the Cheyenne Mountain, and we did it without any battle. We had to do it at the right moment to accomplish our mission and now they are all back home. We left the Grays a little trap underground, not anything harmful, but they got a surprise. We were allowed to do this as long as we didn't hurt them. At first they didn't know the beings were gone but by now they know. We left them holographic images, and it took them a little while to figure out what happened. We like to do fun things, you know.

The beings we rescued are recovering as well as can be expected. We got them out, let's see, it would have been, last Monday, December 23, 2002. They suffered from severe headaches, which caused them a lot of pain. They are still in the recovery stage but as far as we can see will make full recoveries."

Negative Alien Ships

"The negative aliens have, from what we can tell well over a thousand ships in your vicinity. They are here to do the planet and its people harm. There is a certain type of person they are looking for, it is one who does not have much spirituality, to see who they could infiltrate and get to do their bidding.

They are becoming much bolder and don't care if anyone knows about what is happening. They wish to become more public, but the secret governments they are working with don't want them to do that at this time. The aliens even with their advanced weaponry know they can be defeated by spirituality."

Alien Ship Seen Locally In Wisconsin

Two of us saw a light in the sky. The light was about three times the size of a star and would jump and change its shape. At one point it looked almost like a snake and then it would go back to a dome-shaped light. It seemed to have hundreds of lights which flashed different colors, white, green, and red. We were so interested in what was seen that we asked the aliens if they knew who it was.

"It was somebody that we have no knowledge of. We are tracing their path the ship had taken and will eventually trace it back to their home world. They must have been just observing because they left. As a ship travels in space they all leave a telltale marker so it can generally be traced to its home world.

I will try to relate the shape of the ship by something you would know. How about a single-layer cake that is flat on one side and rounded on top. It actually changed positions; it rotated so that sometimes the flat side could be seen and sometimes the concave part was seen. I don't think concave is the right word. It was rounded. There were many lights on the side that had the bump. Oh, I'm getting much better at your words but sometimes they just don't make sense to me." (Monn had a hard time deciding to use the concave or convex word in her description.)

Old and Crashed Alien Ships

During a channeling session we were informed that. "The aliens we work with had lost some ships with beings aboard. They were caught without an escort ship while going to a retreat as a vacation from their duties. We had met some of these beings on board the Peach Ship and worked closely with some of them.

When you are in space, you have to recycle everything including old or recovered crashed ships. The ship that crashed in Roswell, New Mexico was not one of our crafts but in March of 1997 we had a ship crash on Earth in the United State, actually in North Carolina. Luckily we were able to retrieve it before it was captured. Those who saw it go down thought it was a meteorite. Luckily it went down in a relatively uninhabited part of the state.

We did not exactly retrieve the ship whole, we actually imploded it. We made it collapse into itself so it became very small and then we could remove it with another ship.

Accidents do happen, and all personal that were on that ship are in good health. We could have just teleported the crew out of there, but it was the craft that we were more interested in retrieving quickly because we did not want to let anyone on earth get their hands on one of our newer crafts. This ship had an electromagnetic pulse system which malfunctioned."

Captured Alien Ships

"Your government has three alien ships, two that crashed and one that had mechanical difficulty. The one with mechanical difficulty landed safely and then was seized. One of the ships is functional, but your people are not intelligent enough to understand how to operate it. They also have captured aliens, but they cannot survive long on the planet. There is nothing you or we can do to help in that situation, for when we enter the service we are in, we know the risk of not surviving any job or mission. We will not risk a ship or crew for the rescue of one; we cannot jeopardize our true mission here. Life is precious, but we cannot afford losing another ship that could help 10,000 survive. That's why we all know what we're getting into; we all know the possibilities of not surviving when we volunteered for this job. It is for the love of mankind and the survival of this race that we have all offered our own lives in exchange."

Eye Spy!

Government Keeping Tabs On Us

During 1988 while talking to the aliens they said that the government was outside monitoring us. They went on to say that they were in a white truck, like a van. They can hear what is happening but cannot read your mind or ours. After the session everyone went and looked out the front window and there was a large white van. It was then that we realized that the aliens were speaking the truth. They also explained how all of our homes were bugged because the government wanted to keep tabs on us.

Many years later we again asked about the government and the aliens said, "They are still keeping a close eye on you and they know what we are doing. They know where you go, they know who you meet, and they know to whom you speak."

While spending the weekend at a cabin we were talking with the aliens, and they said that. "The government is still keeping a close eye all of you and they were down the road in a beer truck listening to everything that was said."

Listening Devices the Government Has

In 1993 when asked about listening devices the government has, we were told, "The government can hear a pin drop a mile away. That is why they can hone into a conversation that anyone has. They can sit out in a parking lot and listen to what you are saying in the store. That is why they know everything that is going on in these groups around the world."

Satellites Used To Monitor People

The next time we went for a weekend at the cabin the aliens told us that they had a new way of keeping a close eye on us. "The government has a new satellite about the size of a basketball that they could maneuver to any place you could go and it only took about a week to get it into position so they could keep up with your goings on."

"This new satellite that the US has put into orbit cost approximately sixty-two million dollars to make it work properly. It is small, about the size of four basketballs, and very maneuverable. It would take only about two weeks' notice to get it into any position that it would be needed. Say you are normally in your home territory of Wisconsin, to get to Minnesota, Minneapolis/St. Paul area it would take approximately one week for it to get over the area. They can move this satellite to go over the North Pole or around the equator. It is so mobile that they can send it around with the planet going with the orbit or they can send it against the planet orbit. If it rotates around the planet it cannot take a right turn quickly to go in another direction. It must be done slowly. It would take only about two weeks notice to get it into any position that it would be needed to spy. It can monitor approximately 20 miles at a time.

Now they don't have to send out a team to monitor you at your meetings. It can up pick up better audio at its height than what they used to pick up from the ground. We could jam the reception but we don't always want to do that. Most of the time, they record conversations at meetings, so it is pretty hard to outfox them about where you would have your next meeting.

They made this satellite so moveable so they can keep track of quite a few people. This way one piece of equipment can keep an eye on many people of interest."

In 1997 we asked if the small satellite was still monitoring our conferences. Monn whispered, "A OK." (Monn said this just like a secret spy would and she continues with) These satellites used to monitor people would not be visible to you. However you could see it with a telescope. If an astronomer would see anything unusual in the sky they would be told to call a specific government agency. They are then told it is just one of their satellites so they are ignored by the astronomer from that time forward.

Most satellites have an orbit so it can keep its eye on countries like Russia and Red China, while some can even see into underground installations. Some countries even pay for time to use the satellites, but not necessarily with money. Not all countries can afford satellites but some are working on having their own. Some countries even monitor study groups such as yours. Some of the larger Third World countries put these groups out of business rather quickly, they are told to stop or they will be exterminated. You have so much more freedom than most countries and you can't be shut down that easily. Don't get big-headed now because you don't have as much freedom as you think you have."

I always wonder why they just don't come and talk to us, we would talk anytime they wanted. Enough of this cloak and dagger stuff!

Scanning

"If you are hearing a lot of beeping sound, it is probably a small scanning instrument. This scanning is kind of like a mind probe. I doubt you could tell the difference where or who it's coming from. Again, you can use your light as a defense tool but also try to be aware of what you're thinking, think positively not negatively.

This is done with a small circular instrument that is in your atmosphere; sometimes it is at house level. This instrument can understand your thoughts. This is done both by military and the bad aliens. They want to know how their projects are doing. We also tune in so we know how far they have turned up their instruments. There are three instruments that are operational, and a fourth one is in the works. The fourth one has not been installed or set up yet, but it will probably be put under the ice caps of the North and South Poles."

Eye in the Sky

We used to see what we called "eye in the sky" when we didn't see it anymore we asked about it.

"The eye in the sky has been mover farther out so it is smaller and harder to see. It continues to keep track of things but not in the same locations. It has been powered up higher and doesn't have to be as close anymore. Not many people recognized it for what it was. Knowing about this is not a threat to you because who'd believe you if you talked about it?"

Mark of the Beast: Chip or Card

"If you think that a card with a bar code on it is the mark of the beast you are wrong. Credit cards, library cards, check cashing cards these are not the mark of the beast. When you get a card of any type with a thumb print on it, it will be very close to the mark, but, you see it won't be the mark either. It will be a card or a mark on your body that without it you will be stopped on the street and put in prison. In other words, you won't even be able to think or breathe without it. Not only will you not be able to buy or sell, but you wouldn't be able to drive a car or walk down the street. If you don't have this you would be put into prison immediately.

I assume it will be like an ID card but the secret government hasn't made a full decision on what it will be, yet. Whatever, it is a card or mark on the hand or maybe something implanted under the skin and you will need it to function. At first it will look very useful and they will deceive you as to what it really is for.

You could take this card and not know that it is the mark of beast, but once you know then you must make the choice of keeping it or destroying it. If you destroy this mark, you will have to go on the run. With this they can track your every move twenty-four hours a day and you cannot do anything without them knowing what you are doing. They will not tell you in advance about their ability to keep track of you.

Those who are balanced and have their instincts honed very fine will know where to go and where it's safe. To have your body survive is not important; to save your soul is very, very important. What is important is to help other people who are in the same situation and don't have any knowledge.

You could deactivate this device if it is in your body, and eventually your body could expel it or envelop it and then it would be inoperable. This Homeland Security scenario is just a smokescreen to control people. They want to detain those whom they cannot handle. As far as terrorism is concerned, we have no idea who or when it could occur, we just know there are terrorists all over the world waiting for the orders to activate them. Some of them are brainwashed, some mind controlled, and some are chipped."

Evasive Characters and Shady Events

MJ-12

"Shall we say the alien nation is trying to infiltrate and become the ruler of the human race on this planet? They wish to be the rulers and enslave most of the humans that are here. The aliens are playing most of the MJ-12 group and telling them anything that they need to be told so that they can get a foothold in there.

MJ-12 is not out in the forefront nor is it in full operation. The MJ-12 that is under a layer of secrecy is at full force and in contact with the Grays and the Reptilians. They are operating in Colorado at Cheyenne Mountain.

We do not have an alliance with any government body or group to help with awareness. We are relying on person-to-person contact. We are relaying on the foot soldiers the light workers (those who believe in the Jesus message) on the planet to spread our message."

Area 51 and Aurora Type Ship

In February of 2001 while speaking to Eric we asked about Area 51. He replied, "As far as we know Area 51 was a government installation, a secret base. They are not doing back engineering any more in Area 51 because it became too well known. They have moved that type of base to Colorado.

The Aurora ship that many are talking about is old news. It is about three generations behind what the government actually has. This one is newer than the black triangular ones seen years ago. This one can go to the Moon and back without being re-fueled."

New World Order

I had been feeling for a long time that the New World Order was not good for most of us on Earth. It was just a feeling I had deep inside of me and I was surprised to find out that the aliens felt the same way as I did.

"Most people cannot and do not want to see what is going on. Just as the people of Germany could not see what Hitler was doing, most do not see the New World Order for what it is. Many people believe that it is the savior of your planet. I can tell you it is a very well-conceived plan to fool the people into believing what they want you to believe. Be careful of those who bring an olive branch but carry a big stick behind their back."

Y2K

Y2K was all the talk in the Late 1990's, so in the fall of 1998, we asked about it. "The Y2K problem can be handled quite easily but I don't see any place here on the computer where the information is getting out. From what I see here there are three computer specialists who know a way to correct the situation.

If they could get all their options together, Y2K might be a starting point for martial law. After all how many are predicting that 2000 is going to be the start of the end, or the end of the millennium, or even the start of a new beginning? A lot of people are making predictions and most of them won't come true.

What needs to be done is for all of you to get out there and talk to people, talk to your bank, talk to the computer people, tell them you want something done. If the banks don't function, people will go crazy, no money, no food, no heat, or water. Make a fuss because this does not have to happen. You can make a difference."

In 1999 we again asked about Y2K and Monn said, "It is possible that it is not going to be as bad as we thought, things are moving right along. A lot of people and businesses got on the bandwagon and started working toward not allowing it to be so bad.

As far as storing food for a long duration, we don't think that is necessary. But may we say that you all should have at least a ten-day supply of food and water in your homes for any emergency, be it a storm or blizzard as your area in Wisconsin has."

While talking about Y2K Monn said, "I want to ask you this question what would you do if you had a great supply of food and water and people came to your door asking for help, would you give them some or not? Would you shoot them, would you kill them to save your food? Let me say this, if you did not share what you have, you would save your body, but what good would that do, because you would lose your soul.

Terrorists are already in your country and around the world, and I believe that they are hoping for Y2K to happen because it would be an opportunity to cause problems. As for your government it could be an excuse for martial law but we don't really see that happening."

Russia

"Russia has tested equipment they thought would help them to rule the world. Instead, they realized they could destroy themselves and everyone in the process. This was done on a very small scale, but they realized what could happen and are afraid of someone else coming across this destructive weapon. They have also tested a weapon something like the cold burst weapon. This one makes a large explosion with no radiation.

If there were an exchange of atomic weapons, atomic warheads, say more than three, between countries, it could happen so quickly that everything would be over in an instant. If they decide to set off five or six at once, total destruction of this planet could happen. Absolute total destruction of the planet would not be allowed. It is God's decision and the council's decision when and if we the aliens can interfere to prevent the destruction of Earth."

Berlin Wall

In 1990 Monn spoke about the Berlin Wall and the collapse of Communism in Russia. She said, "There's so much negativity that's coming forth now and the negativity has been hidden inside of these supposedly good things happening; the supposed fall of the Berlin Wall, the Russians thinking about becoming noncommunist. Get real, this is all hype. The negativity is hidden in the good things that are happening and the truths are not spoken. These are smokescreens for what is really going on."

Black Helicopters

In 1993 we asked Monn about the black helicopters, her answer was, "They are in training partly for the New World Order, but that is not all they are for. At this time I cannot discuss it with you. Let's just say that lots of the military bases which your government says are closing are not actually closing, and a lot of equipment is being stored in them along with the black helicopters. I am talking about this happening all over the globe, not just in the United States."

Detention Center Moved After Discovery

In February of 1995 we asked about a large fenced-in area just outside of Waupaca that was being called a game preserve. Monn answered. "I know nothing of that area." She asked for co-ordinates and we tried to explain that it was forty-five minutes from Oshkosh and slightly north and west of where we lived. She explained that would not get her close enough to the co-ordinates she needed. We explained further where it was and Monn asked, "What do they call it?" We answered a game farm. Monn asked is that is for pheasants or deer, as it seems they don't have any.

Monn continued, "On my computer screen I can see the area and they have a few outbuildings, nothing that could be dormitory size for holding anything of any size. There's one quite large building that looks like a house. But there seems to be underground storage of provisions and food, I don't have any idea what the food is stored for. The fence that runs around the property has wire on top that slants in and it has fences or gates on rolling wheels. The fence is not electrical but the gates are."

Because of all the talk about concentration camps we figured that this is what it was and were trying to get more information out of Monn, but she would not share anything further.

In 1998 we again asked about it and wanted to know what the status was. We had read that this land had changed hands. Monn answered with, "Yes it has been sold and all the storage was removed."

Not letting it go at that, we asked if it had been used by the military or for a concentration camp. Monn explained how it had been moved to the northwestern part of the state. We of course wanted the exact location and suggested areas that it could be. She then asked, "Do you have the degrees on that location." All we could do was suggest some counties that it could be in. Monn kept insisting on coordinates for the location because she did not have countries on her map, nor did she have cities. Monn explained that, "I have a small map of the United States and all I can see was that it's in the northwestern part of the state." So we never got an exact location of the concentration camp. We asked again later and she said, "It is in your best interest not to know the exact location because the last time we discussed the topic you got into your car and investigated the location and I know you might do that again."

Missing Uranium 1998

"There is uranium missing in your country. It did reach its destination at the depository but it disappeared from there.

As far as India and Pakistan detonating atomic weapons; who do you think gave them the uranium for their atomic power plants. It's only two steps beyond that to the atomic bomb. Your government has shared this kind of information with many, many, many countries knowing full well that they could at some point use what they were given to make weapons out of it.

No one on your planet knows for sure who is controlling these types of things. It's so interwoven and no one can find out who really is in control. The right hand doesn't know what the left hand is doing. You may get a small piece of the puzzle but no one knows everything."

Shooting At the White House

When a shooting occurred at the White House in 1998, we asked Monn if it was a coincidence that a film crew just happened to be there. "They never did say how the crew happened to be there, did they? The shooter had been implanted two years and three months ago. Remember, the people who knew him said he wasn't like that when he left his home area.

This action was done to try to get guns out of the hands of everyday citizens so that you can be controlled. I believe that there is an 82% probability that more of these incidents will occur."

World Trade Center, 9/11

When asking the aliens about the attack on the World Trade Center, the aliens replied, "The September 11, 2001 attack on the World Trade Center was definitely about money and oil, that's for sure. People on Earth have not yet learned you never accomplish anything with war except to cause more problems. But on the planet at this time the beings in power, the beings that want control, want the disharmony that these situations cause because it gives them more power over the small, insignificant beings that they think you are. Of course, that is absolutely wrong; there are no insignificant beings in Gods eye.

I would like to say that the people who perished were not alone when this experience happened. Many who survived were guided out of this horrendous happening. They were guarded, guided out by their guardian angel because their time was not yet to come to an end. For many people it was not their time but they were there and in that case God did not let them perish alone. He sent His angels and He sent Jesus to be there at the time of death to help them in their transition back to God. So these people did not have a long time of fear and disorientation that many people experience when it is not their actual time to die.

We saw the whole World Trade Center disaster from space. There was one Plieadian scout craft in the area. Some humans are claiming to have captured a ship on film although I do not believe one was. I believe the Plieadian ship was checking on what was happening.

There have been many similarities between the Oklahoma City bombing, the World Trade Center, Waco Texas, and Ruby Ridge. These incidents all had a very similar game plan. These were important testing grounds to see how far the people could be pushed. This all has to do with restricting people's freedoms by embracing laws that take away your freedom.

Now don't get me wrong, I'm not saying that Bin Laden did not have a hand in the World Trade Center disaster, I'm just wondering who else had a hand in causing this disaster. That is all I have to say on the topic. I know nothing (says this like they did on the Hogan's Hero television show) I don't want to get anyone here into deep water.

There is definitely a combination of beings behind your government. They are the rich, the elite and bad aliens, but for your own protection it is best not to delve too far into that situation."

Terrorist Activity

"After the World Trade Center I can say that there is a 93% possibility that terrorist acts will be committed in the near future. And there is a 50% chance that it will happen in the state of Wisconsin, although I think Europe has a bigger chance of it happening.

This activity could be the beginnings of World War III. All it takes is for one person to do a very, very stupid action and it could cause an all-out war where probably 40% of the people would not survive.

All of the governments should have been on high alert for a long time before they were. What I'm saying is your government knew beforehand about the possibility of it happening and did not want to alarm you. Many, many terrorists are in place all over the world and not all of them are working for the same terrorist groups they were just waiting for the correct orders."

NESARA

NESARA in this book is referring to the National Economic Stabilization and Recovery Act, which is a legislative proposal for monetary and fiscal policy reform. After hearing so much about NESARA at some of the meetings we attended and reading so much about it on the web we had to ask what the aliens thought about NESARA.

Monn had to say about NESARA, "This is giving hope to a lot of people who are in financial trouble, and then their hope will be taken away. If you are waiting for this to solve your problems, don't hold your breath. Never expect big brother to solve your financial problem's you should be solving them yourselves. This is a big learning problem on your planet. Whenever you expect the government to solve your problems you are giving them control over you. Why don't you look into the process that the Nazis used to convert their people into the belief that caused the death of thousands and thousands of people?

Do you receive social security or government assistance? If you do and NESARA is passed, you will not receive any money. The government will not have the money to run these programs. You see, if no one has to repay any debt to banks and the banks have loaned out the money to people who no longer have to repay the loans the bank will no longer be able to give money back to those who had money deposited. You may not have to pay your debts, but what about the people who will lose their money? Do you not feel any remorse for the problems they will have? Of course, if this does happen, the very rich people will have their money safely hidden from everyone. Could this be a way to destroy the middle class? Is this one way for the super rich to end the middle class in the United States and the world?

The controlling of the food supply and replacing of money, the debt, and credit cards and the eventual chipping is pushing ahead and all should be in place in a couple of years. I am afraid that those who think that NESARA is a good thing are only looking at one side of the issue. They're not looking at both sides. What they're trying to do is take away money so that they can be in complete control, and then the chip will be used. I don't see the Illuminati or the secret government ever allowing NESARA to come about. I don't believe they will ever allow anything that would take control of the masses away from them."

You Can't Fool With Mother Nature!

Tampering with the Water

In 1993 we were told, "Your water supply has been tampered with in areas such as Milwaukee and Sheboygan, Wisconsin. These were relatively small areas. (It was during this time that the city of Milwaukee had problems with Cryptosporidium, which was found in the water treatment plants. It was causing flu and diarrhea symptoms.)

Water is not the only thing that has been tampered with; fungi or mold found in the north woods a few years back caused a few people to die. This was an experiment! Also, Lymes disease, which is supposedly caused by a tick, was played with. It is too bad that this is being done as it might come back to haunt those who are doing it."

New Earthquake Machine

Eric told us in 1995 that, "Russia and our government had perfected a weapon that can cause earthquakes on the planet. If both of these machines are turned on and cause earthquake waves that would cross each other, it could cause an immediate pole shift. This pole shift does not necessarily have to be a natural thing; it could be man made."

What Has Weather Tampering Caused

"Ozone is a thin protective layer that surrounds your planet. This layer used to be very, very thick around your whole planet before the Floods and since that time has been getting thinner and thinner. Since the atomic bomb testing and the increase of pollution it has been decreasing in some areas much more than others. This has also been affected by the negativity of the inhabitants of your planet.

We don't refer to this as ozone depletion, but what your scientists call that situation has actually decreased over inhabited areas. I would say the ozone is actually thinner, mostly in the Antarctic region where it is not doing to much damage. But in the long run it will do more damage because it is going to be causing melting of the ice packs and that will eventually cause a problem.

Tampering with the weather might have caused as much as fifty percent of the sea and vegetation to die in some areas. Even with what you call the ozone problem your sun has not actually diminished, but the sky is darker on average. There are a few places that get more, but on the planet as a whole it is less. This is caused by a combination of everything, manmade and natural.

The ice shelf is melting rather quickly in the Antarctica and the salt content of the ocean is changing rapidly. There is rumbling underneath the Antarctic so there is a lot happening in that area. Many people are clearing out and they are leaving a skeleton crew. That is all I have to say on this topic."

Climate Control 1998

"We have climate control on our ships because it is the only way we can survive. But the weather on your planet is being messed with a lot. By trying to control the climate they are causing many problems which will affect your pocketbooks.

The government is testing out a new chemical and is spraying it in a very few areas, just to see what it is going to do. They can pretty much get it down to, say, half a block, and if you already have a problem, such as a cold or are weak in the lung area, this can cause more problems. They want to know what it's going to cause and how much and whether people are going to seek medical attention for it. Just closing your windows won't necessarily help because it would be on the grass, the bushes and trees so you could come into contact with it. If it would rain the chemical would dissipate quite a bit."

Tsunami of 2004

"The tsunami of 2004 was caused by the tampering of earthlings, Grays and Reptilians. This was a made problem not a natural one."

Star Wars Plan, What It Includes

"The Star Wars plan which includes HAARP and ELF has been in effect for a long time although it is not a threat to space brothers and sisters because it is not as powerful as our weapons. It is more directed for battling each other down on your planet for control of the people. They know what they're doing is harmful but they don't fully understand the consequences of their actions."

HAARP and ELF

ELF is short for extremely low frequency waves that had been used by certain groups in the government. HAARP is short for high-frequency active Auroral Research Project. In early 1998 while asking a question about the changes in the weather, we were given this answer, "There is a volcano off the coast of California by Washington State. Now I'm talking volcanoes in the water, under the water. There is one also off Hawaii. There are two off the Philippines. There are three on the west coast of South America and they are all erupting. So it is raising the water temperatures in the areas. Your government is studying the one right off the coast of Washington.

El Nino is not the full cause of weather changes, but it does have some effect on the changes. There are sound waves that are being used on the ocean floor plus the HAARP waves. This is a combination of all three working together that is affecting your weather changes. It's not that any one thing alone would do it, it's the combination of all. The natural El Nino does affect the weather, but it's not as extreme as what they are claiming. So with the volcano's eruption on the ocean floor, which does add a lot of heat in the water, and the sound waves and the HAARP waves, it's the combination of all.

The volcanoes have been in the ocean for a long time, but as far as I can see on the computer, they have not been all active at the same time like they are now. What did you call it, 'Ring of Fire?' The ring of fire includes the surface volcanoes and underwater volcanoes, and most of them have been rumbling. Also, earthquakes have been on the rise. Keep your eyes on that.

Scientists who are working for the government and those working for private industry have been trying to control the weather, and enhance it. They have been fooling around with the weather, which changes the habitat of humans, animals and bugs. These in turn have caused bugs and animals to carry different germs or maybe I should say plagues. This has caused everything to mutate.

Because some scientists are trying to control the weather, El Nino is acting erratically and this is causing underground volcanoes to erupt, which causes a shift in the plates, which causes the water to warm up.

This has caused the water off the coast of California to warm up about four or five degrees. But your weather will be affected more by the jet stream than the El Nino. If the jet stream continues as it is you will have warmer winters in parts of the country.

I would like to say that your Bible does not say that these end time plagues will be caused by God alone, although many of you perceive it that way. Man is causing his own destruction. So maybe you should not say 'God, why Me, God, why are you doing this to me?' Maybe you should say what are we doing to ourselves?"

By 1999 the aliens had this to say about the weather. "Both the government and the not-so-good aliens have been doing a lot of experiments on the weather. Sometimes even they're surprised at what they have produced. Sometimes it's done with chemicals and sometimes it's done with machinery and chemicals combined. But the United States is not the only country doing this.

The object is to learn how to control the weather without causing much destruction in their home country. This process has been used on other countries just to see what controlling the weather can do. Sometimes these experiments get caught in the wind currents and do unexpected damage, such as the storm in Oklahoma where a natural storm was taken and enhanced with chemicals.

Jet Contrails contain chemicals and viruses that can cause an asthma type of breathing problem. Some of these chemicals cause diarrhea and flu-like symptoms.

By 2002 the aliens had this to say about weather control: "Many of your earth governments and private companies have been doing weather control experiments and have lost control. They thought they had the technology and knowledge to control the weather but did not. So now they are scrambling, trying to take back control and are not succeeding. They think that whoever controls the weather can control the planet. You can only play with nature, you can only play with weather so far and then it rebels.

Anyone, who thinks there is nothing wrong with the weather, oh…how do you, say this, has his or her head buried in the sand. I suggest you keep your eyes and ears open and pay attention to what is going on."

In 2002 we were told that, "HAARP and ELF waves have been stepped up to confuse people more. Another HAARP plant has been started at a new location on the planet. Lets just say that it is on the border between two large countries who usually don't get along; they are doing this as a joint venture."

Bad Boys and Their Toys

Non-lethal Weapons

In 1998 we asked Monn about non-lethal weapons and she gave us this answer; "These are waves that, electrical waves that would confuse the thought process, the thinking process of soldiers, maybe a gas or a spray of some type in conjunction with it. They know their conventional rifle isn't effective, so they've come up with different programs. They've talked about…that in the 'Psychic Warrior' book that Bonnie read, and I guess some of you here tonight have also read the book.

There's a non-lethal weapons program; this would be used to confuse or control both people. I believe this could be used to eliminate masses of people. They might want to use these weapons, at first, to confuse people and cause panic which would give them reasons to take away weapons or anything like that. But when it comes down to the end, my personal belief is that they'll just exterminate people. I'm not saying this is what all the aliens believe. But from what I seen, read and heard in meetings, this looks to me as if that is the way it's going to go. I don't think that these types of weapons would work against the underground nation because what makes you think that with their technical advancement they wouldn't know how to neutralize it.

The underground alien nation is very careful what they hand out. They only give your government what they know won't affect themselves or what they can already counteract."

Remote Viewing

We had gone to a conference where remote viewing was the topic. We asked Monn what there take on remote viewing is, "Remote viewing is the process of sending your mind out to wherever you want to go. When remote viewing, most people are taught to do it with their mind. You should also use your heart and intuition when remote viewing. If you don't, you lose some of your natural instincts and you won't know if you are in danger. Don't do this just scientifically or you will lose your instincts, you don't feel things, you don't back away from trouble, you don't know when something is not good for you, you don't know when you are in trouble, and you certainly don't know when to exit. Remote viewing could cause you a lot of trouble; but if you think with your heart you're going to be admonished for thinking that way because doing it this way is considered unclean science.

Your science is different than ours because our scientific studies are done with heart, mind and soul and with the realization that whatever you do you are responsible for. The scientists on your planet do things without worrying about the consequences. Many remote viewers don't think they're going to get in trouble, and you will never hear about the ones who do.

The government has used remote viewing to sit in on your types of meetings, but not with their super computer, as that is too expensive. Even the basketball (This is a mobile satellite used for monitoring purposes.) works pretty well, but it cannot be in two places at once, so they still use personnel to do eavesdropping on certain people. When you are remote viewing, your ego can get in the way and the viewer can go in the direction he wants to go. The governments and big companies are using remote viewers for spying purposes."

Physiological Warfare

We had gotten so many phone calls where no one was on the line when we answered, so we asked about it.

"It is a way of psychological warfare that some people think works because it takes your mind off what it should be on. Sometimes when a call is between two people and one can hear a high pitched tone but the other one doesn't hear it, it is usually caused by antiquated equipment. I personally do not know any high-pitched sound that is being used at this time."

Weapon Control, Gun Control

"Your government wants to take away your weapons and they may use HAARP and ELF waves to confuse people causing panic even making some of them violent. After all, if they can get anyone to use guns to harm people or even make bombs, they can make people believe that you must give up some of your rights that are guaranteed under the constitution of the United States. This is one way they can control the population. Look at how Hitler used that same premise to disarm the people because then you cannot fight back against an oppressive government."

Cold Burst Weapon

In 1987 one of the members of the group had heard that the Soviets were experimenting with a weapon something like Nikola Tesla had worked on and that it backfired on them. This happened once or twice and a commercial airline pilot saw what he assumed was an atomic mushroom cloud. It had the identical characteristics to an atomic explosion. When the plane landed it was checked for radiation and there was none. It was a large explosion in one of the Soviet ammo or storage areas. We wondered if there is such a thing as a cold burst; maybe there was going to be a hot burst, some place in the country of origin.

New Airplane

In 1993 we felt that the government had a new plane because someone who was at the channeling sessions had seen something very strange in the sky and did not know what it was. So we asked and Monn had to check with her superiors to see if she could discuss with us. She then reported to us, "This is a new airplane the government has."

We felt that the airplane had been back engineered from extraterrestrial technology. We asked if that was true and Monn answered, "The government is trying to develop new types of airplanes from the information they have received from the aliens. But the aliens don't give them everything they need to produce alien technology. It is something like when you are given a recipe and someone purposely leaves something out. This type of ship causes an earthquake-type shock wave noise when it is at full power."

Brain Scans, Sound Waves

"There are two types of brain scans and they are used for different reasons. We do have a brain scan that we use to check and see what your capacity to learn is. Most light workers received a brain scan from us because we had to know how those human brains operate. You use only such a small percentage of your brain. Most humans determine brain activity on intelligence, and you do not allow your heart to teach your brain. Your heart can teach you how to live in the Universe and be in complete harmony with it.

The other type of brain scan alters your cells, and if they alter your brain cells more than once, it will be a permanently altered situation. The negative aliens have tried to use this type of scan on most light workers. If you are balanced, your strength and faith makes it inoperable. That is why it is important to know when something is not right, and if you follow your basic instincts, use your light, and ask for protection, you will be safe. This process must work very quickly because it could be all over in a matter of seconds. So this must be practiced everyday. Practice and think, use it with the minor things that happen to you during the day so that it's instantaneous when you need it.

There also is sound wave activation which affects you temporarily, but once you understand what is going on you can counteract it. These waves can be covered up by other noises but your ears can pick them up if they are directed to you. These sound waves can also be covered up by music; so they can do it to young people who like to listen to heavy metal, as it can easily be hidden in that type of music. It can be hidden in almost any music, including classical or in theme music for TV programs. It is easier to sneak this into canned television programs than on live performances. Commercials are a good place to put these sound waves because it only has to be activated once and it is repeated over and over again. If you are unbalanced, the flickering light you see on your television at night can affect your brain.

I would like you to be aware that there are new sound waves being used that can target an individual. It is a guided wave that they can point exactly where they want it to go, such as over a phone line. These sound waves scramble your basic thinking processes such as not believing what you're doing is hurting someone. But if you are thinking in your right mind, you would know that you were harming them. If your thinking is scrambled, you don't know when something is not right and you cannot follow your basic instincts.

These sound waves set off many of the implants which can be sound activated, and some of the abductees have been given suggestions in their heads. This can be sent through your phone lines, it can be sent out through your TV, or it can be directed to the exact point that they wish it to go to. It works especially well when it travels over a wire because then it can be directed to an individual. If you sent this through the air, it could be intercepted by another person.

If people are abducted, these brain scans and sound waves can activate your brain cells, which have been coded with implanted messages and could alter brain cells for many months. This can also cause confused thinking even if it is used over a phone wire. If you are slightly unbalanced, it will cause you to become more unbalanced and it will cause it to last longer. As a matter of fact, this can also…I'm trying to find the word, cause the fight or flight syndrome to activate in your body so you might do one of two things: go looking for a fight or try to run away.

This new wave action is being used by aliens who have bases underground on Earth. The secret government who has a pact with the aliens is aware of what is happening but they are not cooperating on this project with the aliens. This wave is no way related to the ELF waves."

Thought Senders

Some of us in the group had been having severe chest pains off and on so we asked Monn if these could have been caused by some outside force or psychic attack.

"Yes, these thought patterns were sent by two thought patterns that come simultaneously with ELF waves but neither knows of the other. It's a combination when the two happen to be used at the same time that causes such a big problem. These both were sent definitely from Earth. The two thought senders know each other but I do not believe they're working as a team. They have the same thoughts and are in bodily form right now. You know these people. Remember, I have told you that when you think something it is out there, this is what I mean by having negative thoughts and causing trouble. They are not 100% sure of the consequences. In other words they are aware of the thought patterns they are sending but do not realize that they are being received at the level that they are.

I cannot say who is sending the thought patterns, but they are aware of the negative thought patterns. Let's just say that the persons sending these negative thoughts and the Grays on Earth have this ability and they are both on the same side.

You can use your lights that I have told you about and surround yourself in that light. Do not send evil back. You can reject what is being sent to you but do not retaliate. For then you are on their level. But you have a right to stop it. Try putting up a mirror and letting those thoughts bounce back to the sender. Each one must try to find their way of stopping this. Hone your instincts; trust what you believe to be the best for you, it's part of learning how to survive in these troubled times. The aliens and the government with their thought senders can get into your dreams and often do so with sexual dreams. There are times during the day and night when you're not at full force and are not paying attention to what is going on, at that time they can bother you."

Discussions on the Bible

"Not all stories in your Bible are accurate because your Bible is not 100% correct. These stories have been told and retold and of course they have been changed here and there. I think I should explain that we believe your Bible is the most important book you have on this planet. I do not wish you to think that I do not agree with the book. Many of us have read the book and our understanding of it is just a little different than yours; maybe it is because we're looking at it from a different perspective. We know that as a child you played the game of someone whispering in the ear of person next to you. You keep going down the line until you get to the last person, and when the message is said it is always very different from the original. So too when people hear or see something that happens, they write it from their perspective, from their vision of what happened and how they wish you to understand it. So it is with all books that are written. It depends upon the author and what he perceives to be the most important message to be written down. Almost every book of the New Testament in your Bible was originally written word, for word but things were taken out or changed when translations of the book took place.

We cannot tell you everything that was taken out of the Bible, no, because that is an Earth thing and I am not privileged with every bit of information about what has happened on your planet. If I did, then you would probably think of me as God and I am not God. I am just a being who also is alive and can die. So we as aliens do not expect you to worship us. Do not believe everything we have to say. Our hope is that through our speaking, you will go and search your books and your texts so that you can find the information that you need for yourself. Each of you has something different that is important, each of you has a different path to go down, so please follow what you think is important for you. Please understand that all we wish you to do is to find your own answers for yourselves

Do not believe everything that the church teaches. Do not believe everything that your government says. Do not believe everything that your doctors say. Do not believe everything we have to say. Listen to your heart and go search out your own answers, for you have a responsibility in your own lives. That is part of God's gift to you and He wishes you to use that gift to the best of your ability."

What Is In the Bible

February 18, 1995 we asked Monn if she had any comment about the snow that fell in Alexandria Egypt two weeks earlier. Monn answered, "This is one of the signs in your Bible." Also in February the question was asked of Monn, if there were more than one Adam and Eve. "Yes, you could say so, because there was more than one experiment on the Earth done by aliens visiting the planet. (Then Monn went on to drop a bombshell of information that she knew would blow us away.) Well, all I was going to say was that Adam and Eve didn't come from this planet anyhow, so what difference does it make? Actually, they didn't come from another planet either. They were created here. Oh boy. How can I explain this? I'm looking for the words. (Pause) Aliens genetically changed the DNA of a distant cousin to the ape on this planet. The distant ape was very human like in form so it was an adjustment in the DNA. Let me say this distant ape would have become human eventually as God wanted, but the aliens took the natural evolution and speeded it up. This was implied by the statement in the Bible where it said the sons of God came down and found the daughters fair on Earth and mated with them.

This is a beautiful planet and there are a few factions, aliens as you call them, who wouldn't mind taking over this planet. They want a place to live, to have workers do the work for them, and of course food."

Another question was asked about the sons of God that came down here and mated with the daughters of Earth. We are wondering if they were they Lucifer and his followers. "One set was, you see, both sides did this supposedly for the advancement of the human race."

Elisha

While Eric was talking during a session he told us, "Elisha is reincarnated on the planet at this time as a woman; I know you want to know who she is but I cannot say."

Bible and Bible Code

Lea had this to say about any code in the Bible. "You can find a code in almost any writing, but if you had the original writings from the Bible, the Hebrew Bible and the Koran, then looking for a code might work. So much has been added and subtracted, so I suggest that you be very careful, use your instinct in deciding what to believe or not.

On my computer I see that two people in the Vatican have read the original Bible and they've been reporting to the Pope what they have found. Years ago three other people, also at the Vatican who read the complete version of the Bible, also reported to the pope who was in power at that time.

What they reported would change all of society's thinking on a lot of issues. Most religious leaders don't want to lose power and control, and if everyone had the information, those in power and control of the planet would lose what they have."

We had been discussing the Bible with a group of people and one of them believed that about 98% of the Bible had been tampered with. When Monn started speaking she said jokingly that the percent we had was correct. We knew she was pulling our legs, so we asked what 2% was true. And said she could not resist making a joke and went on to say, "There are thirteen books that were not included in the Bible. I would say basically another 6% was eliminated because it talked about reincarnation and UFOs which took power away from the church.

There are three original Bibles in existence at this time; one is in Rome, one in the lower part of Egypt and one in the United States."

Judas Iscariot

In February of 2001 we asked if Judas Iscariot was considered one of the twelve apostles. Lea comment was, "Let's just say that he was probably the only disciple who was strong enough to do what had to be done for Jesus to accomplish his mission. And to this day he is in his father's fold. You see, sometimes people are called upon to do something that is actually against their nature. Everything had to fall in place for Jesus to be crucified. Judas did not want to do it but was driven to do it although he did not realize what he was doing it at the time."

Magi of the Bible

"There were many spiritual people on Earth when Jesus was born. The three kings were wise, kind, just and generous just as described in your Bible. That is why they were the ones who saw the star and followed their hearts to the point of the birth of a very special being of the planet.

These three kings studied the stars but not the way that many people on your planet do today. These kings studied the stars to find not their own future but the future of the planet."

UFOs in the Bible

While talking with Lea we asked if the Star of Bethlehem was a star or a UFO guiding the three wise men. Lea said. "It was actually a UFO and a star in unison. A UFO moved in the sky to Bethlehem and then it placed itself by a star in the sky. And also a UFO helped to part the Red Sea. The parting of the sea was done by lasers, how else could you part and dry up a sea so they could take their chariots across a water bed and when they were safely on the other side let the water come back. But may I say that the UFO's were working for God. They were doing His bidding at these points in history.

These UFOs also provided the manna from heaven. Now I'm not saying that God did not do this, but God worked through the UFOs to produce this. Also,

God used a laser to write those things on the tablet, the commandments. These UFOs also parted the Jordan River when the Israelites entered Canaan.

The most controversial thing is the ascension and resurrection of Christ. You see, he went up to a UFO in a beam, he went aboard a ship, and He is alive today and He will return in a ship called the New Jerusalem and it will be stationed outside of the atmosphere. He will come down to Earth in a cloud. The New Jerusalem is the most gorgeous huge thing that you've ever seen, and when people see it, they will realize that there definitely is something in the heavens that is far greater than they are.

Elijah's wheel within a wheel was definitely a space ship. So you know also a lot of things were taken out of the Bible that sounded more like a ship than the wheel within the wheel, but they had nothing else to compare it to.

Jacob's ladder was going up to a ship and back down. A lot of people on Earth have also reported seeing beings going up and down a ladder to a ship."

What Is an Apostle

Being inquisitive people we wanted to know about the apostles in the Bible and if any of them were on Earth at this time.

"All twelve of the well-known apostles are reincarnated on Earth at this time and they are here doing a job for Jesus. But remember there were more than twelve apostles and some of them were woman.

Anyone who spreads His word is an apostle. This is anyone doing this kind of work whether it is speaking of Jesus or spreading His word. Do you want to see an apostle? I suggest you put your hand out in front of you and you may see one. If you do good works and are compassionate and loving, then you are seeing the hand of an apostle."

Ark of the Covenant

"The Ark of the Covenant and one of the original Bibles, is at this time being held by the secret government which will in time be headed by the Antichrist. It is in the hands of those who rule your planet right now, and they don't have the key to interpret what it is or how to use it.

The Ark is even more beautiful than it is described in the Bible. It shines with brilliance; even in a dark room it looks as if the sun is always shinning brightly on it. The source of its light is God's light and wisdom.

The dark forces cannot touch the Ark of the Covenant, but they can move it by sheaves, the method that is described in the Bible. There have been accidents and causalities along the way because they did not follow the rules. The Ark has been moved to many different locations on the planet. When it is returned to Israel and set in the new Temple, they will try to claim their man as the true Jesus.

The people are aware of what they are protecting. It is protected twenty-four hours a day by earthlings, but there is a group of aliens who are also keeping an eye on it.

The force in the Ark was given to the people of Earth so they could have something to look at and feel. It was something to hang onto.

The Israelites are pretty sure that the Ark of the Covenant will be home when the temple is built because it was promised to be there by God. He promised that they would have the Ark in their temple, so they believe if it is rebuilt the Ark will come home. But they don't know by whom it will come home. Who knows, maybe the Antichrist will be the one who will bring it home to prove that he is the Christ?

All things are changing very fast and hopefully things will work out the way we hope. If not, we will be coming with Jesus to Earth. We will all be coming in bodily form. You must survive by belief, not by seeing, touching, feeling, or having something to hang onto. He, who asks for proof and does not believe without it is not a saved soul."

Armageddon

"There will be a battle between good and evil on your planet, and this is called Armageddon. How long God and Jesus will allow this battle to go on is their decision. Where and when it will take place is beyond my knowledge.

I am afraid that Armageddon is upon the world; the signs are there if you look. The Rapture that many of your religions speak of and Armageddon could take place in three days or they can overlap. As a matter of fact, what the last book of your Bible talks about could all happen at the same time or not in the same sequence that it is written.

Christ will be at the battle of Armageddon, but He will come as a lion, not as a lamb. I think and hope you understand that it is the Antichrist's decision when he is going to step forward. Jesus will be in command of the forces of good, and all those who recognize him shall be saved. He is your salvation, and He will take the planet from Satan.

We are here to help your planet, we will be there to stand beside the faithful, but will we do your battle for you? No!"

Dead Sea Scrolls

When we asked Monn about the Dead Sea scrolls, she said, "Actually, they were written many years before Christ. They are well guarded, and it seems someone doesn't want to release the information to the public. This is because in all probability it will change the course of religion on your planet. Most of the early predictions have already come true."

Essense

In 1989 we asked about the Essense that are talked about in the Bible as people with higher knowledge and understanding. "They seemed quite extraordinary for their time and had a lot of good strong beliefs. Many who are in the new age groups will be looked upon as Essense but they won't be of any higher spirituality than the person who follows the path of love and light."

Kabala

One of the people at this channeling session felt as if he was with Aaron and that he had buried the Kabala or had hidden it from people. He felt that part of his responsibilities in this lifetime was to make sure it would be shared with the people. When this was put forward to Monn she did not answer the question. There were times when she did not answer our questions or she said that we should go and try to find the answers ourselves because we did not get any points for not learning for ourselves.

Mary Mother of Jesus

"Mary's soul is alive but she is not in the body that she had on Earth. She chose to be here and be the host for the birth of Jesus. She is not an elevated soul and neither Mary the mother of Jesus or any saint has any more power than you do. All you need is the faith that is available to you.

After all does your Bible say not to worship anyone but God? Did not Jesus say not to worship Him but only His Father?

Many people at this time claim to channel Mary or claim to see apparitions of her. Remember, this could be the bad side of the force. Bad, evil, or whatever you want to call them always have a good message at first, but then there is a little twist in their teachings and that could get you into trouble."

Movie "The Passion"

After seeing "The Passion" movie we wanted to know about the suffering that Christ endured in the movie and if He really did suffer that much. Monn answered our question with, "Jesus suffered almost as badly as it was portrayed in the movie but not quite the same. He was taking on of all the sins of mankind so it had to be that violent. Also, the people that were there knew that He could not survive what had happened to Him. They had to realize that no one could live through what He experienced. It was the only way to make His death and then resurrection more believable.

Many people have tried to claim that He did not die, that He was in a coma and then his followers spirited Him away. No, he actually did die. His body died but not His soul, God healed the body so that the soul could reenter it and go on.

It was only a small section of the Jewish faith and the Romans that were against Jesus. Many people after His death saw Jesus and realized that He had risen. Jesus had to suffer terribly, to make His death and resurrection believable."

Melchizedek

"There is an Order of Melchizedek on the planet right now. To join there is a ceremony for pledging your unity to work together for a common goal. It involves a sword that looks somewhat like your cross.

Melchizedek himself is on Earth now. Many years ago he originally came to prepare the way for Jesus the Christ. They are both very spiritual but not the same essence. At one point Melchizedek walked the planet in human form trying to uplift the spirituality of the planet. Remember that if he was male in the past he is not necessarily one now.

Your Bible speaks that Jesus was in the Order of Melchizedek and I would also like to say so was Elijah. The mother of Melchizedek was long in years and knew no man when she became pregnant. Melchizedek was very unique, as are all of Gods children. Those of this order wrote some of the Dead Sea scrolls. They were written in a period of upheaval hoping man would not get into the same trouble again. Many light workers have studied with the Order of Melchizedek in the past, out in space and some on Earth.

The Star of David stands for unity; it is just that simple. David of the Bible will return with Christ just as many of the other essences that are mentioned in the Bible will. The Star of David symbol and the circle within the circle symbol are both representatives of Melchizedek's order."

Star of Jerusalem

"In the Revelation part in your Bible it talks about something in the sky. We call that the Star of Jerusalem. When the Star of Jerusalem first makes its appearance, it will look smaller than the Moon, but as it moves closer to Earth it will look almost as large as the moon on the side that is visible to Earth. It actually might prove to be heavier and more dense and solid than the moon is."

New Jerusalem

In 1995 Monn told us, "The New Jerusalem is a lot bigger than the ship that Jesus is on at this time. It takes an awfully large ship to handle more than 144,000 people. As far as I know it will be visible to most people. But I cannot say for sure because I am not connected to that part of the plan. As your government says, need to know. The New Jerusalem is beyond Saturn at this time."

Prayer

Because so many people had an opinion on how to pray we felt it would be interesting to find out. One of the people at a session said he believed when Christ prayed and blessed food He had His hands open. Now if Christ had His hands open and the energy could flow out freely to remove impurities and bless the food He was about to take in, does clasping our hands with fingers intertwined block that energy?

Monn replied, "By clasping your fingers together, you are making a complete circle with yourself, so that energy is traveling through you alone. Spiritually, it would be far better to leave your hands open, but if you are more comfortable clasping your hands unto yourself; I do not have the power to tell you that is not the way to do it. When you do open your hands you allow your energies to flow to and from the Universe.

When you pray to help someone, you can apply your hands on that person, concentrate your thoughts on helping them in whatever way is needed. Whatever way the sender is more comfortable in doing this and whatever way the receiver is willing to receive the healing energy is the right way to do this. Just remember that a healing does not come from you, you are only a conduit for the healing, and only Jesus and the Creator can heal."

Purgatory

"Your church's version of purgatory, are wrong. I have a real hard time with trying to understand some of your religious teachings. They go a little bit too far.

They go into the physical embodiment of the church and what everyone must have and not into the glorification of God. You don't need all the hocus pocus, jumbo mumbo that many churches teach. It's what is inside you that is important. There comes a time if a person lives a bad existence and do not learn from their mistakes, then they will pay for their actions. Everyone makes mistakes in their lives, everyone errs, and that is a learning process."

Hell

"I know many of your earth teachings explain that hell is in the inner earth. It is not there. We consider hell more a state of mind."

Reincarnation

"Whenever a planet has problems like Earth is experiencing now, a special person is born on the planet to help. Even my home planet Surak had problems way back in its past, and the Son of God was the person who was called on to help. He has also been born on other planets. It is always the same soul that is born; however, it is not quite the same because there were different mothers. Every time a soul is born some of the past is erased and there is new brought in with each birth. Some of the past is lost but some of the new genes of the new parents are added so it is forever changing but basically is the same soul. Souls are like mini microchips, and all these things are imprinted on it, even phobias.

If someone had a very traumatic death that was not planned and they were not prepared for death, more time is needed before they can be born again. During this time they learn why death happened at the time it did. Also, before reincarnation a life review is needed to learn what they did wrong in their last life so they can get back in balance again. If a soul is not in complete balance when it comes back, it has trouble entering into the negativity of this planet and surviving.

A lot about reincarnation has been removed from the Bible so that the masses could be controlled easier. Many of the truths were taken out of the Bible at Nicea, but some never even got into the Bible in the first place.

Christ was born on different planets to help, He needed the covering for His soul to match where He was going. This has been done fifty-seven times. Reincarnation as it relates to abortion is where we differ. Your scientists believe that a soul enters the body when it's conceived. That is not our perception of when the soul enters the body. A soul enters the body as it is being born and the covering can survive on its own. If the body did not survive the, soul would then have to wait for another form to become available. Some souls don't want to wait to be born, so they may enter, their clothes, shall we say and all of a sudden the baby is born prematurely. Sometimes the soul must leave the planet that they were going to be born on and go onto another one because they do not have the vehicle that they were going to use. So other places have to be arranged for, or they can go back to school and learn more and wait for the opportunity for them to be born into the family where they can most accomplish what they were going to do. And believe it or not almost everyone is born with an idea to accomplish something in their lifetime, whether it is to teach a sibling or a parent or to have a child of their own to teach. Almost everyone comes with a plan, a preconceived idea of what they wish to do and accomplish in a lifetime.

Generally, a soul chooses the vehicle and the family it's born into according to what its needs are. Plans can always change, such as, say the fetus did not develop correctly and there was a natural abortion; but say someplace else a couple conceived a child and no soul was ready to go into the body then the naturally aborted soul could go to the other body.

Many people in the new age believe that they reincarnate in the same groups. They like to think their mother is their child, or they were their grandfather or something like that. If you keep incarnating into the same family you are going to have the same problems and the same situations because most families don't learn from their mistakes. They just keep making them over and over and over again. Well, if you learn your lesson, you can move on to another family where you can learn and grow in a different way. So it's not always good to be born in the same family again and again and again.

It is possible for two souls to cross paths in numerous lifetimes. Sometimes a person will see someone and just feel like the person is their oldest friend; it doesn't mean that they met in this lifetime. They could have met in school between lifetimes.

Many times parents marvel at a child's accomplishment, such as a musical tendency. If you are born with this memory you must do something for the good of mankind."

Homosexuality

"Over the years we have come to realize what causes homosexuality and it is not that great a problem anymore. Homosexuality is pretty much caused by a person being born ten times as a man, and then being born a woman or the other way around. This can cause a problem in gender preference but over the centuries we have learned how to handle these types of situations with counseling.

Your soul in each lifetime encompasses everything that you've seen and felt and done in all your lifetimes. When you enter a body the brain does not understand that. The brain must learn like a baby again, but your soul is everything that you've ever seen, felt, touched, and learned. So, yes a lot of your habits, traits and personality will follow you from lifetime to lifetime even when you are born not remembering."

Speaking In Tongues

My daughter went to church with her friend. They spoke in tongues during the service and she became very upset. She asked me what I thought, about the speaking in tongues and who did I think was speaking through them. I told her that I did not know who was speaking but I believed that if it was God or Jesus, everyone would know what was being said. I was wondering about this topic when Monn came through with this response to a question that was not asked of her.

"The New Testament talks about prophesying in tongues, many people feel in a sense this is channeling. But let me tell you that if Jesus or any Christ came to you, He would speak so that you would understand; you would not need anyone to interpret the messages. A Christed being can speak and everyone who hears will understand what is being said, even if they don't understand each other's language. Everyone will understand what is being said because when He speaks, He speaks in pictures and words directly into your head. You will understand 100% what He is saying."

Temple Mount

"The Temple Mount was the Holy Temple built by King Solomon and it was destroyed. Many people feel that the Dome of the Rock Mosque has to be destroyed completely so that King Solomon's temple can be rebuilt. This does not have to happen. All they need is an area where the original altar stood. The actual temples cross at some point, but the actual place that the Ark sat is not under the Dome.

There is now a mosque built on part of this area. To rebuild the whole Temple, the mosque would have to be destroyed by an earthquake or maybe God could take it down. But the Temple could be rebuilt by human hands and still leave the mosque there. You see the holy part of the Temple is actually on Israeli soil, so the Holy of Holies part could be rebuilt but not the whole temple.

Once the Temple is rebuilt and the Ark of the Covenant is placed in it some believe that whoever has control of it will receive the power that was given the Ark because it would be back in the place where it is supposed to be. The real leaders of the planet, the secret government, want the Ark in place so they can receive and be in control of the power.

You have read that some people believe the Ark is a portal to another dimension where God lives, and this is not the truth. Remember that God lives in each of you. God lives in a rock. God lives in a piece of wood. God lives in the stars, God is all over. He's the force. He's the only thing that holds everything together. So His force is in The Temple and The Ark, and it is the force that God gave to the Jewish people, but it is not the place where God lives. You want to go where God lives? You could go there today. All you need to do is meditate and you can stand in front of His throne anytime you wish. True meditation can stand you right before Him.

The Antichrist will head the New World Order, which actually will be run by the secret government. When the Ark goes into the New Temple, they can put their man in to claim himself as Jesus. This is part of his job, and of course, he will be loved for restoring the Ark to its proper place. He will be able to approach and touch the Ark by using magic. He will also perform miracles. This is the only way he can fool people into believing that he is the Christ.

I am not sure about the spear, but the Grail will probably come back about the same time. Remember the story of the Holy Grail and how the lineage is supposed to come from Spain. The Templers will probably bring the Holy Grail back to the Temple so they can prove who the real Jesus is, but they will not have the correct lineage for the rightful one to sit on the throne next to God. It is all an illusion, and I would like to say that this is only a probably, it may change."

Wormwood

"The governments have started to admit to each other that something is coming this way. It is very large and very cold and will affect your planet. One of the names that it has been called is Wormwood.

It is still partially hidden, and if you had equipment bigger than the Hubble Telescope, you could see it. It will be coming from the other side of the Sun; it is coming around it. It is starting to have a pull on the planet but is not affecting people yet. You are water-based beings so it will be affecting you slightly in that manner. It should affect the water levels because it will pull the water in different directions. Earthquakes will happen, which may cause volcanoes to erupt more often than they are, but that is not the biggest problem. Lack of spirituality is the biggest problem and with spirituality you could counteract these things that are going to happen."

Could We Be In The End Times?

"End times are probably the wrong words to use. It is not the end of the planet it is just the end of things as earthlings know it. What is happening now has happened many times on Earth. How and what happens will depend upon each individual and what the leaders of your countries do. If they blast off atomic bombs, there will be radiation poisoning. If the atomic energy plants are not safe and secure at this time, they could leak radiation, which will affect the water. This water will then evaporate into the clouds and rain radiation on the Earth and this would be very devastating. With this atomic energy and the problems it can cause we just don't know if we will be able to help fast enough to clean up the radiation to make this planet clean for habitation.

If this does not happen and there is a natural cleansing of the planet, things will not be so bad. What you have done to the planet is greatly affecting how bad this is going to be. If everyone changed, raised their rate vibration to a spiritual one, this change could be as gentle as a sunset. But without rising the vibrations of the humans this could be as bad as your imagination could imagine." By 1987 this cleansing of Earth was at about 37% percent, in other words we weren't to the halfway point yet. We were told that many light workers decided to be here at this time, trying to make this process gentler.

"We do have ships that are ready to evacuate people if things get bad enough, but I am sad to say that only those who have reached a high enough vibration level will be allowed on the ships. I know that sounds cruel, but when these things happen to the planet it will be at a faster vibration level than it is now. Only the people who have raised their vibration to match our ships would survive on them. Also, your level has to be able to match the new vibration of the planet to survive on it. If we took everyone off the planet and put them back on Earth when it was safe again, the people with slower vibrations could not survive they would die a slow and terrifying death. Those who will be able to survive will be evacuated when and if it is necessary.

There have been aliens collecting all the species of animals, fish, mammals, trees and flowers on board space ships for over two thousand years. Our ships have supplies on them in case they are needed. Because people are always more comfortable with things they've grown up with, we will try to accommodate them with these items. When the planet is inhabitable again we will introduce what is needed for survival including food items.

By the time aliens come down to evacuate Earth, many governments will no longer exist. At that point it will be every man and woman for himself or herself.

I want to warn you that there will also be many negative aliens who will have ships available to take humans off the planet."

Planet Changes

"With the massive shifts that are happening to the planet, the pollution and radiation the planet has received over the years and the killing of the rain forests, you should be very careful and be very aware that even the natural products for healing are not that good any more. So just be aware it is probably not good to advise people to use products that you can't prove are 100% pure. Also, unless you know 100% what the side affects are in natural products, I suggest you don't tell people to try them or try them yourself.

Things that are not ingested into the body are not as bad, but if you smell them they do get into your lungs. Remember, God has created natural remedies for any natural disease, but nothing is natural anymore on the planet. So you are even going to get side effects from natural remedies or maybe what I should say what many claim are natural products. Because a lot of the natural remedies have been destroyed, sometimes medication, a prescription is the only resolve to a problem."

Earthquakes, Volcano's

"Most earthquakes are getting closer to the surface and all it takes is a specific shift of the crust and a major earthquake could occur.

Mount St. Helen is a good place to keep an eye on. All it takes is a shift someplace close and it could blow. Yellowstone Park which is a super volcano, is rumbling deep down and that is natural. But if it gets absolutely quiet and nothing is going on, that would be the time to, well let's just say remove yourself from the area. I also suggest you keep an eye on Hawaii as things are building up there. There is lava flowing constantly, even if it is under the ocean."

Icebergs

"Ice shifting and icebergs of the planet can and will affect the tilting of the planet. Earthquakes can cause ice caps to break off and become icebergs. I think most people think of icebergs as being small, but they can be the size of a continent and that can cause the Earth to shift."

By 2001 the aliens explained how, "Some time ago an iceberg broke off from the main body of ice and was in your newspapers. That one was about the size of Manhattan, but actually there's one that is bigger, about a size relative to Pennsylvania. This is only about 6% of the icecap but the weight is tremendous. If this breaking up of the ice shelf continues, there will be a 62% possibility of the shift happening quicker than anticipated. Also, if the breaking up of the ice shelf continues, it could affect the water and air current patterns. It could also affect El Nino and there will be more extreme weather patterns in the near future.

With the Earth tilting, shifting on its axis there might be a 5 to 10% survival rate for the human race."

Pole Shift or Flip of the Poles

"The pole shift will be very destructive. It can happen two different ways: one is where the North and South Poles just shift a few degrees and cause the temperature to fluctuate greatly and the water to shift in the oceans. During this shift there is a possibility the water from the Great Lakes could come towards Wisconsin, but we don't believe it will happen that way. I know you think sometimes the water could only go east or west but it also could go north or south.

Two this pole shift could also cause a magnetic shift and that would cause the crust of the planet to move. There is a 99% chance of the pole shift and magnetic shift happening simultaneously. When there is pressure under the tectonic plates, you can get pressure from both sides of the plates, and things can get twisting, rippling and opening up or they can slide apart and make crevices such as your Grand Canyon.

If the poles shift and change north to south and south to north then things will get wild. The poles could even wind up at the equator and then the climate will change drastically for the whole planet. What was warm to the equator will now be cold like the North and South Poles. What was cold will then be warm, that is why your scientists are finding animals frozen in the ice with food in their stomachs. It could happen so fast that nothing could survive.

With either type of pole shift, earthquakes will be happening. Almost simultaneously the tectonic plates will shift and tsunamis will happen. The oceans will move out of their boundaries, mountains will rise, and mountains will fall. Nothing will be the same again. Remember, this will not be the destruction of the planet, although man and animals will have a hard time surviving. This will change how the planet looks, just as in the past the shifting caused things to change.

Prior to the shift of the poles some people will see a cross in the sky, some will see ships. Others will see nothing but will instinctively know what is going on. The cross will be shown to nonbelievers to try to get them to understand that this is the Creators world. Maybe things will connect for them so that in their next lifetime they will not have to go through the learning process again.

The North and South Poles will not necessarily exchange places; the poles could shift from a few degrees to halfway or completely. No one knows when this will occur. We can only tell you percentages of when that might occur. Many people on Earth don't recognize that there are changes in your weather. Many of the people that have been working with aliens and have been raising their vibration level on their own are recognizing these facts and they are starting to realize what's going on. As I said, if there happens to be an atomic bomb that goes off during this time period, this could bring it on much faster.

When the poles move only a little amount, many earthlings are going to have a hard time and some will flip out. They won't be able to understand what's going on. They will have feeling of losing control and know that they are in danger. These beings by their negative thoughts and energies will be affecting your vibration level of growth, if you're not strong enough. These negative feelings and thoughts can very easily pull those down who have increased their vibration level. Their fear will be very strong, so you must be twice as strong to keep your own levels. The humans on Earth who have not raised their levels will be the most vulnerable. That is why you are down there, to touch these beings and to help them on the road to a better life.

If you tap into nature and study it, you will know a long time before the flip occurs just like your scientists are recognizing how certain animals can foretell earthquakes. Plants seem to know when it is time to sleep; they know when spring is coming. Even your weather forecasters can't seem to predict your weather because something has changed. But the plants and the animals know, and that's what you must learn to do; feel things, become one with nature, and you will know.

Things have changed over the last few years, and now often the trees and flowers are fooled into thinking that spring has arrived often budding out only to be snowed on or frozen, thus being stunted. There are so many things in nature that tell you when things are going to change. They know, but you know you could also be at that level. Practice meditation; still that mind that seems to run rampant with all those thoughts of everyday life. You must take time to quiet it, to become one again with the Universe.

If the flip were to occur and we couldn't get to some individuals, we would not be allowed to travel back in time to pick up individuals as some people have suggested. If that happens and we can't get to the people, then it is God's decision, not ours. If it is His wish that they survive, they will. It's not our choice to make.

The flip isn't anymore imminent now but is becoming more noticeable, and light workers can feel it more although many don't realize what they are feeling. The polar shift is a natural phenomenon that can be increased or decreased by the people on the planet.

Many people are having dreams of the sky filled with UFOs and that will probably happen just before the planet makes the pole shift. The destruction on the planet will be very bad with a lot of people dying. There will be many ships that come to help to evacuate, and both sides will be sending in ships. Your own instincts will be your salvation, or you could become supper.

You asked about a booklet put out by a well-known church. It talked about end times called 'The Three Days of Darkness.' The booklet talked about staying in your homes and lighting blessed candles. There is a lot of propaganda in the pamphlet, but also there are many truths. When this happens there's going to be darkness, there's going to be high winds of probably three hundred miles per hour, there's going to be a great shifting in the temperatures and the sky is going to be black. Then it is going to be red. You are going to have to be in a safe and secure place, yes. And depending upon where you are will be the degree of the winds, temperatures, and the changes in the climate.

Many people are searching for answers at this time, and what most people need is friendship, someone they can relate to and trust. When the end times have occurred, many health problems will be cured. After all the hard times on your planet, after the cleansing, your life span will increase to approximately 400 to 700 years. We are not here to hinder or frighten anyone. That is why we do not come and join your meetings, because even with the knowledge that most of you have that are here, you would still be frightened if we came and knocked at your door. So be aware of who you're speaking to and how much you're speaking to them about this. And give them only what they can handle.

At one time Wisconsin had a much warmer climate. So with this shift Wisconsin could again have a warmer climate with no winters. One thing I would like you to remember is that when this has occurred and everything on the planet is the way it was intended, health problems will be cured. Look at the bright side of this happening."

The New Jerusalem

In 1998 we asked Lea about the New Jerusalem in the Bible and she said, "It will be a solid object in the sky. It will shine like the sun and it will be about 1,550 miles, square in length, width and height but rounded on the edges. Round edges make it easier to travel in space.

You know a big ship could be on the other side of the sun and could be coming toward you. I don't know if you'd call it New Jerusalem or not, but I am sure you would like to know what your governments are going to do with that one. Your government does not know what is coming from the backside of the sun yet. Part of this object could be seen if you have big enough equipment and you are in the right hemisphere. It would take something much larger than the Hubble telescope.

This could be the New Jerusalem and Jesus will come back and it will be stationed outside of the atmosphere and He will come down in a cloud, there will be a ship in the cloud."

Photon Belt

Because everyone was talking about the photon belt we asked about it and to our surprise the answer we got was not one we expected.

"The photon belt causes more and more questions. It is coming close and a big change is coming. Hopefully, this is the only thing that is going to happen to your system. As I have said before; the changes can be gentle or they can be very, very bad. Everyone's attitude on Earth will make a difference. Just remember that the days ahead are not bleak…nor should they be scary because the joy that these days bring will be the joy of having Christ back on Earth and the rebuilding of the planet as it was meant to be. And if enough people should decide to turn to the light, it could be a very gently process. So do not look upon these times as being sad, dark, or dreary. Look at these times as a way to step into the future where the sun shines brightly, the trees are green, the flower colors are beautiful, all animals love each other, and humans love everything and become the caretakers of all, as they should be."

Natural Disasters

Asteroids and Meteors

"There are many meteors or asteroids traveling through the Universes. In your area there are over a hundred of them, traveling together. If you have a hundred asteroids or meteors in a cluster it could be miles long. They would be individual pieces about the size of a softball or larger. Many of them have been captured in the same orbit and are moving together as one. These could also influence the changes that are coming if they come close to your planet. We are keeping our eyes on them.

Your astronomers had been monitoring an asteroid that in 1989 almost hit your planet. Many believe it has a seven-month orbit. I would like to say that there are actually two asteroid belts with the probability that one of them could hit the Earth or your moon. Whether it will happen or not, we'll have to wait and see. Decisions could be made up here to alter the course.

Meteor and asteroid belts come in all sizes and shapes. They could go from being a little larger than a baseball or about the diameter of a tire. Some meteors are so large that they could be caught in the gravity of a system and eventually become a planet. Because there are so many pieces in a cluster of an asteroid belt, they are as dangerous as one larger one. If they're caught in your gravity, they would spread out over an elongated path, and this would make them even more destructive over a bigger area. The destruction would depend upon the place it hit; whether it is an ocean, desert, or city. If it should hit an ocean, it would cause a tidal wave. Because there could be so many, ten could fall in one area. It would be like atomic bombs going off. This could also cause earthquakes and volcanoes to erupt."

Comets

"There are many comets out in space that your scientists know nothing about and there are approximately three (this was recorded in March of 1997) that could be causing you a problem in the future. Most of these comets have been traveling through space for a long time, but some of them have collided with other forces and their paths have been altered.

Your scientists are becoming more concerned because of the number they see. There will be more comets going past your planet, and the magnetic pull is drawing them closer to the planet. At this time it does not look like an impact is going to happen, but when you're talking millions of miles, a slight bump or nudge from another piece of space material can alter the course rather quickly and dramatically. A comet, if it is large enough and gets caught in an orbit, could become a planet."

Sea Creature off the Coast Of Chile

While at a meeting in Milwaukee, Wisconsin in the fall of 2003, a gentleman talked about an article he had seen in the newspaper about a gelatinous mass that had been found off the shoreline in Chile. So we asked what this was.

"It is a creature that lives in the ocean. This creature is from very deep in the ocean that happened to have died, rose from the depths of the ocean, and was washed on shore. There are quite a few, I don't know the number, but they are very, very deep in the ocean. That's why there were no eyes to be seen on it, because at that depth there is no light to see. There are a lot of animals there that your scientists don't know about yet.

Even our spaceships have a hard time getting down to that depth because of the pressure that is exerted on it. It is actually greater at that depth than pressure we receive while space traveling. So your scientists are a little bit off on calculating the pressure that the spaceships receive. We have trouble getting our ships down that deep, but we do have samples of the species from that depth.

These creatures are being affected by the molten lava that is being stirred up and moving towards the surface of your planet. It is heating up the water and it is stirring it up, which is making the animals migrate more than they have ever done before. They don't like the heat.

Usually a predator eats these creatures before they get to the surface, and that is why they have not been seen before. At the depths that it lived it has no natural enemy. When it was seen and photographed part of it had broken off. You see, there are animals that are much larger than whales and there also are tiny microorganisms that live at these depths. This is a species that has adapted to the pressures at the deepest depths of the oceans."

Dead Zones in the Oceans and Tectonic Activity

"There are quiet a few places in the ocean that have dead zones. That is where there is no oxygen and no life in the water. Everything dies in this type of water. The activity under the planet is becoming more active and fissures are opening up. The water temperatures are rising in places, and that is causing havoc in the water. There are thirty-two places in the ocean where this is happening. Remember when I explained about the animal that came from deep in the ocean? The water in the area was heating up, that is why it was moving from very deep in the ocean, it came all the way to the surface. Things may get worse; we're not sure how this is going to play out.

When the pole shifts, it can shift again, sometimes it moves back, and then it moves a little bit back again, maybe in another direction. Let me put this picture in Bonnie's mind and see if she can draw what I'm trying to explain. Because of this shifting, these fissures are opening and closing it is a very strange movement. A lot of people think that a pole shift is always moving in one direction and it is not, it moves in different directions. It is kind of like a beach ball on the water and how the wind could affect it and turn and twist it in different directions, kind of like wobbling.

There was one fissure that was open for 362 feet in the Great Lakes for a short period of time. There is also one open in Alaska, and there is talk of the ice melting there."

Earthquakes and Volcanoes

"As your scientists are realizing, earthquakes are happening more frequently now on Earth. When earthquakes happen under water, it shakes the water greatly and confuses a lot of aquatic life forms. Use of the ELF and HAARP waves is also disturbing the ocean floors, causing more earthquakes and rattling the volcanoes.

There are many more earthquakes around the globe than are reported. It seems that only the major ones are reported in your news stories. You need all the information to be able to understand what is really happening on your planet.

Over the years volcanoes have not been very active at the same time but the ring of fire is becoming very active, especially on the ocean's floor. Also, the reporting of this activity has become better.

The world would only have to be tilted to make the Earth flip. This tilting will depend upon the ice caps and earthquakes. If the ice caps break off or earthquakes cause great ice caps to break off into icebergs, now I am not talking small ones, I'm talking about the size of continents breaking off and shifting this could cause things to move along much faster. If the Earth tilts, or shifts on its axis, I would say there would be possible be a 5 to 10% survival rate on the surface of the Earth."

Man Made Problems

Viruses

"Many of the flu bugs going around are man made. This flu changes when it gets into your body and your body has a hard time fighting it. These are some of the little experiments going on to see how fast something can mutate, and they have done very well with this one. Your spirituality will affect it to a point, but a virus is a virus and once it attacks your body it's too late. Your spirituality and bubble of protection can help keep you from receiving it but if you let that guard down and it attaches itself, it has to run its course. Try lots of rest and vitamin C."

HAARP, ELF and El Nino

In early 1998 while asking a question about the changes in the weather, we were given this answer. "There is a volcano off the coast of California by the state of Washington. Now I'm talking volcanoes in the water, under the water. There is one also off Hawaii. There are two off the Philippines. There are three on the west coast of South America and they are all erupting and are raising the water temperatures in the areas. Your government is studying the one right off the coast of Washington.

El Nino is not the full cause of weather changes but it does have some affect on the changes coming. There are sound waves that are being used on the ocean floor plus the HAARP waves this is a combination of all three working together that is affecting your weather changes. It's not that any one thing alone would do it. It's the combination of all. The natural El Nino does affect the weather but it's not as extreme as what they are claiming. So with the volcano's eruption on the ocean floor, which does add a lot of heat in the water, the sound waves and the HAARP waves, it's the combination of all of them."

In 2002 we were told, "HAARP and ELF waves have been stepped up to confuse people more. "Another HAARP plant has been started at a new location on the planet. Lets just say that is on the border between two large countries who usually don't get along; they are doing this as a joint venture."

Ebola and Other Diseases

"The negative aliens gave the technology to produce Ebola on your planet. Read the book called 'The Coming Plagues.' It talk's about people being on medications, and this could be part of the trigger mechanism when it's ingested for things like Ebola and some of the other illnesses out now. This can play a part in weakening the body or triggering the disease especially if they're overused. The prescription medications don't seem to be working any more; the viruses are mutating so many of your doctors are starting to combine drugs. Pretty soon two drugs won't work, and then they'll have to put you on three drugs. Man is destroying the natural herbs and foods that could help these diseases. Many of these were found in the rain forests that are being destroyed and lost every day. Some of the natural vitamins, minerals and herbs on the market are being taken off, and some of them can work. I must also say here that if some of these natural products are not used properly and in the right amount, they can be deadly to the human body. I believe they will eventually make natural herb prescription drugs also. But you're killing the forests and plants that could be used to save lives, and when they're gone there'll be nothing left to go back to.

Many of what you call ancient diseases have been around during most of man's existence. Some of these old diseases have been dormant for a long time, but some of them became active again because men is experimenting and trying to change the DNA in them. Some diseases have mutated naturally and cannot be helped with natural medication. Many of these scientists don't realize that what they are doing is not safe. It is almost as if they don't care and proceed with their experimenting just to see what they can do."

AIDs

"Monkeys did not give AIDs to man, this is a man-made disease and it was produced in a laboratory for control of the population. Actually, they had a pretty good idea on how to cure it before it was ever released. What they did not realize was how it would get out of hand and get into the mainstream of society. The scientists have re-worked the cure for AIDs but it keeps mutating.

By having sexual contact with someone who has AIDS you can get it. As a matter of fact, you can call any disease to your body by your low mentality and your negative thoughts. Right now on this planet there's so much negativity that cancer, AIDs, heart problems are running rampant, and they will continue to do so on this frequency/vibration. That is why the frequencies/vibrations must be raised so that you are closer to God and these problems will not be as predominant as they are on this level.

Tsunami of 2004

We wanted to know when the last time angels were recognized for who they were and were surprised by the answer.

"The last time angels were recognized for who they were was when Lot had them come to his residence, but angels have since been to your planet. One was when the twin towers went down, and there were two at the tsunami in 2004. They were at both places to try to help the victims through their fear and to make sure that their souls weren't snatched by the negative beings.

There were approximately 260,000 people who were lost in the area of the Tsunami. This was not a completely natural event, it was slightly enhanced by a Middle Eastern country; that is all I have to say about that. I think they wanted to know what would happen if they did that.

I am not sure if other countries know what happened, but I think they are suspicious. We are not sure why the coast of Australia wasn't affected, and we haven't been able to find out yet. The type of shift in the crust depends if there is going to be a tsunami or not."

Unexplained Phenomena

Bermuda Triangle

"The Bermuda Triangle is a natural fault under the ocean. We have bases underwater in the area where we do research. After all, you have many animals that live in the ocean, and we want to be able to understand and learn all we can about them because they are different than the species we have in space."

The Loch Ness Monster

In October of 2003 Monn said had this to say about the Loch Ness creature: "The Loch Ness creature does exist, but he does not always stay in the lake as it connects to the ocean. The lake is very, very deep and there are two passages that lead from the lake to the ocean way down at the bottom depths. As he travels in and out he is not on any particular schedule that I know of. He travels thousands of miles. There are three of them and they travel together. There are two males and one female, but the female does not reproduce anymore. These are the last of the species. They are going the way of your dinosaurs."

Crop Circles

"Human hands and natural phenomena make about twenty-five percent of crop circles while aliens cause the other seventy-five percent. As far as I can tell there are at least seventeen different alien species that are creating crop circles at this time on the planet. These seventeen species of aliens are not all neutral. Remember the crop circle that looked like a Gray? Well, that is who produced it.

Most of these aliens making the crop circles are trying to get people to be aware that there is something in existence beyond your planet. Many are trying through geometry; some are trying through the pictographs. Most of them are of symbols, some of them are identical to your ancient symbols, which can be deciphered. Some species are even trying to let you know about them by sending back to you what you've sent into space. Don't let the government try to tell you they have sent out one message that told what the planet Earth is like. They have sent out more messages than that one.

So, I guess that's basically all I can say about that except we don't make crop circles. Some of the crop circles are made by those from a system or planet called

Arga. They are the makers of a lot of circles but not all. It will take your scientists a long time to decipher them because they don't look at them with their hearts."

Sonic Booms and Sky Quakes

Many of the people attending the channeling sessions had been hearing sonic booms in their hometowns. There also had been talk about this noise being experienced in the Green Bay, Wisconsin area. The noise was described as an explosion, and nobody quite knew what to call it, so we asked what the noise was.

"In the simplest terms I can bring it down to your level of understanding is it's a sudden compression of the air by fast movement, beyond the sonic boom that I think you all know about. Say there is a malfunction in one of our space ships as we are leaving the atmosphere. With that kind of malfunction there's such a fast compression of air that it's like a…say you drop a stone in water and it ripples out. This is kind of what happens to the air when the body moves."

We then asked if there was something going on in the Valley, this is the nickname for the area we live. Monn answered, "There is nothing, I know nothing, I speak nothing." (It sounded as if she had been watching Hogan's Hero's TV program again and liked the phrase so much she used it.)

Ghosts

Curious about the many people who claimed to be speaking to ghosts or hunting them, we asked about the subject.

"Ghosts do exist but not quite on the level that most of your seers and ghosts talkers feel them to be. A ghost is usually someone who met an untimely or violent death and for some reason or another chose not to go to the light when it was offered them. Therefore they are stuck in a never, never land. A lot of your ouija board people and channelers call on them because they enjoy talking to them, and this holds the ghosts in that realm. What they are doing is holding them back from moving into the light so they can go back to God, so they can go to their next lifetime, mission, or job.

If you are into ghost hunting for pleasure or the excitement of it, you can hold that spirit near Earth and not allow them to move on. A good ghost hunter tries to find a ghost and sends it on its way home to the Creator. If the ghost is not ready to continue on after you've tried to enlighten them on the situation they're in, then you should try to explain to them where they are and that it is time for them to go on. Sometimes they are frightened because they don't know where they will be going; sometimes they are afraid that if they go on they will be going into limbo, hell, the abyss, or whatever your religion prefers to call it. Try to explain to them that God is forgiving and that it is His wish for them to move on.

Ghosts can rattle chains and/or terrify people because as the person was in their life, so they are when they die. So, if they were not good, kind or compassionate in their life, they are not good in death until they have reviewed their life and learned what mistakes were made.

A ghost does not take on a form that can be felt, touched, or give you warmth. While an angel can take on a form, walk the planet, speak, touch and feel emotions.

If an entity comes back and taunts or torments you, it is usually one of the negative side doing their work. They can come as a ghost; they can come as a loved one and whisper in your ear. If you listen even though you know what is being said is not right, you're not listening to your instincts that tell you something is wrong. When you realize your loved one would not say or do what is being said, then you must send that voice, that ghost on their way. Tell them you will not accept what they are saying because if you accept it, they will keep coming back to you, causing trouble.

Sometimes right after a loved one has passed on they may try to speak to you. When this happens it is usually because there had been trouble between the two of you or there was some unfinished business, but it is very rare.

If you perish unexpectedly and don't move on, you do not go on to review your life. You do not go on to learn from your mistakes, and you certainly do not become more enlightened or spiritual than you were in your last lifetime. So I have this to suggest, all of you who hold on to those that have departed, tell these beings to move on so that they can be with the Creator. They can then fulfill their mission on Earth and go on to learn from their mistakes so they can go back to the Source. Many of these beings have been trapped for hundreds of years because people won't let them go.

We all mourn the loss of our loved ones, be they alien or human. What we have learned over the years is to mourn their loss but to thank them for what they have given us, for the lessons they so gladly endured to teach us. When we have mourned them we can happily send them on their way if they have not already done so."

Gulf Breeze

After reading a book about Ed Walters who had taken pictures of the crafts in Gulf Breeze, we wanted to know if they were real or not. So many people had said that this whole thing was a hoax and the pictures that were taken were faked.

When we asked the aliens, they had this to say. "Those ships sighted around the Gulf Breeze area in Florida are real and some of the good guys are piloting them but some of the not so nice guys are also there."

MIBs

When asked in 1993 about who the men in black were Monn had the following to say. "Most of the MIBs are robotic in their movement, and that pale skin is a dead giveaway. The skin is synthetic as they haven't quite mastered making the skin look natural yet. Because they are robotic in their thinking, you can trick and confuse them by just telling them you're their master. Confuse them just as you would try to confuse the negative Grays."

Things Associated With New Age

While asking questions associated with the new age community the aliens said in 1992 that, our ideas and theirs were becoming separated more and more. They suggested that we move ourselves away from them. Following are some of the answers to questions we asked, about what some people were doing.

Rituals and Incantations

"Rituals and incantations are a way of focusing your energy and power. Let's say the dark forces use a lock of hair, burning a candle, or a chant to focus their energy/power. These are all ways of focusing your energy and your power. We in the Light do not need that; we should be able to learn to focus our energy to the point we want without props. Many people in the New Age community use crystals to focus energy. When you use crystals, a lock of hair, or nail clippings to focus the energy, we prefer to call this witchcraft. You see when you're dealing with magic, it can be a way of focusing your energy to that person or being.

There is power and it all comes from The Source, but how we use it determines whether it's good or bad. It is a God-given power/force and it is there for everyone to use. It is up to you if you use it for good or evil. Only remember that for every action there is a reaction, and if you use the force for, not very nice things will be coming back to you ten fold.

When using crystals or talismans, lock of hair, or nail clippings to focus energy, you are not using the power that God has given you. You are showing the mustard seed of doubt in Him. Those things are only a way of focusing your energy to a person or being, and it is not trusting God.

We as light workers cannot initiate anything against anyone else to cause them problems or harm, but we do have the right to stop any force that is thrown against us with equal force. There is never a time when negative incantations or rituals are acceptable."

Crystals

In March of 1990 Monn had a few things to say. "I think maybe we should clear some things up. People are going to be coming at you with lots and lots of questions, and it may be a little hard to tell them what they wanna hear. Sometimes you are going to have to tell them what they don't really wanna hear. But I'd like to get something straightened up about crystals. Crystals are what we like to call a gift; God creates everything including crystals. Many people are interested in crystals and some people liken crystals to a God. There's nothing wrong with crystals, if you use them as a focus to go into yourself. Some people need something more tangible to focus on; something they can see and touch.

Crystals do absorb energy; they do absorb negativity around you. They can have calming effects on you but you really don't need them. As a beginner you may need crystals to focus on as a human, it's much easier to use them as a beginning point. So when people come to you with the idea of should I wear a crystal? You can ask, are you comfortable with it? Does it help you remember something in your life? Does it make you feel secure? Does it make you feel comfortable? Then use that. Anything that gets you to focus, to look inward is good. It doesn't have to be a crystal. It can be a stone out of your driveway or a piece of China that you like or something that reflects the light through to you, anything to focus your thoughts on, so that you can learn to turn inward."

11:11

In 1995 there was so much talk going around about the planet making ascension at 11:11 that we had to ask Monn if that was so. "So many people have been stating that the planet is already in the fourth dimension and is rising to the fifth. No. Can't you tell by all the negativity around you on this planet, all the fighting and killings? When you're in the fourth dimension and heading into the fifth, people should be calm, loving, caring individuals and would be willing to work together for a common goal."

We then asked, now the New Age community is talking about 12:12; is this a façade also? Monn replied, "Its kind of like, saying look at me, I know what is going to happen and you don't. They may even throw in Melchizedek to make it more believable."

Souls

When asked about New Age and their take on souls Monn said, "I know many people claiming to be New Age feel that a soul can split into many pieces and live at least seven or even more existences. They claim to live in different areas all at the same time, and this is absolutely false. You have one soul and it does not split apart."

Urantia

For years we had people tell us about the Urantia book. A man encouraged us to read about Jesus' life and especially the section called The Lucifer Rebellion in the Urantia book. We read these parts in the book and were not so sure about what it said so left it drop. Many years later we met a group that studies The Urantia material from the book and asked if the book, which talks about Jesus' life almost year by year, was fairly accurate. We asked Lea because she knew a lot about the life of Jesus and thought she might know about the Urantia book. She replied with the following, "I have not read the whole Urantia book, but from what I understand just a percentage of it is the real truth. A writer puts their own ideas, their own philosophies into what they are writing, so as with anything please read and look for the pearls and then look for confirmation from another source."

Tidbits of Interesting Information

Energy Flow

In December of 1988 Monn had this to say. "Many times when you sleep you may feel the need to turn around in your beds and face another direction. This could be caused by the energy coming through your home differently at that time. As you become more aware of what's going on around you, you can recognize which way you need to face to be comfortable. Sometimes you have to shift your body for the energy flow to go through your body easier. In other words sometimes you can collect energy from everything that's around you but you need to let it flow through your body as that is healthier for you."

Astral Traveling

"When you astral travel the soul keeps in touch with the body; you are connected by thoughts not silver cords. When you astral travel the soul leaves and your body runs automatically on very low power. This means the body slows down very much, body temperature drops, breathing rate slows and the blood pressure drops. The longer your soul stays away from the body the greater the risk of something happening to the shell.

Walk-ins don't have silver cords, actually, nobody does. Having a silver cord connected to your body is one of your earth ideas. Actually a lot of people have the idea of a silver cord connected to the body when a soul leaves and if that should break the soul would not know how to get back to the body. Did you ever think about what would happen if all the silver cords got tangled up? I think this is a hilarious idea! We also have heard about angels having wings and that everyone has multiple angels with them at all times. Just imagine if everyone one on Earth had three angel's with very large wing all beating at the same time. Can you picture that in your mind, can you see the wings beating each other."

Middle East

In 1990 Monn had this to say about the Middle East: "The Middle East does not look good at all. Bush seems to want to push Hussein into a corner, and if he tries it's not going to work. I don't know if you would call this WWIII, but there's going to be an awful lot of hot spots in the Middle East. I can't say how long this will last, but it might be for some time. All I can fathom is a guess on how you people think. It will not be an easy thing to settle. It's going to last a long time, except if they start using the gas and terrifying chemicals. If they do, then I'm afraid quite a few of the governments will just walk all over them and end it rather quickly.

The Arabs are very, very religious, and if anything is done for religion they are willing to follow. They have been oppressed for such a long time. One of the plans is to keep this area in turmoil until the Antichrist can step forward with a peace plan.

Even in Africa it is not looking so good, brother killing brother. How can you get along with aliens, when you can't get along with your brothers who are from the same planet?"

Hitler

"It is going to take a lot of time and a lot of repentance and forgiveness on the Creator's part to let Hitler come back into human form. He is going to need a long time and a lot of schooling on the other side to learn his errors and accept the fact that he did err, before he is going to be allowed to be born again.

Next time around he may be the oppressed one and may have to live through many horrors. Another lifetime can be a learning experience, and many don't have a choice of where you go or to whom you are born if you are so negative. There comes a time when you are put back on any planet in the Universe for a lesson. There are not a lot of people like that, but there are some who must come back and live in poverty or under conditions that are subhuman in order to make up for something that they have done in a past life. If a person is willing to accept the responsibility for what they've done, acknowledge that they have erred, and are willing to try to make amends for the things that they have done, they then could be reborn to make up for those mistakes. Remember karma, you always pay for what you give out."

Karma

When asked about Karma, the aliens shared with us the following information. "The law of Karma is; what you put in is what you get back. What you sow is what you reap. Negative emotions can be like a mirror reflecting back at you but if you send love it can be also have the same effect. If you send love it will reflect back upon you. This is very simple but is one of the things that everyone has to contend with. If you think you do not have to pay for the things you do, you are wrong.

With the instincts that God has given you, you know when you are incurring karmic debt by your decisions or choices. I know myself if I get a sinking feeling in my heart when I realize that I'm doing something that I shouldn't be, and I'm going to have to pay for that at some point. I'm not too sure that humans could recognize that fact, but I think if you make wise choices and then realize that you made a mistake and try to correct your mistake the karmic debt would not be carried over. God is forgiving if we recognize the mistakes we've made.

If you feel you are in danger and someone is threatening you with force, that force can be met with equal force. Force can only be met with equal force but no more than necessary or you will have a large karmic debt to pay. When I say force, it could be a physical force but doesn't necessarily have to be. It can also be a mental force. If somebody is bugging you, you can bug them right back, but you have no right to initiate a force of any kind.

It is never acceptable to take ones own life. No one can stop you, but when you face your final judgment you are going to have to have another lifetime and do it all over again and with more karma added. The Heavenly Father does not accept suicide. If you commit suicide, you will not be allowed to enter the kingdom until you atone for your mistake, and then and only then it is forgiven.

With your technology today you can keep the body alive long after the soul has departed. Suppose after a week of extraordinary medical attention everything is stopped and then you die. The ones doing these extraordinary medical measures to keep the body alive will have a big karmic debt because this is stopping God from having the soul return to Him. It keeps the soul in limbo. This is even worse than committing suicide because many of your scientists are tampering with life in laboratories and that is going against nature. The ones doing these extraordinary medical measures will have a big karmic debt. This happened in Atlantis and Lemuria, and look at what happened to them.

We may have to decide if we will intervene in the course of the planet. We may have to let the people know who we are. If that happens, the outcome of the planet will be very different and we would be going against our principles and God's principles. We would have to pay for our actions, but sometimes it's worth the risk. We have decided that if we have to we'll let people on Earth including your government know who we are, and then we'll have a karmic debt to pay for doing so. However sometimes it's worth the karmic debt to win the battle."

Eric in 2005 stated that, "If the common person would ask for help from the aliens, they could and would help us in the troubled times ahead. By your asking for help we would not incur a karmic debt."

Look to the Future

"Many of you are searching your past relationships and your past incarnations thinking it will help you with the people you come in contact with today. It is not necessary for you to search out all the answers. Sometimes you might come across people who affect you certain ways; they are drawn to you or you're drawn to them. That might be interesting for you to look into it because it's affecting you heavily in this lifetime. What is important is what you do with this lifetime because the past is passed. Look to the now, look to the future. What you do in this life will affect your next incarnation."

Lecture on Our Loose Lips

Monn had been sharing some information with us, and we shared the information with other people who were not ready to hear it. We thought it would help fix their problems, but Monn had other ideas. "If you do not stop sharing the information I give you with everyone I will be sent home. You all seem to be so busy fixing someone else you forget to fix yourself. I plan on staying. Therefore, when something is in the wind, something is planned, I will not discuss with you, anyone or anything else again, until we can see that you realize that by telling someone too soon can push them over the edge and we lose them forever. We realize and you know how short time is. But everyone cannot hear or understand too quickly.

If we ask to speak to someone please do not go to them and say, you're on the ship with us and you are in our group. Please let us handle it as we might also send them over the edge, but we have slightly more knowledge on how far we can speak to these people. It is probably a good thing to try to get everyone together to sit and realize that among all of you there is a mission and there is a job. But everyone must do and accomplish it the way that they were meant to do it. Even if you don't agree with what they feel, please be understanding of that person. Tell them you don't understand but you will support them anyhow. If someone asks you to teach them something, help them, be patient with them. Don't put them off, don't degrade them, and don't turn your back on them. Embrace them because we all have many things to learn. We all have lessons and we all need someone to take our hand and help us. We all should be learning what each other is doing so that if you should become incapacitated or if something should happen to you physically or mentally that you cannot do your part of the job, then they can help you. And in the same token if they have a problem, then you can help them through that situation.

Understand that the Creator loves all of you the same and you should also love everyone no matter how many times they irritate you, how many times they get under your skin. You should love them because they are teaching you patience. Do not think that all jobs are quick and easy. Sometimes jobs can be tedious and slow and it's much easier just to get up and walk away, but you must be willing to sacrifice your time even when it seems useless.

We all love you and we think we can understand where your feelings and emotions are going. But you don't decide things outside of the meeting and come to the meeting and say, oh, we discussed this and it was decided…I wonder when it was decided that this job was done by a majority rule. I don't understand that. We believe that it's God's rule, not the majority of a few people.

From where we stand, we can personally see four, five, six, seven, eight light workers are teetering on the edge of walking away. These are the core of the light workers in Wisconsin. If all these people walk away, I will be leaving the service. I'm not saying this to upset you guys. We want you to know the facts on how things are happening, how things are tumbling. The dominoes are falling. They're falling quickly.

You have lost respect for each other. Where did it go? You can see it happening to other people but you don't see it right here in this room? (Ten second pause and the rest is said with a trembling voice.) We hope that you can build back your respect for each other. You know each other's weaknesses, so instead of snide remarks why don't you help that person? We, we just want you to know that we're rooting for you and maybe it's time that you're willing to share with other people that you also have shortcomings, you also have problems, and maybe you can all help each other. Are you setting yourselves up to look like this is a wonderful group with no problems? Maybe if other people understood, maybe they could try to be more understanding of each other."

About a month later Monn had this to say, "I had hoped that last time I spoke about this that we would see some changes, but we haven't seen it. We have seen the sniping; we have heard the little slams here and there. There's where you lose your spirituality. Please understand, this is not a group of five, this is a group of people in Wisconsin who must learn to understand each other, to love each other. Who cares who's right and who's wrong? Maybe explaining about your shortcomings to other people might help them understand that you can survive all things that earth can throw at you.

I am going to have to speak more authority, when I speak to you. It is not a job that I relish doing, nor is it in my contract, but I shall do it if it is needed because I refuse to go down without a fight. And I'm fighting to keep every single one of you in the light. Don't speak of the negative and don't speak of the dark because that brings it to you whether you realize it or not.

I hope that we can all continue on our job, on our mission. If you do not wish to, I will understand. The only thing that I ask you to do if you do not wish to continue in your mission is please turn in all the material that you have in your possession because if you do wish to leave, you may use the material in a negative way. If you have a problem and a situation that you are not comfortable in, then I suggest that you leave. We can't have dissention and continue to go forward. There are a lot of bridges that are going to have to be crossed and we don't know if they can be mended.

No matter what, love is the solution. Love is what makes the world go round. Remember what you probably have accused others of doing, is what you've done yourself. Think of what you have accused old members of the group that have left of doing and right now you are probably doing the same thing. Open your eyes, open your heart, open your soul, and let the sun and the light shine in so that you can allow your radiance to shine so that others can see it. (Monn takes a deep breath.) We will not let any of you fall without a fight, and we expect you here on Earth not to let these other people fall without a fight.

We have never demanded anything of you, but I am saying to you now, fight, before all is lost, before your connection with your past and your future is broken. We will fight from this side, but you must fight from that side, too."

Time Differential, Between Earth and Space

Monn in 1989 explained, "When we are in space we do not have the sun rising and setting because we are not spinning around a sun. In space we basically have a six to eight hour resting mode and approximately sixteen hours of awake time. The confusion turns into converting it from your time to ours, let's see, sixty minutes make an hour. We have a hundred and eighty minutes to an hour. Now I'm trying to convert our time to fit into your span of time. We have more time modes than you do.

Our time differs when you are off the planet and depends upon how far you are outside the atmosphere. If our ships are inside earth's atmosphere, time would be speeded up about three to one. If you were on board a space ship and you were outside of Earth's atmosphere, in approximately one hour of your time you could accomplish eight hours of work at our vibration level.

Now this has nothing to do with spiritual enlightenment, as enlightenment has nothing to do with time. You see, just like us, when the bad ones come down to your planet they can only stay there for a short period of time. You can go into another dimension and stay there for a short period of time. You cannot stay for an extended period of time unless your levels are equal to that to which you were going, but your body can survive for a short period of time."

Solar Cross

Eric explained, "The Solar Cross has no beginning and no end. It is a silver-colored cross...I believe is the term you would call it. It has two lines that cross and blend into one, it sort of looks like your religious crosses. The part that goes up and down is longer than the one that crosses over. On the top there are three suns peeking from behind, one at the top and one at each side, and at the ends of the cross-over there are also three. At the bottom of the cross it comes to a point. It looks a little like the swords that the knights-of-the-round-table used.

It's the symbol of unity and joining as one to become a stronger force. There is a ceremony with it for pledging unity and to work together for a common goal. It is the joining of two to become one, be it people, nations, systems or Universes.

It is the symbol for the command of Lord Michael and his legion of the Solar Cross. Michael has been on Earth many times but always in small ways and not in names that you would recognize."

Physical Problems

"We cannot interfere with any of the physical problems your human bodies have. You knew what body you were entering and knew of the physical problems it would have but you entered anyway. I suggest if you have physical problems to go to an earth doctor. We are allowed to assist surgeons, maybe guide their hands, but we cannot interfere with them unless it's needed."

Shots, Injections

"The measles inoculation is going to be mandatory for everyone very soon. Many who are entering certain levels of school have already been inoculated. It is a evil plan to ensure that everyone has an implant, a computer chip in them. This is one way that they are insuring people get implanted through vaccines.

Many times you cannot take a newborn home without them having shots in the hospital. Accept the fact that it has to be done, remember at this time not all injections carry an implant. You can make any of these foreign bodies inoperable. Implants are so small now that they can be shot into the body with a regular-sized-needle."

Microchip

"A small microchip is a foreign object that is put in the body for a purpose. Some babies are being implanted with a chip at birth in hospitals without the parents' consent. These people want to see how long the chips function and how tractable they are. This is in a test market, yes! There also is a chip scientists are working on to control your mind when implanted in your body. But first they will try to control you with a card with a bar code on it; then they will break the money system. From there they could make a one-world government, with a one-world police force.

If your government makes you pay taxes to keep it running give your share, don't give them your soul. That is yours, give it to God. When you go solely to cards with a bar code, credit cards, library cards or the volunteer cash cards, these are not the mark of the beast, yet. When you get a card with a thumbprint or iris prints, it will be very close to the mark of the beast that your Bible talks about. This will be a card or mark on your body. and without it you will be stopped on the street and put in prison immediately. You will you not be able buy, sell, or drive a car without this mark of the beast. You won't be able to exist outside of a prison without it."

Flickering Lights on Video Games and Cartoons

In 1998 there were articles in the newspapers and news on television reporting about seizures of varying degrees in Japanese children who watched cartoons. We asked about them and this was their answer.

"There is a flickering pattern of light that can be used to cause seizures and it doesn't affect all brains the same. In other words, two people could watch the same flickering light and one would be affected much greater and quicker than another. If you ever notice in children's cartoons especially they use a lot of color and movement which can cause flickering light to affect the brain more than usual.

I wouldn't say it's done purposely, but they do know that it can cause seizures and they still repeat the process. This can also happen with your video games, and many children have had seizures while intently watching them. If you want to see what I'm talking about, go to a video arcade and watch the children playing games. You will almost see their bodies jumping in spasms. This can become addictive to them. They become so involved in the game, in the lights flashing and their muscles contracting and contracting, that it can cause seizures. Because of the lights flashing and intensity of their concentration, I would suggest that you limit exposure to these things."

Indigo Children

Having read a book on indigo children and hearing about them at a few meetings in 2000 we asked about Indigo children.

"Many people are talking about indigo children with a triple DNA helix but there is not yet a change in your helix…in your DNA. There is a change in the souls that are coming, but DNA has nothing to do with how your souls react or how they behave. Your DNA is the makeup of the physical body, not the soul attached to your body.

This is nothing new; these types of souls have been on the planet since the beginning of time. The souls coming here now have chosen to be here so they can advance with a leap in their spirituality.

Indigo children usually have a more spiritual soul, but along with that some souls are being born more negative. So again you have that balance. Many souls choose to be here at this time so they can experience what is going to happen to this planet."

Alzheimer Disease

"Alzheimer's is caused by lack of good nutrition and the environment. Your fruits and vegetables are no more grown naturally and have been treated from before the seed is planted until you receive it. The animals that you eat are injected with chemicals to make them bigger and more resistant to disease, and these chemicals deteriorate the value of the food that you put into your bodies. Those of you that are balanced do not have as great a probability of receiving this disease because your body is in balance and can counteract the effect of the food upon your body. Saying a prayer about your food before you eat also helps because there are many chemicals used in manufacturing that contribute to Alzheimer's disease. So be cautious in what you put into your body and what is in your environment."

Blackout on the East Coast and Canada In 2003

"Just recently the blackout you had started with a problem in Ohio and went both east and north; it was caused by a malfunction in a transformer. I'm afraid that there could be more of these because the grids are so connected with each other that they could all go like the domino effect.

The problem with the transformer was not caused by human error, it was caused by an alien error. The aliens had their force field on surrounding their ship and got too close to a transformer. Please remember accidents do happen. Remember what happened when Derrick's ship got a little too close to Bonnie's house: the lights got brighter and then dimmer.

A short time after the blackout in your country, England's secret government caused a power outage. England was saying that the outages could never happen to them. This was a message to let the people in power know that they are not as safe and secure as they think they are."

Dreams

"Dreams can sometimes be your subconscious having memories. The dreams bring them to your conscious mind by relating to it the only thing that makes sense to your conscious mind, such as a dream of a train engine noise could be a memory of the noise that you heard on a space ship."

In December of 1988 we asked if dreams could be a memory of what we do at night. Monn replied, "A dream is often just a rerun of what has happened during the day, often it is just bits and pieces all jumbled together not making sense. But a memory of something that you do at night as a light worker will be in full color, it will look real and it will make sense. There will be smells and sounds that are so real that you know what you remember is really happening. If you want more memories of what you are doing at night with the aliens, ask for remembrance when you go to bed. Try to hang on to what happened, even just one thing, when you come back. If you can bring one little thing back into your wakening period, you should be able to remember it all day. I suggest upon wakening to write down what you remember. Try to figure if it relates to what happened to you the day before and what does not.

We do not believe full memory would be good for you because then you would have a hard time living on Earth. Try to pull up one memory because if you can pull up one thing, then you should be able to pull up more memories as to what you as a light worker are doing. The dark side aliens and the government have often infiltrated those who have full memory of everything that happens to them. This means that they report what the aliens and government want them to say about what they remember, which will make everyone in this field look foolish.

On the other hand, if you are honest and tell those doing an interview, be it a radio show or whatever, they will believe what you say is 100% accurate. If you have one flicker of doubt that what you're saying is true, people won't believe you. So work on that. Work on that very, very hard. You need that for stepping forward. People can feel the questioning in your soul. A memory does not have to be 100% accurate. But if you can pull back two or three things and know the difference between reality and a dream, people will feel it. If you try to talk with authority and you don't have good memory and you don't believe what is happening to you, frankly, people will think you are nuts."

A person who attended a channeling session had a reoccurring dream. It was a dream about a locomotive engine coming right towards them. Eric was channeling and this is his explanation of that reoccurring dream.

"That is not a dream of locomotive engines, it is the sound that the engines on my ship makes that you are hearing. Your conscious mind puts it into a form that it can relate to. That is why dreams are so important to remember. Try to put them in perspective because a lot of times things that you have learned at night, things that you have done in meetings, projects that you have agreed to take on, you generally take only part of the memory back to Earth. Your subconscious mixes reality up and tells you it was a dream. So please write down your dreams and try to understand what your subconscious is trying to tell you."

What??? The Aliens Actually Have Humor!

In 1989 we were asking questions about where we were from and what part of the Universe we came from. Monn got a little impatient with us about that question but she did answer a few other questions. Being persistent we again asked the question of where we came from and she said, "Oh, well, what star system do you want? Pick one, we'll let you be from there."

In 1990 Monn said that many times they look down at us and laugh at our thoughts and mistakes. Later in August of 1990 we were camping in tents, and it was raining and thundering and lightening during a channeling session. As Eric was speaking, he said, "It sounds just like God is bowling and you have all the liquid you need in the campground."

We had been told to keep track of all the sessions. We should make hard copies and spread them out so that if something happened to one set there would be another available. Now, I am very bad at keeping things neat and in order. In 1991 Lea made a comment about my filing system. She said, "Now that's what I call a great filing system. Can you imagine us running a ship like that? Every time I go into Bonnie's room and look at that computer stand I just throw up my hands and walk away. Once she files something away it is lost forever. This is at its worst! Hey, come on, people, get your act together. Then at least you will be able to put your hand on it if you need to."

The aliens were in a good mood during a session in 1995 session. We were at a hotel and could hear the clanging of the water pipes in the next room. Eric asked, "What is that noise?" We explained that it was water in the pipes. He answered, "What, they haven't perfected that yet!"

We were talking about ice skating; Eric commented that he would never ice skate. "I'd have to have my wings flapping just to stay alive." He went on to say, "You aren't the only ones to make jokes, we also can joke. After you went to bed last night we partied!" After a few seconds he said, "No, I'm only kidding, this weekend we are having meetings and round table discussions on how to prod light workers like you to get moving forward."

During a 1996 session while talking to Monn we asked if we could we make an audiotape message of anything that they would like to share with humanity. She answered the question with, "I would have to bring it before the council as to what could be said." We told Monn we would leave it up to her. "Oh fine," she answered, "I thought I was going to be shuttling people around this time. Talking to people was not in my contract. Oh, good lord, I have to work with you people!!!"

On December 26, 1998 again we asked Monn if she had read the stories about our leaders meeting with the aliens. This had been reported in one of the famous rag magazines. "I just love those rag stories, especially about John Glen being a space alien and the one where President Clinton met an alien every once in awhile. We got our hands on that one and laughed like crazy. They haven't had a real good alien story lately."

During a session we were also told that people sitting in a bread truck were listening to us at this meeting. When we asked them if they could buzz these people and scare them, Eric, answered, "We're good people. We don't do that." We then made suggestions about what the aliens could do to make the people in the bread truck less bored, and Eric answered in mock disgust, "Earthlings!"

Another time Monn told us we should send them some funny little tunes because we have a lot of them, "You know little ditties. You know, I really liked Cheech and Chong in the movie 'Up in Smoke.' It is funny."

In 2001 Monn gave us this runaround when we asked what we thought was a reasonable question. We asked when and if they could send us some help. "Could be."

Would this help be a conference? Monn answered, "Could be." Or maybe a book to open new ideas? Monn answered again with, "Could be." The question was then asked if she would answer our questions? Monn again said, "Could be." It was then said that everyone was trying to stay alert to things going on around them. Monn answer with, "Well you could try harder. Just try to be more alert."

In early 2002 Eric was talking about how, "Many of the people on this planet feel that they can control everything. Your government has known for years of the aliens and they have traded with them knowledge and understanding. And, of course, the aliens did not give all truth, only bits and pieces of it." The question was asked if something would happen in March and Eric answered, "*I know nothing!*" (Vocally impersonating Sergeant Schultz from the TV sitcom Hogan's Heroes of the 1970's)

It was Christmas time in 2002 and Eric was channeling when he had a huge smile on his face. He wished us a Merry Christmas and explained why he was smiling, "I'm smiling because it is warm here." (A fire was going in the fireplace and I was sitting right in front of it collecting all the heat.)

We asked if it felt good or if a fan was needed to cool him off. Knowing how we sometimes refer to him as a big blue bird (chicken) he answered with his quick wit, chuckling all the time. "Now I know how a rotisserie chicken feels. It's warm, I can feel the warmth come through. It is really warm. Monn has explained to me about the blinking Christmas lights that you used to use for decorations, but I don't see any today. Don't you use them any more?"

In October of 2003, when asked why we were so stupid to volunteer for this job Lea gave this funny explanation, "Before you came here many people were standing at attention in a line. Then volunteers were called for to go on a mission to Earth. Everyone standing in the line backed up except those of you who are here. So you volunteered for this mission. That is how you came to do the work here." Lea was laughing as she spoke because she was making a joke.

In October of 2003 Monn told us about Eric's reaction to watching a presentation we had seen about UFOs in Milwaukee. The producer wanted to sell his production to television for a special and had used part of the presentation that I had given at a UFO gathering in Wisconsin.

When the picture of Eric was on the screen, the producer called him a big blue chicken, which I thought, was a slam to Eric but evidently not so to him. While talking to Monn about the presentation, she explained, "Eric had a hilarious reaction to the comment about being a blue chicken. (Monn was laughing as she told us.) You should have seen Eric, for a couple of days he walked around and went *cluck, cluck,* bobbing his head up and down just like a chicken. It was hilarious, and then he had to put on a straight face and go into serious meetings. I don't know how he could turn it on and off like that. We were laughing in the hallways and he looked so straight-laced. (Monn continued still laughing) I believe he wanted to make fun of himself first before anyone else did. That's why he's captain, he's one step ahead of everybody.

It is hard imaging a big blue bird in the sky, and you know some people are going to be very shocked when they start seeing some of the different aliens, but some of the aliens will look at you and go, oh my God!"

Monn also had this to say to us, "You know it is very surprising to us when we see people running around with those yellow cheese things on their heads like some of you do in Wisconsin. I know you don't all do that, but you can see how we all get preconceived ideas of what is going on. Many people, what do you say, stick their heads in the sand, they either have their heads in the sand or they're hollering Chicken Little."

We asked many questions over the years and every so often did not get any answers. Like in 1987 when we asked for an explanation of a black hole is. Monn replied, "A black hole is something that you could not understand even if I explained it."

In 2003, when asked if planet X is inhabited by the Annunaki, Monn told us, "no." We then asked who occupied it. Monn replied, "I don't think it would be wise to answer that question at this time."

When asked about the New Jerusalem, would it be visible in our sky. Lea answered, "I do not know. I am not in the chain of command to know that."

When asked about the location of an underground base in Wisconsin, Monn replied, "I cannot answer that because it could put you in danger." We again asked the question in an attempt to find out more, she rephrased her reply. "There is an underground base in your area close to the border of your state. It would be too dangerous for me to tell you which border it is located on."

Someone wrote to us and asked us to find out about his father who had been fishing on Lake Michigan and got caught in a whirlpool. His father had put his boat in full speed, and the boat was almost in an upright position getting out of the whirlpool. This happened somewhere in the middle 1980's, was as close to a date he could come up with as to when it occurred. Monn replied, "I cannot answer that. I do not know." They keep telling us they don't know everything but we still ask the questions just in case they will give us an answer.

Monn admitted, "I blab more than Lea does, Lea is all business. If she knows something she just tells us, and that has gotten her into trouble." Monn went on to explain, "Sometimes I have people standing over my shoulder watching and listening to what I say to you. I know you want to know who is with me tonight but (Monn growls) you would like to know wouldn't you? It is not a female but I won't tell you who it is because that would get me into trouble."

Our Solar System

Jupiter

When asked about the Shumaker-Levi impact on Jupiter in 1995, Monn told us that the beings had been evacuated from Jupiter before the comet impact.

So later in 1995 while talking to Lea we asked her to confirm that the beings had been taken off Jupiter, and this is what she had to say; "Our people to some extent had a hand in the evacuation of Jupiter. They have been taken to another planet in another solar system. I know you want the exact number of survivors, but let's just say it took quite a few of the ships that were here on standby for the evacuation of Earth. It took quite a few of them to do that. As long as we were in the area, it was our job to do it. It is hard for them to adjust to a new place.

When Jupiter was hit with the Shoemaker-Levi meteor, it was not an isolated incident. It has happened many times as there have always been meteors traveling through space.

There were life forms, human, life forms on Jupiter's surface at the time of impact, and they were evacuated to a different section of the Universe. The beings on Jupiter breathe a different atmosphere than on your planet. If we go down to the surface of the planet we must wear suits to survive. There were also beings underneath the planet that had to be evacuated. These forms are at a faster vibration and your eyes cannot comprehend them. Some of our ships in this area helped with the evacuation as it happened so fast.

It may be a long time before the planet stabilizes again. There are a lot of earthquakes underground so that area is also being destroyed. This has to stop before anything can be done to help the planet. There were also firestorms on the planet, and your scientists observed this. And your government got some wonderful photos with the help of the Hubble. The planet is in pretty bad shape, and it may take years before it is inhabitable.

There have been many close calls with your planet Earth, and there have been many times when it has been hit. I hope that your people never ever send an atomic weapon out into space to destroy one. I know some people on your planet are talking about using an atomic weapon in space that could be the destruction of the whole planet. If Earth was going to be hit by a meteor and if man would counteract that with a nuclear weapon strike in space, it probably would not destroy the planet but it would destroy almost all life forms on the planet and would mutate that which was left. This would also affect other planets in the system. Right now there are a few meteors out there that a slight change of coarse could put them into a collision path with your planet. Some people believe that Death Valley was caused by meteorite eons ago, but it was not."

Venus

"People on Venus have a much higher vibration than you do, yet they still have a form which is more human like. You cannot see their trees, plants, houses, or anything else on the planet because everything vibrates faster. People are born on various planets, but I know of no one who has been born on all the planets."

Mars

"There actually is a population on Mars and they had a cataclysm shift that is exactly what Earth is going to go through. Because of this, the people on Mars went underground for survival. Your governments have a small group, a very limited amount of people...researchers on Mars. The Grays also have a base on Mars although they do not relate to the other groups that are there or the original occupants."

In 1995 Eric explained, "The United States and Russia were working together to get a base and colony established on Mars, but it's kind of gone the way of the back burner.

The Mars rover is getting people more accepting of what is real. It wasn't too long ago your government hardly thought there could possible have been any life on that planet, but now they are slowly easing people into the knowledge that there might have been life on Mars."

Planet X

"We are going to let ourselves be known by your governments with radio signals because Planet X is coming. Most of your higher echelons are aware of it, but a few of the smaller countries have not been informed of its coming nor the consequences of it moving into the area. Although Planet X is coming there is another mass that is coming from behind the sun that may be of more concern.

This object on the other side of the sun coming towards Earth is an object that you should be aware of. Your government does not know about it yet and I wonder what they are going to do with that one. This mass is not closer but it's a much faster moving object. It is not a companion to Planet X. I don't know whether to call it a comet or a planet because I don't fully understand your meaning for either. If you are doing it by size, it is approximately twice the size of your planet.

It is going to come from behind the sun and will cross, kind of on the opposite elliptical plane of Planet X. It has come your way before but is faster moving than Planet X. Last time it came through later than Planet X in your time and happened about six to ten thousand years ago. These two have never passed this close together time wise. The last time these two passed so close together there was some devastation but not much.

In 2002 they were not causing any changes in the weather patterns because they were not yet close enough. This object is not being dragged along with comets as it moves on its own power. It has a name that we have given it but it is nothing that you can say or recognize.

This object on the other side of the sun could pass within about thirty-five thousand miles of Planet X. This is not a great distance but could mean the difference between something hitting the planet and not hitting it. All it would take is something to bump either one in space and make them make a change in their present course.

We hope that Planet X will pass you first because if they both get here about the same time, it could be very devastating. The moon could be altered by this action as well and it could also change the whole solar system. If they pass close together only divine intervention could prevent devastation."

Sun

"Many people think the sun has diminished, but it has not. Your planet is receiving less sun. This is caused by a combination of man's tampering with pollution and putting chemicals into the clouds.

We don't refer to this situation as ozone depletion but that is what your scientists call that situation. The layer has decreased somewhat over inhabited areas but it is thinner in the Antarctic region where it is not doing much damage. But in the long run it will do more damage because it is going to be causing melting of the ice packs and that will eventually cause a problem.

You see this thin protective ozone layer that surrounds your planet; used to be very, very thick before the floods and since that time it has been getting thinner. Since the atomic testing and the increase of pollution it has been decreasing in some areas much more than others."

In 2003 a friend at a channeling session asked about a spot or anomaly on the sun. We were told that, "There are actually three spots on the sun, two are natural and one is not. The spot that is not natural was caused by a negative species shooting at the sun with something close to your neutron bomb. This has been causing major eruptions on the sun. We don't understand why they did this, except that it was probably an experiment.

Sun flares are causing increased solar energy, and that's creating bigger hurricanes, but your government has learned to intensify and move the hurricanes. There will be many more hurricanes this season. (This was given in the spring of 2004.) The planet axis is off by eleven degrees; this is why your seasons are off. If it gets to around twelve degrees, the planet could flip. So far the light workers that are on the planet are holding the flip off."

Moon

"The Earth had originally two moons that were destroyed. Approximately five hundred thousand years ago the object you call your moon was artificially nudged into the orbit it is in. That is why it doesn't rotate, it is artificial. The moon is not hollow but is not a solid body. Your moon doesn't have the normal mass of an object that was captured into an orbit.

There were aliens who were using this object as a ship that traveled through the sky. They were explores and their planet/ship malfunctioned so they had to abandon it. It was at that time they left it in an orbit around your planet.

There are three active bases on the dark side of the moon, the backside of the moon: they are Russian, American, and alien. Even the astronauts saw ships lined up watching them when they landed on the moon. One base is definitely an alien base and there is a base that's representative of Earth. There is another base that I'm not free to delve into at this time. This is why you have not been back to the moon, you were told not to come back. Earthlings will not be welcomed into space until you change your ways. We would just escort you back. We are here to raise you to the spiritual level so that you are able to come into space, and we're here to make sure that the humans survive if tragedy happens. There is a group of aliens here who wish to take the planet for their own and don't want you coming into space either.

Before you were told not to enter space your government touched down on Mars with a recovered alien craft, which could actually go to the moon and back without being refueled.

I saw the special on your television about your not going to the moon; it was rather interesting, but what better way to put doubt into people's minds that you even got there."

Earth

"As I have explained before, God has a very special place in His heart for Earth. It is one of the most beautiful planets. You can destroy yourselves, and many things on this planet can be destroyed but He will not allow the destruction of Earth. It doesn't mean Earth would not get into trouble, and things could get rough on the planet, but it will never ever be completely destroyed.

The planet has been wobbling for oh…my goodness since 1978. It wasn't very much before but now it's starting to wobble enough where people, are noticing that the sun isn't quite right in the position and yet in another day or two it's back where it should be. Also the magnetic pole has been moving. It's kinda like a rubber band when you pull on it. It kind of goes back and then it pulls out and then goes back and then all of a sudden…it breaks. There is a comet coming that is also giving a little bit of a pull." (See Planet X)

Pyramids

"The pyramids are about 20,000 years old. At the time the pyramids were built they had a cap on top which was used as a homing device or a beacon for space ships coming in. There were not such nice beings also on the planet at the time, and they wanted to be able to home in on their own people. You see they had quite a large civilization here at the time, except a short time later most of them left. When they left they buried a space ship at the base of a pyramid, and there are also a number of records buried that would give man knowledge of levitating, which is exactly how the pyramids were built. The blocks were levitated to where they were placed. These things were buried after the pyramids were built, and the people who were left on the planet lost the knowledge and their civilization declined. Because of this gradual loss of knowledge, many people of Egypt were buried in the pyramids hoping the aliens or gods would come for them. They believed they could be brought back to life when the ships returned or, as some believed, they could leave in the flying ship and go to heaven.

A space ship was buried on purpose after the pyramids were built. You see, the Egyptians knew of space travel and had a lot of advanced technology that they learned from the aliens. The aliens had quite a large civilization in Egypt at the time and when most of them left, the technology was lost and the civilization that was left behind declined.

We hope that earthlings do not uncover these things yet. There are agents who help protect these records and the spaceship from archeologists and whoever else may be looking for them. As some of your people think now, this knowledge would not be used for good, but should this information get into the right hands it could be very, very good for your people.

If the ship that is buried underneath the pyramids is uncovered it will change man's course of history. It will probably be uncovered, and whoever uncovers it will decide if this change will be good or bad.

The chambers inside the Great Pyramid are kind of like a record. Many of your people have come up with all kinds of ideas of what they are, such as, the 365 stones, the sun when it's due North shines in and all that kind of stuff. But basically it was to try to fool the people, should they enter, as to what it really stands for. The common person didn't understand what it was all about.

The Great Pyramid had a casing or shell on the outside, which was removed years later to build other buildings by the local people. If that outside casing on the surface of the pyramid were in place and got hit with a laser, it would give you the history of the planet. It told the story of your planet, and the only way to see it was with a laser. It really isn't a laser light, but it is kind of like a laser light that would reflect the story of the planet and the beings who had visited it. It told of the rise of humans and the reason why people fell. This would be projected in pictures not words; it would be like a single frame of a film so that if you moved the light from stone to stone quickly, it would almost look like a moving picture.

There are more pyramids on the planet than in Egypt. Like the Great Pyramid, there are information and records stored within each of them. South America has one of importance and so does Central America. China had one with information in it which could not be figured out, and the message it contained was destroyed. There is also a pyramid in the state of Ohio, but it is in a place where white people can't get at it."

Hollow Earth, Inner Earth

"There is another civilization under the crust of the earth. They believe, like most people do on the surface of the planet, that if they keep their heads buried in the sand, thinking if they don't see or hear something, it does not exist. There are many cave dwellers who moved underground when Atlantis sank, plus there are the beings that live inside the hollow core of the planet. These are the ones that Admiral Byrd found."

Ancient Civilizations

"Beware of those who claim to be from Atlantis or Lemuria. The Lemurians and Atlanteans were both great societies long before the pyramids were built.

Both of these societies were doing genetic experiments and cloning. They created half-human and half-animal beings mostly as beasts of burden. This is where the mythology of half-human and half-animal came from. They received a lot of their knowledge from space beings that had come to visit the planet. Your planet is much older than you think, and this was not the first time the planet was visited by any means.

Lemuria was destroyed before Atlantis, and when Atlantis grew up they also started down the same road of decline, going against God's will. They were also destroyed. A few of the Atlanteans became cave dwellers on Earth, and their skin has a light blue tint to it.

You are almost at the stage that Atlantis was when it was destroyed. It is the creating of life and the changing of DNA that is the problem. They both took to becoming gods by creating life as they saw fit. It was not only the creating of life but also creating a mixture of beings, as many of the aliens did when they came here thousands of years ago, just as some of the aliens here at this time are creating hybrids between themselves and humans. The ones who claim to be creating hybrids do not work on the light side of the force. The cloning that some of your scientists are doing has us all very upset shall we say.

The Summarians are not really responsible for building the pyramid and the sphinx, but they did get a help from the space brothers. The Sumerian culture actually became the Egyptians.

The pyramids weren't built to be tombs for their leaders. Another interesting fact is the pyramids were built in an almost perfect alignment with the pyramids on Mars but are off 1/100 of a degree."

More Interesting Topics the Aliens Had a Lot to Say About

Dimensions and Vibrations

"I consider a dimension something that you cannot see at your level of existence; it could also be called a vibration level rather than a dimension. It is just another form living in the same space but you cannot see it. In other words, if you raised your vibration level, if you vibrated at a different speed, you may not be seen either by those around you.

A dimension or vibration is a little like your radio waves they can be very close together and yet separate, like when you're tuning a radio and how they sometimes join together and you get nothing but squawking, but if you move the dial just a hair one way or the other you get different stations.

You are in one dimension on Earth, and as you rise to a different vibration level, you also go to different dimensions. Your vibration level would determine the dimension you are in. It is very hard to explain. I think that is the closest and the best I can do at this point.

Very often now, as you begin to realize that other dimensions exist, you will see the shadows that they cast when they are near you. As you become more aware of what is going on around you, you get glimpses of other dimensions. Sometimes you can see and hear the other dimensions if you become one with the Universe.

Earth is on a lower vibration level than we are. If you were on a higher/faster vibration, you would see and feel things happening earlier. The faster the vibration, the faster time seems to fly by. That is why when you come to our ships you can get a lot done in a short period of time.

You need to be at the right vibration level to be able to leave the planet for any reason. If you don't match the vibration of the ships when the evacuation occurs, you will not survive. The planet is going to raise its vibration and when it is ready to be inhabited again everything has to match the vibration of the planet or it would not survive. To change your vibrations you also must raise your consciousness.

Many aliens have the technology to be space travelers but they have not raised their vibration level, so they are as vulnerable as humans to low life beings because their consciousness has not improved. They have the knowledge of space travel, but they have not raised their spiritual levels. We wish to protect people of your planet and help where we can without interfering straight out. As you guide your children, you also push and prod them but if you want them to grow, you also give them the freedom of making their own choices and mistakes. We are working to expand people's minds, to raise their vibrations and that is done with openness and love and the sending of light to all.

Many workers who are on the planet at this time may want to consciously remember everything that is going on when speaking to aliens or visiting ships in space. For the protection of the contactees we work with, we don't allow them to remember everything as it would not be good for their mental well-being. You have all the truths of the planet and the Universe in your soul. For the time being it is put in storage. When the time is right, when they are needed, these truths will come out into your conscious mind. We would like to see the salvation of all the people of the planet, but unless people raise their vibration level of their own free will, there is nothing we can do to help. We can give the media ideas like movies that come out, so people realize what is happening. I am afraid that many people hear and ignore these things. I hope that you can understand and realize our dilemma in this situation.

When the changes in vibration start, there will be many earthlings flipping out. They won't be able to understand what's going on; the feeling of losing control and the knowledge that they are in danger will overtake them. They, by their negative thoughts and energies, will be affecting your vibration level of growth if you're not strong enough. These negative feelings and thoughts can very easily pull those down who have increased their vibration level. The fear will be so strong and you must be twice as strong to keep your own levels. The humans on Earth who have not raised their levels will be the most vulnerable. That is why you are down there to touch these beings and to help them on the road to a better life.

To travel dimensions is hard, and taking your body with you is even harder. It is kind of like going through a doorway but not as easy. It is much easier to go in the spirit form, and the body does not fall in a pile or heap on the floor. The body waits for you to come back. I am not a dimension traveler myself, but from what I understand it is like opening a door and walking through. There are times when you may hear a slight noise from someone in another dimension, but a touch or a breeze is hard to accomplish, and it is only through sheer will power that this can be accomplished.

I like to keep track of all people who come up to our ships, and their levels are rising. I tune into the soul records on the soul computer, and we know where you are, what you are doing, and what your levels are at. We do not interfere in your lives. We can nudge you, point you in new directions, just subtle things. Sometimes thoughts are sent out and received, but we're not allowed to interfere too much. It is important that each one of you realize that to become one with God, you must become one with the Universe. You should become in tune with even the smallest things on your planet. You should be able to feel the emotions of everything and everyone around you. It is possible to do this with practice. It's going to take a lot of work, but you can learn to become compassionate with everything in your life, even what you think has no feelings such as a piece of furniture, new carpeting, and the animals in your life. They all have their own auras. A piece of furniture was once wood that breathed and was one with the Universe. It may not be living now, as you assume life is, but if you tune into it, it still has vibrations. If you can tune into that, you can also tune into God. Practice is the essential way of going about this.

When you are in tune with the planet's vibration, you will feel the Earth's wobbling, its pain, and try to help, I don't know when or if this will happen as I am no fortuneteller. Many of the aliens that are here now vibrate at a different speed than those on earth do. If we wish to walk on your planet, we must lower our vibrations. This we can do for short periods of time. You cannot stay for an extended period of time anywhere unless your levels are equal to where you are going.

There are many places in this Universe that do not have the negativity this planet has, and they too, make mistakes. We too are learning to get back to God. That is our ultimate goal to be back with Him. It's a lot of hard work and it's learning many lessons. Isn't it the recognition of the errors and the willingness to change that is important? God can forgive almost anything if you recognize your mistakes and your errors and try your best not to do it again. He is a forgiving God, I can vouch for that."

Channeling

"Channeling is a process of one being using another person's voice box to speak through. Now there are many different types of channeling. There's one thing I would like to say: many, many years ago when the prophets and seers worked, if these prophets and seers did not produce, if they were not correct, they were killed. What would all these so called psychics, prophets, and seers do today if this were the case? Would they be so willing to speak out if what they said did not come true and they were put to death? Anyone who gives you dates, times, and places, please back away from.

The type of channeling that is going on here is a little different. Bonnie met us years ago on a craft so she knows each person that she channels. To do this we had to meet each other physically so that we'd recognize each other and it could be done more easily. We are in solid physical form and we would never channel when she is not in good health. The type of channeling that we do is done with a blending of souls. We let Bonnie know when we want to channel; no, we are not at her beck and call all the time because we all have work to do on board our ships. Bonnie then gets into a meditative state and lets the soul who is going to channel come into her body. It is her choice if she wants to continue or stop at anytime. Once we enter her body, we get to speak to each other. She then leaves and is able to go to anyplace she wants to because her soul is free of the body. When she leaves we use her vocal cords to talk to those present. The voice is Bonnie's but we do have different patterns of speech, and after awhile most people can tell who is speaking. We keep track of her bodily functions and even know when she has to use the bathroom. Keeping her breathing correctly can sometimes be a problem.

It was decided that this channeling would be done to get the message out that there are two types of aliens here at this time. One faction does not care about humans and have their own agenda. Their agenda includes abducting humans for experiments and producing hybrids. They do not care what happens to the human race as long as they get what they want. Then there are those who are here to help the planet in the troubled times that are coming."

In 1990 many of us had been discussing various types of channeling and had a hard time finding any information about the type of channeling that I do. So many people channel discarnate people or spirit guides, and it was asked why I channeled a living alien being during a session. Monn answered, "Well one of the reasons is because Bonnie is not from this Earth; most light workers are not from Earth. Therefore, many of you have come from a higher vibration level. Many light workers have met and talked with aliens aboard space ships and the souls are connected, even if many of you don't remember. That is why many of you have aliens for guides.

Many people think they are channeling someone when in fact they are only getting in contact with their higher self. Oh, how I hate the word higher self. I have gone with Bonnie to meetings where this has occurred and the things that were said were good and beautiful, but they were only going into their inner being and connecting with that. It is a shame that these people do not realize that they are so powerful and spiritual. If only they could accept the fact that they are the ones with the messages.

Many of the people on your planet call talking to the dead when channeling and we often wonder why you would even want to talk to the dead. When you contact the dead again and again, you don't allow them to move on to another lifetime. This is not good because each soul has many things to learn, and if you hold them in-between lives you are keeping them from the process of learning. We aliens also wonder why you think that these dead people have any more knowledge and answers to questions after death than before death. They aren't any smarter in death than in life. If they screwed up their lives, they have to go to school and learn about the mistakes they made so they don't repeat the same mistakes.

Another type of channeling is when a person is possessed by a nonentity. They don't even know who is speaking through them and they never question to see if what is happening is good for them or leading them down a path that is not good for them.

One of the things we want everyone to know is that we don't have all the answers, we certainly cannot predict a place or time when something is going to happen, although we can give percentages of when and how something could happen. You see, everything and everyone has free will and anything can change in an instant if you make a change.

If a channel were to ask for a higher life form, they could channel an alien instead of a discarnate. You must have already attained an equal vibration, in this or a previous lifetime, to channel a higher life form. If they do not request a higher form or if the channel does not reach an equal vibration level of the being they want to talk to, this cannot be accomplished.

All people who are true channelers when they start channeling have a period of I think you would call it rebellion. Many think that the channeling is taking over their life and they are losing control of their lives when the channeling occurs. When they won't channel, they are exercising control over their lives, and a good being will not interfere with that choice. This is especially true with a young person, as they don't have many life experiences to fall back on. A spiritual person will realize there is a responsibility that goes with the channeling. There is a choice that everyone has to make. They can walk away at any time although the negative side will do anything to hold onto a channeler.

If all things are correct, channeling does not make your lifetime shorter. I am very careful, and when Bonnie is tired or not feeling well, I will not channel through her. When I speak through her, she is actually giving her body to me so I can speak with her voice. Her soul actually moves over and allows me to come through. When she does that, if there are bacteria or an infection in her body and she is not there to protect it, it goes on a rampage.

You know some people want the glory of people looking to them for their answers. During channeling sessions, many channelers give people advice on what to do with their life or are making decisions for people and that is frightening. They relish being in the spotlight that the channeling affords them, never thinking that they are responsible for anything that comes out of their mouths. So they had better be sure who they are channeling and whose side of the force they are on. Most of them don't realize what they are doing. The law of noninterference is applicable to this planet; these channelers are taking a lot of karma upon themselves."

Because many people were claiming to channel Ashtar and Jesus, we asked in the fall of 2000 how many people were actually channeling them as if they actually were. Monn replied, "At this time from what we know there are approximately 4,000 people who claim to be channeling Jesus. At our latest tally I see there are something like 3,200 people channeling a being called Ashtar, but these numbers changing daily and they are growing. Most of these people are not channeling who they think they are and should be very careful about who they are channeling."

In 2001 we asked Monn again about so many people claiming to channel important people, especially Seth. Monn said, "For an old soul Seth really gets around. According to our computer there are 327 people now on Earth claiming to channel him. Now you have to admit he is a pretty busy dude. There are 673 people who claim to channel Mother Mary right now, and they're not. That is not who they're talking to. This is a lot of people thinking they are channeling someone when they are not, and many of them are being mislead.

Please at all times question, question whoever is channeling and follow your instincts about what is being said so that you are not fooled.

Many of the channelers and their original messages are true, but when you try to make money or profit from channeling, it ceases to be truthful."

Cloning

In 1992 because so much was being discussed about cloning in the paper and on television that we asked if the aliens knew whether a human was cloned yet and for what purpose was it done.

"Your scientists tried to clone some very important people, but those were not a success, so they have been trying to clone the scientists that were doing the experiment and have succeeded in one but that was not quite genetically perfect, so they will try others.

The body is just a covering or housing, and in order for it to function properly it has to have a soul; it needs a soul for it to function completely. If someone is cloned, a soul must enter that body or it cannot be a living, breathing thing. It's almost like a person in a coma; it cannot move. Sometimes with coma patients the body doesn't get a chance to shut down enough for a soul to exit and the soul is actually trapped in it. So a soul is snatched from a dying person for that purpose, and if you are not a spiritual person this could happen to your soul.

I am afraid that these cloned beings would not be spiritually advanced. This would probably be all right with most of the people cloning because many of them would be trying to make an army out of the cloned. The clones would be bewildered because before you are reborn, while the gestation period is happening, you become acquainted with the family you are joining. You become acquainted with the body you are going to enter, and it is an easy natural process, while cloning is just a bang and there you are in another body."

In 1993 we were informed that "Cloning is 45 % perfected. The scientists on your planet have just about mastered the genetic code, and once that is mastered they can then create a human body. They have not created a viable human clone yet, but they are about 72% close to accomplishing it. The errors in the cloning process have been mostly genetic which have not produced a sturdy offspring. If the scientists were to allow the experiments to come to full term, they would have a soul but not a spiritual soul. Yet they consider these clones to be lab rats and extinguish them when they are not what they want."

During February of 1995 Monn told us, "Cloning was about 85% perfected. It is perfected enough to fool someone for a short period of time. So make sure you know who you're talking to. You have not had contact with clones yet. A clone cannot shape shift because they are specifically grown to be the shape they need to be in."

In 1996 all the newspapers had the story of a sheep called Dolly that was cloned. When we asked about this happening, this was the aliens reply. "When an animal has been cloned, like the sheep called Dolly, the soul has been, let's say for your understanding, it has been snatched from another animal at death. When Dolly was cloned, it had a sheep's soul, but it would not have the original soul, so their personality would be different. It would be more bewildered than normal because while the body is in gestation it becomes acquainted with the body it's going to enter, and this is a natural process. However, with cloning this doesn't occur. Clones would have normal instincts because it would have a sheep's soul, just as a dog would have a dog's soul and a monkey a monkey's soul, but they would not have the same personality of the cloned animal. It could, however, take on the habits and personality of the new soul."

In 1997 we asked if our scientists had cloned a human yet, and this is what Monn had to say about cloning a human. "Your scientists have tried to clone some very important people, but those were not a success. So then the scientists tried to clone one of their own who was working on the cloning experiment and have succeeded in a clone who is genetically perfect, so now they will try others."

In 2001 we asked for an update on cloning, and this was the answer: "In the case of cloning, a soul needs to come into the body to make life but that would not be the gift of life from God. As a human you were given a gift of choice, you do not live on instincts alone as an animal does.

It is very, very important to understand that these souls that enter into a cloned body have not gone through the process upon death of learning from their mistakes made in the previous lifetime. They have not processed what they have been through nor do they understand what has happened to them. Generally, these are lower types of souls. I shouldn't say really lower, maybe I should say a soul that has made the wrong choices in their previous life. And these types of soul can be snatched upon their death and forced into a cloned body, and this can be very dangerous. The only type of soul that can be forced into a cloned body is not a soul of a high vibration. Now by vibration, I don't mean the rate it vibrates, I mean that its understanding of God and the Universe is not good. Your scientists don't even understand this yet.

The growing of a clone is an accelerated process as the ones doing this can't wait around for it to grow normally. They will be used in the government or any-place else they are needed to get in and do a job undetected.

Unless you engage them in long conversations and that type of thing, you won't know it is a clone. A clone would not know everything of the person they look like; they would only be given enough knowledge to get by.

A clone grows from one cell, from an egg that reproduces itself. How fast it reproduces depends on how much electrical stimulation they use to get it to start reproducing itself. A clone could be brought to full size adults in a short period of time. Actually this could be in a matter of a few days. Now it takes about five years to produce a body from one cell that divides, but don't forget they will be improving on their technique every day. The cloned bodies grow much faster than the original and it depends on how much electrical stimulation they use to get it to start reproducing. As you can see this, growth can happen very quickly.

Who knows, a clone could be used to incriminate someone of a crime, such as a convenience store robbery, but I wouldn't sit up nights worrying about it. Just be aware of what's going on around you so if something should come up, you have knowledge of it so you can reason out what is happening. Or if you see something or someone that you know and they are acting and behaving differently that you might recognize it for a clone, especially if it is a leader, a very high official. How do you know what these people will try? We can't even fathom that. I mean the probabilities are immeasurable.

Many of your scientists and fiction movies talk of soul snatching and it is kind of like a process like that. Upon death your soul leaves the body. The soul is almost like a light source but does not look like a spotlight. The soul is very soft, very small, about the size of a tennis ball, kind of relative to the size of a baseball. As it leaves the body it prepares to go back to school for lessons, to the place where it must study or must relive the bad things that it has done so it can understand how that hurts people.

A soul transference, which has been accomplished by earthlings, is always done at or near death. What they want to do is to be able to snatch souls that are negative and have not yet reached completion of their training in-between lifetimes. So if they have been negative in their last lifetime, they do not get their full retraining to try to bring up their vibration level of the soul. So it is possible to have an army of very negative beings.

If a soul is very loving, compassionate and understanding (spiritual) it makes one leap within an instant to where it needs to go. It cannot be touched by anyone or anything. Now a soul who had a very hard life is very troubled or very disturbed and can be snatched by the evil forces, or as some people on your planet say, Satan and his forces. As a matter of fact, these negative souls are generally the ones targeted by negative beings because they are easily snatched and placed into a cloned body. So those who want to make an army of clones are going to get an army of exactly what they want. They would not have much trouble doing the killings they would be trained for. They would be trained from the time they entered this cloned body until they are put into action for only one thing and that would be death and destruction.

Those of us who work for the Creator do not clone as it is up to God to produce a body and give it a soul. This is one action that makes God very angry. Just because you can clone doesn't mean you should.

You know, it says in your Bible that a being will be mortally wounded and will have a miraculous healing. I would like you to think about this. Suppose the Antichrist got a lock of hair off a hairbrush and cloned a body to its full growth. Then this person is mortally wounded, the bodies could be switched and an evil soul would enter the body. Could this be what the Bible is talking about? It doesn't take much to get that DNA sample.

Sometimes if a person is killed violently this causes them confusion. When someone gets pregnant that is not planned there is not a soul prepared for the birth. So a soul has to enter the body without preparation, and this sometimes causes anger, resentment and violence in the newborn.

God is the only one that can make a soul, and generally a soul is snatched at death for a clone to be produced. Your scientists can do soul transference and have done so for some time.

It is very important to understand that the souls who enter into a cloned body have not gone through the natural process upon death of learning from the mistakes they made in their previous lifetime. Only a soul that does not have a high vibration can be forced into a cloned body, and it will probably repeat the same mistakes or maybe even do worse things.

The Grays and Reptilians are cloning and have it perfected. The aliens who are cloning think of them as lab rats and just extinguish them if they are not 100% to their liking. I am speaking about clones that have come full-term and have a soul.

Aliens, meaning the Grays and Reptilians, can clone humans off the planet but not on the planet. All they need is the DNA, then take it to their laboratories and produce the clone. They have the ability to snatch negative souls and put them in the clones or they can transfer the soul near death."

In December of 2002 the Raelians claimed to be the first to clone and successfully deliver a human baby. This interested us so much that in January of 2003 while speaking to Eric we asked if this was true and he gave us the following information: "Your scientists have been trying for a long time, but it has only been in the last three and a half years that it has been accomplished to the extent it has been now. Before, shall we say, the clone was not a whole viable being.

The Raelians were given this information by their alien contacts to try cloning. They were given enough information to go ahead, as they have done. But do not think that all those on the planet are going to accept it as an accomplishment because they themselves want to be the ones to step forward with the first human clone.

Everyone wants to be recognized as the first to accomplish cloning. Most people on the planet do not believe that it has been accomplished yet. And of course, just like UFOs, they are always easily explained away. So do not think that everyone will believe this process has been accomplished, but I say to you, it has been.

I wish to tell you that I have never seen such a pained expression on the face of Jesus as I have seen since this has happened. He is well aware, as most of us here are, that this is one of the final things that God cannot accept from the human race. One of the other things that God cannot accept is the arrogance people feel that they can have a war and win. Many feel with a war they can put anyone that they wish in power. Little do they realize that a force much greater than them will step in and take that power from them."

Hot Bed of UFO Sightings in Wisconsin

Dundee, Wisconsin, the Ships That Have Been Seen

Dundee is where we often go to see UFOs. There is an establishment called Benson's Hideaway and it has alien and UFO paraphernalia throughout the bar. Every third Saturday in July there is a get-together where people can talk about the topic of UFOs and aliens to strangers and not be afraid of ridicule.

In July of 2000 a handful of people were present when a blue craft was seen that looked like two pyramids with the flat bases together. As we stood near the shoreline behind Bensons, we were facing south over Long Lake. It came up about half the length of the lake when it started to tumble end over end and also rotated clockwise.

The first chance we had we asked for an explanation of what we had seen. What follows are Monn's comments. "That ship was not one of ours, it belonged to a group that is from the Sirus System and, we don't work with them. Your planet has a variety of humans on it but the Universe has a wider variety of beings. These are not negative beings; they are observers. In other words they don't want to participate in helping your planet but they aren't necessarily here to cause harm, either. They showed themselves to see what reaction people would have. They are trying to observe and understand you better. We've been observing you for a long time and still don't understand you. Everyone needs to see and feel other species. Look at how you go to your zoos to see different species and observe them."

On July 21, 2001 approximately fifty witnesses saw three amber colored lights appear one at a time over the southern horizon to the left of Dundee Mountain. At approximately five-minute intervals the second and third lights followed the first just over tree tops along the east side of Long Lake. When the first light was half-way up the lake, it dropped a small amber light from its bottom. The second and third lights followed the first and continued past the northern end of the lake until they just seemed to disappear. A little later another light came up the center of the lake. This object had two smaller objects which seemed to dance around the larger one. Suddenly there was a popping noise, the larger light split apart and fell from the sky, while one of the smaller green/blue lights broke away and shot off to the north over the horizon in about five seconds and disappeared. The other green/blue light was still in the area when I went to bed. The next day I was told the light stayed in the area until 4a.m. The last object was different, and everyone there felt that it was not the same as the other three. When we asked Eric about this sighting, he said, the last one was definitely partially man-made and alien made which they were going to use to make things a little rough for anything that was seen that night. Eric also told us that, the craft at Dundee were there to wake up a few people, and they did their job very well. These craft are actually stationed on Earth. The last craft was not 100% a hoax, part of it was man-made. The two bouncing around it were not manmade. They were checking it out and decided to make it inoperable. Eric told us that he was not at liberty to tell us who the green lights were.

On July 21, 2002 in the evening large lights appeared from the northwest over the trees and proceeded in a southeastern direction. Each of the lights pulsed getting brighter and dimmer. We asked Monn what we saw and this is what she said, "These were not the same beings that were there in 2001. I can't tell you everything, but I can tell you this: the first two ships did not belong to anyone of the Federation, the next three did, the last one did not belong to anyone of the Federation, and the seventh one was a definite man-made object coming from the south. I believe that the ships that had the stobing lights were partly from the Federation. It was raining that night and many of you did not get your cameras out and then when you did you had to keep your cameras from getting wet.

The six lights all pulsed; this was caused by the changing atmosphere and the propulsion system they used. There was also a little showboating by all of us. Many also dropped balls of light. A lot of times when they come in that close they put a perimeter around the craft for safety reasons because you never know when the government is going to show up. With the propulsion system working in that enclosed environment, you sometimes get a dropping of the lights. It's actually like an electrical discharge, I would say impulse.

We were there to make sure a mass abduction did not take place. They would have gladly done abductions if they could have. They were planning on coming down really close, but they knew that we would not put up with it.

No one from the Federation was communicating with anyone attending as we had no reason to do so. We knew they were going to make a show, and once it started we had to react immediately. It's like everybody was waiting to come on stage. We all looked like the same craft; it was just easier for us to come that way. We liked seeing the reaction of the crowd. I found it very enlightening myself. We did not want to show our force and the other ships weren't coming in to do damage, but they were coming in for a show the people wanted. We just thought we'd come along with them to make sure that nothing happened.

A few people went looking to see if they could find where the lights were coming from but then didn't find anything. Then the following morning they went looking and found objects that they believe were the lights. I am not at liberty to say who planted them last night, but I will say the ones who found the evidence weren't using their heads very well. I defy anyone on Earth to make anything that looked like the ships that appeared. Many said they found a plastic bag that had holes in it and candles which were used to fool the people. I say this is false.

Some of the people who were there are military personal. You don't think that a place like Dundee is going to be unobserved. The last one was a man made object, it was going with the wind."

In 2003 we saw no ships, but a lot of people got orbs on their film so we asked Monn what they were. Monn said, "A lot of people got orbs on their film, and that was caused by the flashes that the people were producing in the rain, so it was not necessarily their own flash but somebody else's. It was very quiet that year but a gas was dissipated over the area by military aircraft during flyovers earlier in the day. It was something on the order of confusion gas; this was done to cause confusion, creating a different atmosphere, a different feeling among the people who were there. You could say that everyone was part of a science project. No one really connected their feelings with what was going on. This is a type of gas that would not affect a lot of people negatively, you know, make them aggravated or anything. But just think what would happen if they did that over a large city with the negative-feeling gas. This was done during a basketball and football game a number of years ago."

By 2004 there were more people there than we had ever had. Most of the people had left when we saw only one ship up close. It was the most awe inspiring object I have ever seen. This was a Y-shaped object that was so low I felt that if I had a good arm I could have hit it with a small rock. I could see an outline of a craft with lights on each appendage. These lights were a bluish green and there was one yellow/white light in the center where they appendages met. What was strange was that as it got almost overhead the object looked like a cross. All this time there was no noise and it just slowly floated above us.

Monn confirmed the appearance of this ship which she said was a Y-shaped craft that looked like a cross when it was overhead. "There was also a second blue-lighted ship and that was a Reptilian craft. The white light was the Gray's craft. These Grays and Reptilians were neither evil nor bad, just neutral they were just passing through taking a look. What you didn't see was an orange-colored craft going from the west to the east. We had three ships in the area, one was Derrick's, one was Lea's, and I was there, also. I believe you could have seen Lea's craft because it is a much larger craft and only about three miles up."

In 2005 some video footage was taken of a few craft. However most of the craft were seen by the naked eye but not by the cameras present. This was frustrating those operating the cameras. When you looked through the view finder on either 35 mm film cameras or digital video camcorders, you saw only the black sky. What was also very strange was almost everyone remembers seeing some green and red balls in the sky but no one that I talked to could remember what sequence they appeared in or how many were seen.

Monn explained, "There was a total of seventeen craft in the area, but I believe the most anyone saw was seven. Many of these were too far out to be seen. The red and green ones you did see had a block on them so they could not be filmed. I believe there were four government ships that look something like UFOs in the area. You see, the government now has the technology that can cause them to look different, just as we can. So please be more aware of what's going on. These followed the same flight path east of the lake. These were not made by the citizens who live around the lake. These were made in Houston, Texas. I don't believe you could have gotten these on film if you had used a different color lens, but it might have worked with an infrared film.

Some of you saw a white light over Benson's off to the west, and that was my craft. I made a circle from Fond du Lac almost down to West Bend, I was patrolling the area to make sure nothing happened."

Except for 2001, there were many cameras taking pictures and footage as proof of what was seen. This is not a detailed report of what has happened in this area, but there has been regular activity in this area. Regularly people come to the bar and tell what they have seen as it is well known that this is the place you can tell your stories and not be laughed at.

More Information about Myself

When asked about one incident Monn said, "In 1989 Bonnie was walking down the hall in her house and something hit her on the back of the leg, she thought it was her cat but it wasn't. It was, shall we say, a lower life form that tried to invade her territory and space. I don't think any of you here really realize the strength of your lights. The only time that these negative things can invade your space is when you allow this to happen. It's your choice.

These lower life forms are able to touch you when you're thinking negatively or when your guard is down. That's what attracts them. If at the time you are in a very weakened state, they could do some damage but that is not what they want to do. They do more by giving you fear. If your light is not strong, they can reach you and you become frightened, and then they can reach you more. As you become more frightened they can get to you. Do not become frightened. Just remember with whom you are joined. You are one with God so have no fear."

On December 24, 1987 I was shopping with my husband in a local store and we separated to do our own shopping. I noticed three men following my every move. So we asked if Monn could tell us anything about the incident. Monn answered, "I think the word best describe them are aliens from another system. They were trying to intercept her so she could not do her job that night. An outside force was not protecting her. The greatest protection that you can have, are the ones that God gave you. It takes a little training to be able to recognize them. And those are the instincts that you are going to have to learn to live with and to survive with. Follow the instincts, which is a God given gift. Use them please, I can't teach it. But between Gods light and Gods gift of that inner instinct you can survive almost anything."

In 1997 Monn said, "Bonnie knows more than she is telling and some day she will be willing to explain to you more about what life is like on the ship. It can't be done until you get your acts together. There are more memories in her head than she wants to remember. And she wants to tell you but knows that this is not the time. So, it may come tumbling out of her mouth sometime in the future although we keep trying to tell her to hold it back. Every once in a while something slips out and then she has to clam up real quick. A lot of times you don't even catch it. And then she apologizes to us and we say, "Stop it." So just hang in there and when the time is right she will share more information."

One night after a meeting I had about twenty minutes of missing time between the car and the house. Monn said, "It was Reptilians who were testing her just like all the rest of you are going to be tested, they want everyone's soul. The only problem is you won't even know if you have sold out to the negative, and that's the sad part. They tried to take her, but because she was balanced and had her light shining they could not. They tried to stop her and did for awhile, but the light was stronger than their negativity so it won out."

In February of 1996 there were red spots on my neck. When Monn was asked she had this to say, "It was an altercation which was partly physical and partially a psychic battle. It seems that she was protecting butts of some of the group members. Somebody was getting pretty close...maybe I should just lay it all out on the table. The negative forces were hot on your tail; Bonnie stepped up to the line for you. She met them face to face and it hurt her body. It was a draw between them but she did this because she doesn't care about her physical body. The point is she will do it over and over and over again until she can't anymore."

On February 6th of 1997, I woke up with an ugly looking scar on my neck which went away after about a month. Monn explained, "Bonnie was being herself and others up on board a ship. In the process of doing this received a laser burn. She was going up physically to the Peace Ship and was intercepted. An altercation occurred, and instead of keeping her seat like she should have, she got into the middle of it. Being that she was in her physical body, the injury went home with her, as a reminder to keep her nose where it belongs. It was the Grays from under the shell of your earth that were the cause of this problem. They know about her and the light workers, and they are the ones who get into your dreams negatively."

I recalled that I was involved in the retrieval of important artifacts from a crashed ship on Monday, September 16, 2001. In the fall of 2002 Monn gave me some more information to fill in the gaps. "Not everyone was involved in that retrieval. Records are kept in a book, and the book was lost in the crash of a space ship. It had to be retrieved and retrieved very quickly so that the names of the light workers on the planet at this time would not be revealed. That is basically what happened. The ship had a malfunction of the drive system. And even though our technology is a little advanced over yours, we still do have accidents that happen, including people being hurt. Having higher technology does not necessarily mean that accidents don't happen.

I know Bonnie has been concerned about this, but she did not bring back the full story. She knew something happened but was not sure and it has been bothering her. Things have not been going well on the planet. If the money people get there way and if another war is started, it could preempt the Third World War, especially if atomic weapons are used. She was here at a meeting we had and expressed our concern about what could happen. We are trying our best to be prepared for anything that could happen. We have actually one alert that is above red alert. And if that should happen, that's when Jesus will send his, shall we say his soldiers forth and I want you to know that light workers are part of His foot soldiers. And if you are not ready, you will have a harder time. So we would like you all to be more aware of what's going on around you. Please watch the news more. Please pay attention to what's going on. Please when you talk about things, recognize when people are becoming frightened. The object of your job is not to make people believe as you believe but is to plant a seed. Maybe it will take you ten tries to get the message across. People can accept only what they are ready to accept. They only can understand what their mind, body and soul can accept. And it's not your job to try to make the decision of what they can and cannot understand. Please, if you are seeing people reacting negatively or hard, become compassionate enough to back away. As Christ said, 'There's always another day to shine a light upon a soul.'"

In the evening of March 18, 2005 I went to bed at my normal time. After I got up on Saturday, March 19, 2005 I went to the kitchen to get a glass of apple juice. It was when I was filling my glass that I noticed a large red mark on my middle finger close to my hand and, it looked strange.

As I looked closer, I realized that the finger was swollen and my ring finger was also swollen but had no pain. Going into the living room I decided to try to remember if anything had happened during the night. As I sat in my chair, a memory came of being on a small ship when there was a flash of bright yellow light and then there were people lying on the floor. I know they were injured and I needed too stay and help them. That is all I could remember.

We were going to Milwaukee for a UFO meeting in the afternoon, so I bandaged my finger and showed them my hand and asked if anyone had any idea what it was. One person said that it looked like a radiation burn.

By Monday morning my hand was swollen past the knuckles on my hand. My ring finger was so swollen that I could hardly get off my engagement and wedding rings. My husband took one look at it and then told me to go to the doctor's office and get it looked at. Well, you know how hard it is to get to see the doctor, so I went and asked to see his nurse because I needed her to look at something.

When she came out to the waiting room she asked what I wanted her to see. I showed her my hand and she asked to me come into the area where the doctor's office is. She then had another nurse look at my hand, and they asked me to have a seat in the nearest office, the doctor would be in to see me shortly.

When the doctor came in he looked at my hand and asked what had happened. I told him it happened during the night and I did not know what had happened. I certainly did not want to tell him what I thought had happened because I did not want him to think I was crazy.

He told me that it was probably not a spider bite because it was too early, although he did ask if I had been cleaning out the basement or closets. I told him no, but I had been in Nevada the week before and wondered if maybe I had been bitten by something there. He said, "No, that a bite would have been noticed immediately." He also said that it did not look like a normal burn. Because of the swelling and being hot he thought that whatever it was the wound was infected, so he decided that I needed an antibiotic and prescribed Cephalexin Cap 500 mg three times a day for a full week. He gave me an antibiotic ointment to put on the wound so that it would not get infected from outside. He also told me that if the swelling got worse, I should call and he would send me to a hand specialist. He scared me so I took all of the medication as prescribed.

When I finished the medicine, the wound was still red and looked infected but the swelling was down. After another week the top layer of skin started to peel away, so I decided to cut it off. When I did that, the air got at the wound and it was the first time that the wound hurt. Let me tell you that I am a baby when it comes to a burn. Often if that happens I walk around with my hand in water for a day or two. What was different about this was that there was not a raised blister like you would think a burn would have.

By April 5, 2005 there was still some infection in the wound, but it seemed to be healing from the inside out. I could see that there were at least three layers of skin involved and it was still red. There is not much infection coming out as there was in the beginning. I was still putting on a bandage with the antibiotic ointment and the swelling was down. However, I could not put on my rings yet as they were still a little tight.

In July 28, 2005 I woke up with my foot injured. It was bright pink in color and covered the top of my right foot. By the second day it was not as bright red and had a slight green color on the right side of the wound. By the 30th of July most of the pink color was gone, but where my toes and foot connected it was discolored in a light purple color. In the middle of the wound was a bump that was sore to the touch. I could step on the foot and had no soreness or pain. The total of the discoloration was three inches across the top of the foot and 2 ½ inches from the toes to the ankle.

In August of 2005 I woke up with a black and blue mark on the outside of my left leg. It was a large bruise about three inches wide and about four and one half inches from the top of the knee to the bottom. This took about a week and a half to heal.

I knew something was different, something had changed. I knew that I was not being abducted and felt no fear with it. I knew I had been doing something that was important. These types of things continue to happen, and when I asked Monn about it she said, "No, you were not abducted. You see you have entered another phase of why you are here. There is a war going on in the heavens, one that is very important to the survival of the planet. There has been an influx in the negative aliens and ships and the system of Love and Light is keeping them from entering your space. You have heard from some people that all the aliens in the underground bases have been removed from the planet and this is not true. It seems that those that are here already are staying, and it is up to the human race to either get them to come into the light and raise their vibration or to send them on their way, out of your space."

Even with all of these things going on in my life, I have great faith in the human race. I believe, if we work together with the love and compassion that we should have for each other, we can become much better as humans. We were made in God's image and have the power to become as he intended us to be. We don't have to allow the aliens to enslave us or use us as their experiments. We don't have to allow them to use us to bring a new species into the Universe. We have the power to take our future into our hands and carve our own future.

My only hope is to give the human race knowledge and hope that we can survive this desperate time. We can survive if we remember that we have the strength and knowledge of the Creator, but we must have 100% faith or we will fail.

About The Author

✦

Bonnie Meyer

Bonnie has always considered herself to be an ordinary person living a normal life until UFOs interrupted it. She was raised without any specific religious affiliation but was given a belief from her parents that she I could have a strong relationship with Jesus and God. To this day she does do not attend church on a regular basis, but considers herself a spiritual person.

Bonnie is a very shy person and it has been difficult for her to do some of the things that have come her way. For about a year Bonnie and two friends did a UFO television program. There have been numerous radio interview shows along the way. She has been featured in many newspapers but time and again she was disappointed because she was often misquoted. It seemed as if the newspapers were looking for shocking stories and hers was not one of them.

During her years of research she acquired an extensive video, audio and book library on UFOs and related topics. She read everything she could get her hands on. Trying to learn everything she could so that she could understand what was happening during her contacts with the aliens.

Bonnie has attended many UFO conferences across the country trying to see if anyone was talking about aliens who did not cause fear. She was surprised to learn that only abductions, where horrific things were happening to the abduct-ees, were being brought forward. Bonnie wondered if hers was the only contact with a positive outcome, she wondered if her experiences were in the minority. Maybe there were there other people like her, who were not sharing their experi-ences. The aliens had suggested writing this book and it took almost thirty years to bring it forward. The time is right for the positive side of alien contact to be heard.

Bonnie hopes that this book will give you some insight into the fact that there are good aliens here at this time. They believe in the same Creator of all, as she does. It is time for the positive side of alien contact to be heard. Each individual should be able to hear what the benevolent aliens have to say, so that they may decide for themselves what the truth is. Her only desire is that you will read this book with an open heart and mind.

Index

978-0-595-38404-
0-595-38404-8

Lightning Source UK Ltd.
Milton Keynes UK
UKOW02f1854070916

282472UK00001B/168/P